ALSO BY DANIEL ROBB

Crossing the Water: Eighteen Months on an Island Working with Troubled Boys—A Teacher's Memoir

SLOOP

Restoring My Family's Wooden Sailboat –
An Adventure in Old-Fashioned Values

Daniel Robb

Simon & Schuster
NEW YORK · LONDON · TORONTO · SYDNEY

Simon & Schuster
1230 Avenue of the Americans
New York, NY 10020

Copyright © 2008 by Daniel Robb

First Simon & Schuster hardcover edition June 2008

SIMON & SCHUSTER and colophon are registered trademarks
of Simon & Schuster, Inc.

For information about special discounts for bulk purchases,
please contact Simon & Schuster Special Sales at
1-800-456-6798 or business@simonandschuster.com

Designed by Paul Dippolito

Manufactured in the United States of America

1   3   5   7   9   10   8   6   4   2

Library of Congress Cataloging-in-Publication Data
Robb, Daniel.
Sloop / Daniel Robb.
    p.   cm.
Includes bibliographical references and index.
1. Boats and boating—Conservation and restoration. I. Title.
VM149.R63   2007
623.822'60288—dc22   2007045164
ISBN-13: 978-0-7432-0239-8
ISBN-10: 0-7432-0239-2

The names and identifying details of some individuals in this book have been
changed. Dialogue has been re-created, and some characters are composites.

All photographs are by the author.

For Alexandra

Contents

SLOOP

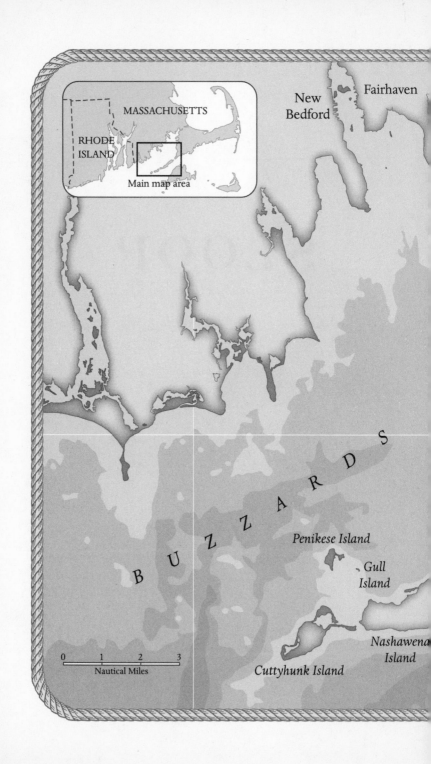

MASSACHUSETTS

RHODE
ISLAND

Main map area

New
Bedford

Fairhaven

B U Z Z A R D S

Penikese Island

Gull
Island

Nashawena
Island

Cuttyhunk Island

0   1   2   3
Nautical Miles

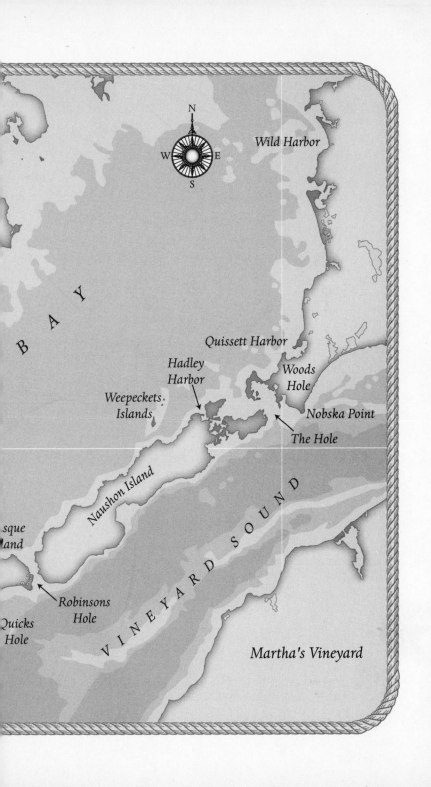

1. Sloop

I SAT ON A roof in Marion, Massachusetts, on a December day. I wore heavy overalls, a blue wool sweater, a grey wool hat, brown leather boots, and a tool belt. Occasionally I worked on roofs. I did this as a way to pay bills, or as a favor. I didn't mind the work, once in a while. The view up there was usually good, and it kept me present—there was always the slight danger of falling off.

This day I was venting my cousin's roof to alleviate condensation in her attic. It was just below freezing out, there was little wind, her two dogs were shifting around on their leads down in the driveway, and I was thinking about what I might write next.

There was a low-pressure system coming in, and the dogs could feel it. One, a short-haired pointer, kept pausing to nose an old sailboat that sat across the drive. I, a lifelong sailor, tried not to be distracted by the boat, which lay in a weathered wooden cradle on a rusty trailer. A faded yellow tarp covered her. On top of the tarp was a scattering of pine needles.

The pointer would pause to sniff the air. I found myself doing the same, up on the roof, pointing my nose off to the west beyond the oaks and the road. Like the dog I could smell something sharp in the air. Snow was coming.

I still had a couple hours of work to do. I had to roll the

heavy plastic mesh along the ridge, over the narrow slots I'd cut through the roof on either side of the peak. Then I had to nail down the hundred-plus cap shingles that would curl over the mesh, covering the ridge. At the end I would drive four nails into the last cap shingle and cover their silvery heads with tar.

Then I'd climb down the north valley with a canvas bag holding flashing, nails, saws, and pry bars. I'd ease down the heavy staging planks, bringing them to the ground one end at a time, take down the roof jacks—slim folding triangles of wood and steel that supported the planks—pack up the tools, and load the truck. Which was an old white Saab coupe with a roof rack. I'd do all that when I was done. But not yet.

As I worked, the dog kept at it too, nosing the old sloop. He'd sniff her stem, sniff her keel, nose her rudder, then lift his head up and try the air again, auguring something there. Perhaps the scent of her white cedar planks changed for him as the barometer dropped.

For my part, I tried to concentrate on the work. But my eyes, as I sat astride the roof, kept leaving the nail held by my left thumb and forefinger, kept rising to look at the boat down there. "Maybe," I thought, "I could write about rebuilding her."

Once this thought had arisen, I looked at the boat for a moment, gazed at the curve of her white hull under the edge of the yellow tarp, and at the powdery green of her old bottom paint. Eventually the wind swirled a leaf in the drive in front of the dogs, and I came back to myself. "Nah," I said softly, and, "You gotta be nuts," and looked again to my hands and the work as the wind moved through the oaks to my left, between me and the road.

· · ·

But she had been a *beauty*. She had been drawn by a man spoken of along with Burgess, Crane, Rhodes, Alden: *Herreshoff*. She was right there, shrouded by a thin lemon-yellow tarp. She had been in my family since 1939, when she was built. Clearly she still had form, although it was hard to tell from the roof how much of that was rot.

Daphie was her name. My mother had grown up sailing her with her brother and sisters during the 1940s and '50s out of Quissett Harbor, just north of Woods Hole on Cape Cod, on the eastern shore of Buzzards Bay.

The Cape at Woods Hole is not quite at its most poetic. It does not reach far out into the cold waves of the Atlantic, the way Provincetown does at its other end. Rather, Woods Hole is a blunt southern corner that juts down into warmer waters. Currents swing with the tides through tight channels there, and islands pepper the waters to the south. One of the beauties of Quissett Harbor, though, is that on most days in summer, just beyond its mouth, a strong southwest breeze comes up around noon. This breeze almost always matures into twelve to fifteen knots of reliable wind, building short, sharp waves that (if you know her) *Daphie* will handle better than any other small boat. Or so I have always thought. She was made for that place, that wind, those waves.

More than twenty years ago (as a large boy) I had cared for her and sailed her for a few summers. Now, she'd been with my cousin for some years, and spent ten or more of those years under the trees alongside which I worked. My cousin was a good person with too many things on her mind, and the boat had suffered.

Place a cap shingle (one-third of a shingle, cut down to resemble a child's drawing of a house—a square with the top two corners trimmed off) on the mesh covering the ridge vent. Place it so it half overlaps the last cap shingle. Grab three nails with your left hand out of the pouch on your left hip; hold the hammer in your right hand, which is cold despite the half-finger gloves you wear. Nail the left side of that cap shingle down. Bend the shingle over the ridge. Nail the right side down. Slide forward, squeezing the roof between the knees. Place another cap shingle so it overlaps the last by half. Nail the left side down. Reach for more nails in the pouch. Bend the shingle over the ridge. Nail the right side down. Slide forward.

"Hey Danny, you want a coffee?" yelled up Carlton, who worked with my cousin. He stood in blue coveralls, squinted up at me.

"Yes thank you, Carlton," I said.

"How you take it?" he yelled up.

"Black. When's the weather gonna hit?" I asked.

"Two–three hours, max. I can smell it comin,'" he said, and then, "You better come down off that roof, man. Weather's comin' and it ain't waitin' on you."

He disappeared into the house.

The wind moved more strongly through the grey branches of the oaks that rose to the west of the house, and through the needled branches of the several white pines around the boat. About an hour later, after driving the last nail and covering its head with a smear of tar, I brought the tools down the valley, and just as I eased the staging planks down, snowflakes began to fall.

By the time I was loaded and driving down the narrow New England roads, away from my cousin's house, the snow was heavy, and I could hear it crunching beneath the tires of the Saab, which, with its heavy engine mounted over the front-drive wheels, seemed unconcerned. It was an old faded-white car, not fast, built for safety and snow handling, two-doored, with a maw of a trunk that swallowed the tools I needed to build a house. I thought a lot of that car—it was just simply capable.

The snow fell steadily, driven across my path as I drove south on the highway. I kept the speed at fifty-five, and eased over the bridge at Bourne, onto the Cape. Was I to rebuild that old boat? Shit, I didn't know.

Once off the bridge I traced the twenty miles of back roads home as snow eddied in the wake of cars in front of me. Along some stretches of road I could look left or right into consider-able woods between the summer homes and old farms.

Finally, just before I came to the long hill that dropped down into the village of Woods Hole, I turned right, and coast-ed down the side of the moraine, almost to sea level, and then stopped at the mouth of my lane, and looked to my right. Be-tween two houses I could see a beach with Buzzards Bay be-yond. Dark grey seas were crashing there after their long fetch down from Wareham to the north. There were four-foot swells now, square and breaking hard on the sand. There was power in them, and it was growing. I was glad not to be out in that.

There were two inches of snow on my lane as I drove in, and no tire tracks—just a couple of sets of footprints, and the staggered periods of a steadily walking cat. My place, a cot-tage with a loft above, would be cold, I knew, and I'd left Ted out—those were probably her prints. She'd gotten bored and gone visiting.

When I opened the Saab's door the hinge groaned, and as I stood my knees did, too. I walked to the cottage door, and went in.

I made a fire in the old woodstove, put the kettle on, settled into a chair, and felt the north wind shake the house slightly even though it was passing far overhead. In the twilight I knew how the snow would cut visibility at sea to several hundred yards. There were fishing boats out in that mess, more than a few of them from New Bedford, struggling back off the banks toward Vineyard Sound, toward their last hard fetch through Quicks Hole. I knew that trip.

They would have steamed southwest toward shore for a day or two, then west through Pollack Rip, just south of the Cape, then onward through Nantucket Sound and Vineyard Sound in relative shelter, then southwest as they passed Woods Hole, and then northwest to slip through Quicks Hole (between the islands of Pasque and Nashawena) before the last six-mile stretch across Buzzards Bay to New Bedford.

But if the tide were against the wind, the sea at the north end of Quicks Hole could be vicious, a hundred-yard corduroy of square waves that would swamp even a large fishing boat if it lost power and got turned sideways. That had happened to one boat several years ago, and it had gone down with all hands right in Quicks, not more than a hundred yards from shore, and within sight of home. Most New Bedford fishing boats had to pass through that gauntlet before crossing the bay and coasting into harbor, and what a tough thing that would be—to come all that way back, within sight of home, and sink.

The kettle boiled. I made tea, lay down on the old wooden couch with a book, and listened to the low note of the wind passing overhead. An hour after dark I awoke to Ted scratching at the door. I let her in, and saw the snow coming down harder still. By 10 P.M. there were four inches of white on the ground, and the note of the wind had deepened.

•   •   •

On Saturday morning, as I looked out on the new snow through the kitchen window, I wrote out a letter longhand to my editor, detailing some of the notable aspects of the Herreshoff Twelve and a Half, or H-12½, as the boat under the yellow tarp was known. I had a good feeling as I wrote. The weather outside was still grey, but inside, somehow, something had changed.

2. A Proposal

"THE NUMBER REFERS TO its length in feet on the waterline," I explained in the letter, as I wrote of *Daphie's* history, her pedigree, her beauty.

"This is a boat that has long been thought the apogee of American small boat design, and the man who designed her (in 1914, late in his career), Nathanael Greene Herreshoff, is known as a genius of American design and engineering. From his drafting table came many early America's Cup defenders, which were then built to his specifications at the family boatyard in Bristol, Rhode Island, where standards of workmanship were second to none. To this day, "Herreshoff" is synonomous with the highest quality in both design and workmanship. What I am proposing is to write a book about the renewal of what amounts to an American icon (at least in the rarified world of small boat design), but more particularly the renewal of a family icon.

"My grandfather was Benjamin Harrison Alton, a surgeon from Brookings, S.D., who went to Harvard Medical School, served in Europe in the Army Medical Corps during WWI, and then settled in Worcester, Massachusetts; my grandmother, Elizabeth Moen, a mother and domestic engineer, was the daughter of a wealthy industrialist from Worcester; they bought the boat in 1939.

"Not much remains in the family, in terms of things from that time, other than this boat. In some significant ways it is what is left of a former age, a vehicle in which generations of Altons transported themselves away from the land, singly and together, out onto the ether, and discovered something—out there."

I continued, "The children raced this boat in the local club, testing themselves against others, seeing if their version of the American family would stand up, whether their stuff was good enough to get them around the buoys faster than the Careys, the Tompkinses, the Swifts. And now, all these years later my grandparents are gone, as are all but one of their children (my mother). I, among the various first cousins sprung from the Alton-Moen marriage, am the only one moved to restore the boat, and I guess, when I think of it, it's as much about the family as it is the boat—this process of restoration."

I proposed to write a book about rebuilding her. In the freshness and the quiet of the morning, writing this letter seemed entirely the right thing to do.

Then I walked to the post office and mailed it.

Back at the cottage, I sat at my desk, looked out over the frozen front yard for a minute, and then examined my hands, which were rough from recent work. There was a gouge in the left palm that had finally closed up, and the knuckles had a few dings—white streaks that marked recent scars; the pads near the base of the fingers were thick, and the fingers themselves were broader than they had been a few months ago.

I wondered how long the proceeds from the roof vents (and a porch I'd rebuilt just prior for a lady down the street) would pay the note. Not long enough. It was winter. It was becoming more deeply winter. I didn't want to be scrambling outdoors any longer. My knees were talking to me. "No more ladders, and no more squeezing roofs, please," they said.

On the following Wednesday I called New York City, and there was an answer: "Yes."

Heck. Now I was in the soup. I had two fears:

One: That I wouldn't have the skill or stamina to rebuild the boat properly—that it would wind up at the back of the garage, gathering dust, after several years of well-intentioned but pointless labor.

Two: That I wouldn't be able to write about the old bucket. It was just an old boat, after all, sniffed at and peed on by attendant hounds, left to rot for ten years under a white pine tree. Did I really want to pour the next year (or more) of my life into her?

Son of a gun.

3. Perseverando

A WEEK AFTER I finished the roof vent I was back in the Saab, driving to my cousin's house in Marion. The snow had melted, and autumn had returned in December, as it often does on the Cape, as the sea cools gradually.

•   •   •

All was arranged. My cousin, whose life had become complicated recently, was ready to have the boat taken away and cared for. A boat mover would arrive later from Cotuit, hydraulic trailer in tow. It was seven o'clock in the morning. As I drove up the sandy drive the two dogs bounded around, desiring play. So we dodged and feinted for a couple of minutes (barking being important nourishment for the soul of man and dog) and then it was time to look her over.

I hadn't examined *Daphie* carefully yet, which upon reflection was daft. I should have looked her over better, looked the *whole* situation over more carefully.

Maybe the old girl was so rotten she'd just come apart, planks separating from ribs during the overland jounce to the Cape. In that scenario her planks would litter Route 25, and I might be able to observe them fluttering off her in the sixty-knot wind of highway travel. At some point it is good not to imagine too much, and I was at that point. I began, then, instead, and for the first time in many years, to touch her.

Besides her name I knew a few other things about her, among them that my grandfather had ordered her from the Herreshoff Manufacturing Company in 1939 through Charlie Eldred, who ran the Quissett boatyard then, and that she was built by Herreshoff in Bristol, Rhode Island, and brought overland to Woods Hole, probably on a truck.

It was also possible that she arrived on a train, which in those days came right down to a terminal on Great Harbor in Woods Hole, where the ferries for the island of Martha's Vineyard still dock. If she had come on a truck they would have delivered her straight to Quissett boatyard, where she would have been rigged, and perhaps caulked and given a coat of bottom paint.

Her name was for the four children: Dorothy, Alison, Philip, and Elizabeth—my mother and her siblings. They all sailed and raced *Daphie* hard, through the '40s and into the '50s. The houses of those years had by now been sold out of the family, as had the other boats. *Daphie* was what remained of those days, the 1,471st boat produced by the Herreshoffs, according to the shield on her transom (an oval plate of bronze covered by many coats of varnish). That was most of what I knew about her, other than my own recollection of maintaining her and sailing her in the 1980s.

I looked her over for quite a while, and then tested her planks, leaning in on them with my fingers, seeing if there was play where a fastening (a bronze screw or copper rivet) had given way to corrosion, or where a frame (a rib) had softened with age. I also probed carefully for rot with an old screwdriver, nudging its rectangular head into each plank in several places.

As I did this, the wind moved lightly through the trees. I reckoned Mr. Cooper (the pointer I'd watched from the roof) had done a thorough job of peeing on her, but this didn't seem to me a problem. Perhaps his urine would act as a preservative. In any case, her planks seemed okay, at least below the waterline. Still, there *were* a number that moved in and out when they shouldn't have, which meant trouble beneath. Fastenings had corroded and parted in there, or ribs had deteriorated and let go of screws. And there was a sizeable gouge in one plank at the waterline amidships where I imagined a truck had backed into her. She just looked a little worn down.

I cleared bittersweet vines out of the struts of her cradle, and carefully pulled out an arrowwood stem that had climbed up through her open bunghole (an inch-wide drainhole) just above where her keel joined the hull, amidships, on the port side. This seemed to me a particularly rude invasion, and it was clear that soon she would have been encircled by the thicket, and reclaimed by another sort of steward.

As I continued my examination, I found that there was some dark rot in her transom (the stern, or back of the boat, where the tailgate would be if she were a pickup) that looked almost charred. Odd. But the lower parts of her keel (the deadwood, so-called, which is beneath the hollow part of the hull) seemed sound enough. I was going by eye, though, and what my screwdriver and thumbnail could tell me as I pressed them into the wood. I wasn't at all sure what I would find when I began to take her apart. Then the awful thought—that perhaps I would have to rebuild her piece by piece—arose. Which would mean at least *several* years of work. I felt my heart beat faster, and my hands grow cold. I wasn't ready for a marriage! I put that thought away, and instead turned to the immediate: the two trailer tires.

It took twenty minutes to dig them out, submerged as they were in five inches of earth and roots, and then another fifteen minutes to trim back the brambles that encased her cradle, and then another ten minutes to stand around and wonder about the wheel bearings in the trailer's two wheels—whether they were frozen, and whether I would be able to turn the trailer if they were.

To pivot the boat so that Jack the boatman would be able to back his trailer up to her bow was my greatest task for the morning, and it had kept me awake for a couple of hours the night before. I had played out various scenarios in my head. In some there were come-alongs and block and tackles stretched from the tongue of the trailer to different trees, but each time, as I tried to haul the trailer around, the great strain put on these mechanisms broke them. In my imagination the chain would snap with a metallic "clink" and my arm (in a Monty

Pythonesque montage) would be severed from my body, or my legs would be, or my head.

Or the chain would stretch from the rear bumper of the Saab to the trailer's tongue, and I would be inside the car gunning the engine, and then the tongue would bend and break and the Saab would lurch forward through the wall of the little barn, cut a gas line, and flames would engulf the building. The three horses my cousin boarded would then gallop out of the barn, leap the fence, and disappear into the mist-shrouded woods . . . I saw this film play out in my head until I drifted off, still chasing horses through the trees.

Standing across the driveway from *Daphie*, having cleared the brush around her, and faced with this ultimate task of pivoting her, I thought (in a moment of heavy-lumber inspiration), "Let me just see what that four-by-four can do to clarify things." On impulse I had thrown a weathered ten-foot-long four-by-four on the roof rack as I left in the morning, and something told me it was time now to bring it into the picture.

I found that by slipping its snout under the nose of the trailer and lifting the other end, I could nudge the nose of the trailer over . . . three or four inches at a time! In ten minutes I had the boat turned to face the mouth of the drive. This had been my Olympus, my great task, and I was done in ten minutes. What an anticlimax! Now I had two hours to sit around and wait.

So I seized the opportunity to get *nothing* done for a while (something that experience has shown is a big part of boatbuilding) and sat on the stone wall across the dirt drive from the boat for an hour. The dogs thought this a wise course, and came and curled up on either side, and fell asleep in the middle of their meditation. I sat and watched the sun come on, gradually gaining height among the trees to the south, which were five months from leafing out.

Occasionally one of the dogs sighed. Or I heard chickadees in the juniper bushes on the far side of the yard, whirring and chirruping. Or a pickup would pass on the road, tires hissing. Once I heard the high whistle of a killdeer from open ground beyond the house. And *Daphie* sat there, before me, mute old sailboat on old steel trailer between two pin oaks. Three young white pines rose to her right, straight and tall, with branches radiating like treads on a circular stair.

And then, about an hour into this consideration, a big picture of a steaming cup of coffee rose up before me, and quickly I was in the car and down the road toward the coffee shop.

And I did appreciate very much as I drove the fact that I (at the age of thirty-eight) had finally learned to carry a ten-foot four-by-four with me on *faith*. Surely this was a sign of evolution.

At Sudden Coffee—an old farmhouse converted to a coffee shop—there were several Mercedes and several beater pickups in the small lot. I parked and walked over the crushed clamshells into the former living room, and ordered a coffee and a Bear Claw.

There were six other men in the shop. Three looked like golfers, and had the body language of the dedicated golfer, bearing themselves with stiff, masculine dignity. Their hair was short, and their polo shirts and khaki pants and Windbreakers were clean. There were also three other men, at a table by a window, who had the look of hammerers, with leathery complexions, sinewy forearms, small, hard potbellies, and the sloping, broad shoulders of those who carry a lot of wood. They, more than the others (though I do golf), were of my guild. But none of these, golfers nor carpenters, was my cousin's ex, who had built the house with the unventilated roof.

I had wanted to talk with him, ask him some questions. I'd always liked him, and thought I might find something out if I ran into him at coffee. But there would be no dialogue here about soffets and rafters and vent schemes, and how he had intended to vent the roof back before he had split. None of that. So I drank my coffee from the blue paper cup.

And then it was ten to ten, and I knew Jack the boat mover would be on time, so I drove back to the house, and back to *Daphie,* who somehow in the interim I had come to accept as the new focus of my life, as my present work.

4. *The Boat Mover*

JACK IS THE SORT who would survive happily if he were set down in the middle of the Yukon in his shorts with a penknife and a pack of Marlboros. Six months later he would emerge at a trading post, dressed in buckskin and fur, buy another pack of butts, and head back into the woods because he was having so damned much fun.

He pulled up at 10 A.M. sharp and backed his long trailer down Hilary's serpentine driveway in one try.

And then he was jumping out of the cab.

"You takin' the trailer?" he asked, standing six feet tall, in battered jeans, work boots, a flannel shirt, and a faded blue jean jacket.

"No," I said.

"Good, 'cause we weren't going to get it on the truck this trip anyhow."

I offered my hand in greeting, and received a hard grip and a shake that jolted my shoulder as he walked by to look things over.

He eyeballed the boat from a couple of angles, and then in fast motion began jacking her cradle up a few inches at each corner, sliding a block or plank underneath, then repeating this on the other side, then at the rear. Despite his speed he was careful doing this, for two reasons: because he took care with his work, and because even though *Daphie* (at fifteen and a half feet overall) was a relatively small wooden boat, she weighed about fifteen hundred pounds, half of it in the lead in the bottom of her keel. She could crush a guy.

Eventually, after Jack's ministrations *Daphie* was eighteen inches higher than she'd been, her cradle was sitting entirely on blocks, and with the trailer now free, he pulled it out from under her by hand, and ran it off to the side of the driveway. The dogs and I watched from the low stone wall; they were a little intimidated by Jack, recognizing in him a large fierce animal on a mission. They were happy to sit back with me, and observe.

"That ought to do," Jack said finally, leaping back into the truck cab and proceeding in one smooth motion to back his own trailer under the boat with inches to spare on either side. Then he was out of the cab and working the trailer's hydraulics, moving its four padded arms, one after the other, against the underside of *Daphie,* and elevating them slightly until she was off the ground and her cradle was free.

Then he braced her from below by sliding a five-by-five under her keel, pulled forward a little, and he and I threw *Daphie's* cradle on the back of the truck. *Daphie* was about to move, and it had taken him all of fifteen minutes to secure her for this new journey. She was to him, at the moment, something that stood between him and lunch. For me, however, a new lifestyle was about to be delivered to my small yard.

I had intended to stay behind him as he drove east, follow at a little distance to be sure nothing flew off the boat, that she was not shifting dangerously on the arms of the big trailer as it bumped along. But he lost me in the midmorning traffic on the two-lane state highway. I pulled over and bought some gas, and when I came down the little road to my cottage he was already there, leaning against his truck's grille with his arms crossed, waiting.

I pointed to where I wanted *Daphie,* and he put her where I'd indicated in one shot, and got busy lowering the boat onto her cradle. I went inside to heat some coffee. When I came out again, he was in a rare state of stillness.

"I need more cinda blocks," he said.

There were a few out back, buried under leaves along the foundation, and I got them for him, watched him stack them. In five minutes the boat was deployed, his rig parked along the street, and I was heading inside.

"I just gotta get my checkbook, Jack. Can I get you a cup of coffee while I'm at it?" I asked.

"Sure," he said.

"How d'you take it?" I asked.

"Black."

I headed inside and came back out with two cups of coffee.

"Gotta have a smoke with a coffee," he said, and fished a pack of unfiltered cigarettes out of his breast pocket.

"Jack, you've been moving boats around for fifteen years or so now, huh?" I said.

"I guess so."

"I hope they pay you well, because you're good at it," I said.

"Not much to it," he said, taking a drag, and looking toward the end of the lane for a moment.

"Nice little marsh you got down there, huh," he said.

"Yeah," I said. "You're from around here, right?"

"Yarmouth," he said. Yarmouth was a few towns farther out on the Cape. "Family's been up there three hundred years or so," he went on. "Course, they're trying to drive us out."

"How do you mean?" I asked.

"We own cranberry bogs and a bunch of bottom lands, me and my brothers, and they want it all for the water district, to keep it clean, but we're looking into selling the development rights so we can hold on to it." He took another drag on his cigarette, and a pull on the coffee.

"We used to do everything out there," he went on. "Grew berries, of course, but we'd hunt and fish in the river, and just live wild up there in the summer. That's all changed. The whole place is changing, what with all the new construction, and all the folks coming in and building a house where they have no idea that it used to be a farm or commons or Indian land or good oysterin' or whatever."

He paused to take another drag. I had never really spoken with him before.

"Three hundred years, huh?" I said. "My family's only been around here since 1928."

"Yeah, we're originals, do what we can to get by."

"You have some other line of business?"

"Oh I do some carpentry." He paused here and took a drag, and squinted at the sky where it was faintly lighter around the sun. "I used to fish a trip now and again, but that's a dead end."

"Fish are all gone, huh?" I said.

"All gone for guys like me. Some guys still find find 'em but you have to have spotters in planes for the swords, and side-scan sonar for the rest to track 'em well offshore, and the near-shore trips don't pay, and the herrin's mostly gone, not much of a run anymore. We used to eat a lot of them, years ago."

I noted that his cigarette was nearly gone. "Well, good luck holding on to that land," I said.

"Yeah, I think we're gonna do all right," he said. "We're getting something in the mail from the Nature Conservancy in a couple days. And I must go."

He finished his coffee in a gulp, handed me the cup, stamped the filterless butt into the sand alongside the road, took the check I offered, shook my hand, and leapt into the truck. As he did so I thought, "There goes a relic. One of those yeomen who Jefferson said would be the basis of the new nation."

But we on the Cape are losing these independents, who spend their time outside, working the land, or the rip over Horseshoe Shoal. Our meal is ground elsewhere.

5. Bill and Rafe

IN THE MORNING THE first thing I did was go see Bill Mayhew. Bill is one of the people around here who makes his living working on wooden boats. He builds them from scratch once in a while, and he repairs them. He keeps old ones going for a number of families around here. Not much has changed for Bill, who is in his early fifties, although when he was coming into the trade there were still many wooden vessels used for fishing of one kind or another. Now, his work is almost entirely on pleasure craft, and that's okay by him, as far as I can tell, because it's all wood and boats in the end.

Bill's shop is tucked back in the trees off Senegansett Road. Really what you have to do is get off Senegansett onto a small road that isn't signed, right by a big copper beech, and go up that road about four hundred yards until it turns to dirt, and then take a right and there you are. The number of buildings out there depends on what's in the yard. He might have a fifty-foot Alden something-or-other in there for a while, so he'll build a shed around that, and then after a couple years she's done and down comes the shed until the next boat comes along. Usually he has at least one big project going on, and several smaller ones to peck away at when the big one hits a snag. Then beyond the periphery of the jumbled boat sheds, which come together at odd angles, are various craft becoming more and more rotten, woebegone, and diffuse the farther out into the meadow they lie.

I pulled the old Saab into his drive at about eight-thirty in the morning, allowing him time for a cup of coffee and to figure things out with Rafe, his partner, before I entered. There were three big beech trees in the yard, noble and stolid, their trunks elephantine, smooth, subtly rippled as though muscled, and I could see that Bill and Rafe were both there—Bill's newer Toyota truck was parked in front of the house, and Rafe's green Dodge van was there too. Roland, Bill's sleepy English bull terrier, greeted me from the threshold of the house as I approached, and followed me into the main shed.

"Hey Bill," I said. "You back here?"

I was in a long, wide, barnlike room with morning light coming through seven old eight-over-eight-lighted windows mounted in the wall to my left. Under the windows ran a long workbench, about two and a half feet wide and thirty feet long, with wooden drawers underneath it. To my right was a big lathe, and beyond that a big planer. The machines were staggered in the space so that long objects could be passed through them, and I could see several hatches in the far wall where long objects could be passed through if they were longer than the room.

Next beyond the lathe and planer was an ancient drill press, and an even more ancient-looking band saw. I knew if I looked closely I would find the blades of these machines sharp, and that they would hum smoothly if turned on, their brushes and bearings fresh. At the back of the shed was an old wooden dinghy sitting on horses, in the midst of being refastened. It looked like it had been there awhile.

Under the machines on the floor were wood shavings, sawdust, and small scraps of wood. I could smell oil paint, gum turpentine, cedar, epoxy, pine tar, and (strangely) fresh bread. In the distance I could hear news on a radio.

"Who's there?" called out Bill, and I heard his feet approaching on the soft board floor.

"Dan Robb here, Bill. Just hoping to ask you a quick question or two."

Bill appeared at the far end of the shed, entering from another wing that went off at an angle to the left. He had a spare frame, stood about six foot two, with sandy blond hair, most of which remained. He kept it short, allowed to arrange itself. He wore jeans and light hiking boots, a sweatshirt over a heavy canvas shirt, with a battered down vest over that, patched in places with duct tape. His hands, the most remarkable part of any boatbuilder, were large, tanned, and expressive. He had all of his fingers.

"Dan. How are you? What's new?"

"Not too much," I said. "I've got a new old boat on my hands. I was hoping to ask you a question or two before you got a head of steam up."

"No danger of that this morning. We're meeting with a client who thinks he might want us to build a Rozinante, starting this spring, so we're just waiting on him till he can haul his carcass out of bed."

"He from around here?" I asked.

"Somewhere outside Boston. He's in a B&B over in town with the wife. Thought he'd be over around nine."

"You guys are giving the place a good cleaning then, huh?"

"Oh Jeez yeah," he said. "We were just putting a little bunting around the table saw. Come on out and have a cup of coffee and talk to Rafe," he said, as he retraced his steps and I followed. "He's bored and needs someone to gnash his teeth at."

We were now in another shed, this one about fifty-five feet long, with a high arched ceiling, roofed with clear plastic sheeting, built to accommodate a Concordia yawl off of which they had pulled the bottom two planks. It looked like they were refurbishing some of the frames in her.

"What's this, a forty-two?" I asked. I knew Concordia had made boats of varying lengths, many just over forty feet long. I could tell she was a Concordia by the shape of her hull, which was long, lean, beautifully sheer, and powerful.

"Thirty-nine," said Bill. "She looks bigger when you're looking up at her."

Rafe was standing by a drafting table that was set up at the end of the shed, looking at some drawings there, leaning on the table with both hands. He looked up as I walked in.

"Now tell me, Dan," he said as I walked in, "why in hell do you think that some of these guys don't want to get those town bogs along the Coonamessett out of cranberry farming and back in town hands as open space?"

"Mornin', Rafe," I said.

"I mean, where's the downside?" said Rafe. He was about five foot eight, had a big beard, deeply set brown eyes, and looked like a man from the old West, or maybe a holy man from an older time. He was fifty or so, wore brown duck overalls, work boots, a clean flannel shirt, and over that a worn but clean canvas work jacket. As he spoke he began quietly to count off his points on his fingers. "We take the leases back, there's no more pesticides going on the bogs, the bugs can come back, the trout can come back, the osprey can come back and fish there, the people can come back and fish there and get their dinner when they need it, people can walk along the river because it's theirs again, there's no more nitrogen fertilizer going on, so we get rid of the algae, the herrin' can get all the way up the run to spawn again, so that historical fishery is renewed and we can get a feed off that, too, the river's clean again, there's less *E. coli* in Great Pond to make swimmers ill, plus we can farm the bogs organically till the cows come home. I mean come on, where's the downside?"

"The downside," said Bill, crossing his arms on his chest, "is that somehow along the line taking care of the river got confused with being anti-Bush, and being a liberal, which is dumb, but that's how they're painting it. They're just mixed up, but that's how it's playing out."

"I know it," said Rafe. "But what I don't get is how being a conservationist came to be so mixed up with liberal politics in the first place. Teddy Roosevelt was a conservationist, not a liberalationist. He preserved Yosemite and Yellowstone and the Badlands and a whole bunch of others, and he was Republican through and through. Rock-ribbed. We've forgotten all about that side of things."

"You're right, Rafe, but the problem is that you're antibusiness. There's a farmer leasing those bogs, and he wants to keep farming," said Bill, glancing at me to see if I was attending the joust.

"I am not antibusiness," said Rafe, his eyes flashing. "I am probusiness. I am pro–making the place lovely so people frickin' flock to it, and it draws 'em in, right past the fish restaurant parking lot, where they drop seventy on dinner. That's the business end. And the bogs'll be in better shape for it—more flushing, more water, more trout, more fishermen. I tell you, the antiriver people are just foolish!" He folded his arms across his chest, stood straight up and relaxed, and looked us both in the eyes. He was looking for a friendly game of push hands.

"What do you think, Dan?" said Bill.

"It's a tough one," I said. "I can see both sides of it. I guess I'd like to see the river cleaned up. I lived in a cabin one summer in the woods right along the side of the river, in Hatchville. The bullfrogs were still loud at night, and every day the osprey worked a pool right upstream from me. It was a nice piece of water even then. Of course, at about that time a cleanup crew from the airbase in Bourne had put in a bunch of monitoring wells to track the plumes of benzene and jet fuel that were coming down from the old dumps, which are, what, about ten miles uphill. And then they put in wells to pump the plumes out of the ground before it got into the river. But the osprey didn't seem to mind—just kept fishing out there. Of course, I don't know how their chicks did."

"What about you, Bill?" asked Rafe, quietly, an amused look in his eyes.

"I'd like us to stop taking the side of one team or the other in this town. We're always on one side or the other. It's like we never got beyond playing football. 'You're with me or you're against me.' That's a junior high perspective on the world. We ought to be able to farm, preferably organically, and have a clean river, herring, osprey, trout, the whole deal. To say one defeats the other is horseshit."

"Okay," said Rafe, moving smoothly back to leaning over the bench. "I got my ya-yas out. You ought to watch your blood pressure there, Bill. Take a look at this boat, Dan. This boat will shut you up."

Communicating with Rafe was often an adventure. We turned to the drawings on the table, which showed the offsets for L. Francis Herreshoff's slim twenty-eight-foot ketch *Rozinante*. We all just looked at the lines of the boat for a minute or two, which in me produced a taste at the back of my tongue like sugar in darjeeling tea, full and sweet, complex. L. Francis was the son of Nat, the man who designed my boat, and in the opinion of many it would be hard to find a better-looking, better-sailing boat than the Rozinante.

I broke the silence after some moments.

"Has your man decided he definitely wants one?" I asked.

"Seems like it," said Bill, sighing. "We haven't signed anything yet, but he's talking strongly about it."

"Does he know how small she is down below? I mean, she's really only built for very simple living down there," I said.

"I'm not sure," said Bill. "He's reading *The Compleat Cruiser* this weekend, so we'll see what he has to say when he comes in. But he sounds like he really wants one."

"Would that keep you busy for the year?" I asked.

"Yup," said Bill. "It's not a big boat, but she's just as complicated as any other twenty-eight footer. Besides, I'd have to fix all of Rafe's mistakes."

At this Rafe's eyes widened.

"You gotta be kidding me," he bawled, smiling. "I'm the one who's always going out to find the chisel you heaved out in the grass after you split the what-and-so-ever." He pointed out to the boat bone meadow as he said this. I had seen the kind of work that Rafe could do, and knew that these two regarded each other as equals, but that Bill was willing to run the business on his property. Rafe, on the other hand, climbed in his van and drove to the harbor at the end of the day, rowed out to his boat, and left the paperwork behind.

"You want a cup of coffee, Dan?" said Rafe then, looking at me with one eye closed.

"Yes, please," I said. He took three steps, grabbed a battered mug that read "morning edition" from the shelf where it sat next to an epoxy dispenser, upended it to get any dust out, poured it full of black coffee from the pot that warmed on the counter there, and then said "Resin?" as he held the cup under the nozzle of the epoxy dispenser.

"No thanks, Rafe. Tryin' to cut down," I said. There was no offer of cream or sugar.

He handed over the cup of coffee, and then said, "So tell us what brought you out here this morning."

"Well," I began, "I've got a couple of questions about this boat I just put in my driveway."

"Shoot," said Rafe, leaning against the counter that held the coffeepot.

"Well, it's the old family boat, and I've got a deal to write a book about it. So I'm going to rebuild it, what of it needs rebuilding, and I wanted to ask you guys what you look for when you take one of them apart."

"First thing," said Rafe quietly, shaking his head slightly, "Don't do it."

"What do you mean?" I said.

"Just walk away," he said. "Leave it alone. You're doing fine. You don't need to get involved in all that. It'll suck you in and before you know it you'll be standing in a cold boat shed every day in the middle of winter breathing lead paint and fiberglass dust, and you'll die of black lung and silicosis and emphysema and everything else. Just back out."

Bill rolled his eyes.

"Rafey, he's just going to fix the one."

"Put the saw down, that's what I say," said Rafe. "Step away from the boat. These things have a way of gaining steam. Once the thing starts, it'll snowball, and then he'll wonder how he ever got into it."

Bill motioned me wordlessly over toward the Concordia.

"Take a look at this boat. See what we're up to here?" He pointed to the port side of her hull where they had begun to take out the old screws.

"Most boats of a certain age are the same. The fastenings start to go, and they tend to go fastest near the waterline. But they all go," he said.

"What we're doing with this one is replacing all the screws in her planks, putting one size larger in their place, and replacing some of the ribs where they've gotten a little rotten below the waterline."

At this he knelt down and pointed into the bilge of the boat, which we could see into, because they had removed the two lowest planks on either side.

"In a boat like this it's pretty common not to replace an entire rib," he said. "We'll just replace the bottom six feet or so. On a twelve-and-a-half, where the frames are so much smaller, we'd usually replace the whole frame, and, what year's your boat?"

"Nineteen thirty-nine," I said.

"A young one!" he said. "Yup, she's still probably going to need all new frames. Or most of them. And the transom will probably need some help. Why don't you get things opened up, give us a call, and one of us will come on over and look at it with you."

"I'll pay you your rate," I said.

"That'd be fine."

"I still think you'd be better off just not getting into it," said Rafe. "Concentrate on the writing."

"That's what he's frickin' trying to do, Rafey," said Bill.

"I know, Billy." Rafe's eyes widened a little again as he said this. "I'm just trying to argue so he can see if he really wants to get into it. See, if he hears me and then decides he still wants to go ahead with it, then he's that much more resolved."

I laughed at this. Rafe was a good guy.

"Hey, I'll let you guys get back to work," I said. "I'll give you a call in a couple of days. Thanks for the coffee."

"No problem. We'll put it on your bill," said Rafe, who then seized the post in the middle of the room, which ran up to the ridge, and held himself out horizontally, which position he was still in when I walked out the door.

"I can still do it today, Bill," I heard him say. "Better not mess with me. Try me tomorrow. Maybe I will have weakened by then." I bent down to tie my shoe, next to the drill press, and as I did so I heard him ease himself down from the post with a groan, and then say to Bill, "You know there's no frickin money in this," and Bill was then saying, "There sure isn't if we don't sell this guy his Rozinante this morning."

I found my way out through the two sheds, got in the car, backed out, and was just turning right onto the main road when a BMW pulled in from the left. Their client, perhaps. And I had gotten what I needed. I had made contact with the underground stream of boatbuilding energy that runs around here, and up and down the coast, made just enough contact with it to keep me going for the next few days while I got the boat unpacked and the shed built. I had the promise of a visit of inspection by one of the guys, and that would give me my initial direction. I could do this. Go out, make contact with persons in the know, accrue knowledge and resources, do the job. I could do this, this odd mission I didn't really understand. Maybe.

6. Resolve

I DROVE HOME FROM Bill and Rafe's along the three miles of sandy back roads, and by the time I was nearing home, everything about the boat project felt slightly wrong. Perhaps Rafe was right. I would be wed to this spit of land for at least another year (and maybe two) by this project, unable to leave until the boat was complete, scraping by on odd jobs while the words gathered and new ribs went in. I had already written a book about these parts—the hills and streets and thickets and beaches and waters around here—and revisiting the subject, even tangentially, well, the idea made me somewhat queasy.

I rolled down the window for the last mile, letting the cold air play over my face. As much as I loved the place, I felt hemmed in by it, by the deep history of my family, which dwelled also in the hills and shoreline. I needed a walk.

I pulled into my lane, coasted past the several small old frame houses (two capes, a bungalow, and a cottage smaller than my own), pulled into my drive, jumped out of the Saab, walked back out the lane and then to the left, downhill and toward the sea. I'd just stretch my legs a little.

The road was quiet, with marsh on either side and an occasional house vacant for the winter—it was my old paper route from boyhood, a route I'd jogged a thousand times—and led me after a quarter of a mile to a small beach.

I walked along the water's edge for fifty yards, and then walked out on a jetty that stuck thirty yards out into the waves; I stood at the end, looking across Buzzards Bay, and then down through the clear, faintly green water. Six feet—a fathom—below there was white sand.

I had by now mentally consigned two years to this boat project. I had to be reasonable: It might take that long. Maybe even three years. What of other plans, other ambitions? How had a boat so quickly become the center of things? I looked down into the water some more; it came onto the jetty with an irregular surge, small waves meeting their end there, rushing past the barnacles that gripped the brown rocks, falling into gaps between the stones to end in a jumble of water that receded and then rose again with the next wave. I watched this for ten minutes or so, and then turned and started back toward the beach.

Someone was walking toward me along the sand. A strong gait, toes out, slightly stooped. It was Conrad Burns, an older man, maybe eighty-two or eighty-three now, a local I'd known for years. He wore a corduroy cap, and his grey hair stuck out to the sides in tufts. He studied salt marshes, fiddler crabs, ribbed mussels, spartina grass—their interconnections. He was out for a walk as well, and stood at the base of the groin as I returned to the sand.

"Hello, Dan Robb," he said, "Find anything out there?" His English accent, from the north, near Newcastle, was light.

"Lotta water out there, Conrad," I replied, and then asked, "How are you, Sir?"

"Fine, thank you," he said, "You?"

"Fine as well," I said.

"Hmmm," he said, "Just out for a walk?"

"Considering a project," I said.

"What's that?" he said.

"Book about rebuilding an old wooden boat, its provenance, the craft of it."

"That's a hard one to sell," he said. He pushed his hands farther into his pockets. The wind picked up a little. He was about my height, but broader, thicker, rather more ursine. I had always respected his opinion.

"There are so many books out there about boats," he went on. "Better find another topic, something with more life!"

"I've already sold it," I said.

"Ah, that's good then," he said. "No need to question then."

But he already had, and I, out of respect for an elder, had allowed him to do so, and taken the subtle arrow in the chest, could feel the shaft sticking out through my shirt, the fletching trembling in the breeze. He leaned back on his heels, looked me in the eye. He had meant no harm.

"Hard life, that of the writer," he said.

"Not so hard," I said. "I skip out for a walk on the beach anytime I like."

"Ah but it is," he said, and his small brown eyes searched the sand at his feet.

"When I was in the British Army during the Second World War, I was never more content. I knew every day where to be, what to do, that my work was needed. Now, I'm my own boss. I keep on studying the little crabs, their respiration. I can go for walks anytime I like. Enough to drive you mad."

We talked a little more, and then parted ways, I retracing my steps, he continuing over the base of the jetty and on down the beach. Somewhere along the way I pulled the arrow out of my chest and threw it in the brush near a fire hydrant. I trudged most of the way home, stopped at another little beach, looked out at the water there, and noted that the small waves volunteered ceaselessly. At home, forty minutes after driving back from Bill's, I made a fire in the stove, lay down on the old green couch under the front window, and took a nap.

7. The Old House

I AWOKE AT TWO in the afternoon. Sleet was ticking onto the glass of the window above me, the sky was a deep grey, and I could hear the wind chimes in the front yard dinging in the wind. Another low had approached without my knowing it. Which was fine. I often ignored the forecast, preferring to look to the sky. I had ignored that as well.

I got up, reheated some soup, and thought some more about the boat. As I'd slept, I'd dreamt of an old family house up on Gansett Road. In the dream I stood in front of it, on a day as grey as this one, looking out to sea. Okay then. It was time for a walk to that house. Perhaps that would clarify things.

I dressed warmly—wool pants over long underwear, a Gore-Tex shell over a wool sweater, my ski hat, construction boots, a pair of heavy leather mittens—and when I walked out the front door there was a boat in my yard, by god.

As I came to the end of the lane, I felt the full force of the wind booming up from the little beach across the road. Thirty-five knots of wind easily, heavy with salt, and I had to lean into it until I was around the corner and into the trees. I wound north, up the road: the sky darkened and the wind thrummed through the telephone wires as the evening came on.

After a quarter mile on old tarmac, I cut over to the shore on a public right-of-way through the woods, and came out on the back of a small beach, where I headed north again, along the lumpy wrack line of eelgrass, sticks, and pieces of plastic rope. The tide was low, the waves came hard onto the gravel and coarse sand at the base of the beach, and when I raised my eyes from my feet I could see the breakers ahead, bashing themselves on the boulders that made up the rest of the shore I would walk. Then I was up on the boulders, stepping from one to the next, occasionally stepping over a tree trunk, a tangle of lobster fishing tackle, or a hump of eelgrass thrown high by the wind.

It wasn't far on the boulders—another quarter mile on their tops. The waves came on, breaking hard below me and sending mist into the air, and soon I saw the narrow path up the side of the bluff, and was quickly on top, and walking now away from the wind across a lawn toward a family house I had never lived in.

The house was big—a behemoth built in 1928 by a maiden great-aunt of mine. She had traveled to Spain, and liked the style there—stucco and green roof tile—and came back and built the house, the first on the road, a grand Mediterranean manse. And then she died.

There was also a smaller family house, right next door, built by my mother's parents in 1954. They'd sold the big house, and when my grandmother died in 1974, my mother and I lived in the smaller house for eight years, and then it too was sold. Now we, the surviving generations, lived in other smaller houses with no water view, and closed off parts of them in winter, and heated with wood, if we could, and sometimes recalled the grandeur of those former days.

As for these old houses, we looked at them now from the sea, gazing back at the shore from boats.

This perhaps was the crux of it, I thought, as I looked up at the big place, its windows reflecting some of the light still left in the western sky. Two green shutters had come undone, and opened and shut on their own across upper-story windows, banging in the wind. This was the place which many had worked hard to create, particularly the generations that came before the great-aunt "Sophie" who had built it.

Those ancestors had built steel mills in Worcester, had made what sacrifices that required, had used the labor of men to amass wealth, had moved the nation toward industrialization, had made wire to fence the range.

And both houses were gone now to others. I was trespassing on a lawn my mother had played on as a child. Turning back to the sea, I could look out on Gansett Bight, a small embayment formed by a point arching out to the southwest. Buzzards Bay lay beyond, dark blue-grey and raked by six-foot combers.

Once, in fall, I had been out in conditions like these, on a last sail in my old eighteen-foot fiberglass sloop. I had been running for Quissett, and was surprised by a squall which came down fast from behind as I gazed ahead. Suddenly the squall was driving the boat so hard I couldn't head into the wind and lower sail. I decided the rig would take the strain of the long reach in, but towards the end, as I rode down a long wave just off this stretch of coast, my starboard spreader had crumpled. This left the shroud on that side slack and the mast in danger of snapping. I came over quickly onto port tack (to put the strain of the sails on the port shroud) and lowered both sails as the boat pitched hard in the following sea.

Then, to steady the mast, I took the main halyard (the line used to raise the mainsail, which ran to the top of the mast) off the mainsail, shackled it to the starboard chainplate, and took up hard on it. The mast steadied enough not to break—by some grace not having sheared in the intervening minutes—and I raised the jib (the forward sail) again and scurried in on that alone, and then sat on the boat, now tethered to its mooring in the cove, and was thankful I had not been dismasted, that the boat had not swamped, that I had not had to swim for it through the storm. It had been close.

That happened right off the shore here. Those waters out there were mine, as much as anyone's. But this house—no. Nor the other smaller one, where I remembered my grandmother sitting in a green overstuffed armchair with the television playing *Lawrence Welk* and *What's My Line?* as she smoked Parliament cigarettes and blinked hard, her feet puffing out at the instep from very proper low-heeled shoes.

"Put the screen across the fire, won't you, Dear?" she would say, and "You must finish your soup, young man, or there will be nothing else for you."

She had died, as my grandfather had (before I was born), and their children had moved away, and their grandchildren had gone to other parts of the country. One cousin who grew up here (just down the road) called the other day from her home in Atlanta to say she was getting married. Atlanta!

The wind was relentless, now blowing sleet hard enough that I could only look at the ocean for a moment before turning away. History along here was relentless, too: Through much of the 1800s there were saltworks on this land near the shore, windmills pumping seawater up through hollow logs to begin a week's descent through evaporating tanks, 360 gallons of seawater eventually reduced to a bushel of salt. The locals had been forced to the industry—needing salt to preserve the fish they caught—when the English blockade during the American Revolution had cut them off from their salt trade with the West Indies.

All of this land then was woodlot and rough meadow, leading down to the saltworks by the bay, long before anyone in my family showed up. Before that it had been hardscrabble farm, and prior to that woods where Manomets and Nausets and Narragansetts lived, took game, and looked across the bay.

I walked up closer to the house, which I'd worked on several years before, reconditioning windows for the present owner. I peered in through the French doors that opened onto the patio. The entrance hall was bare but for a great dark Spanish chest, and a couple of big wooden arm chairs. The stairs, I knew, would resonate hollowly if I were walking up them now, and I would feel uneasy on the second floor, as if someone were watching me walk down the hallways, as the wind shuddered outside.

I turned and looked out at the bay again. Long windrows of foam lay on the waves as they came down from the northwest, stretching across the bay from New Bedford. They broke out of sight, below the brushy lip of the bluff.

Daphie was pretty much all that was left of that life: summers on the Cape, the men in khaki and loafers, the women in sundresses and espadrilles, playing croquet; or, the men in fishing hats with a fly or two hooked in the band, out on the twenty-five-foot fishing launch *Notla*; or any of the above people racing *Daphie,* or having cocktails on one patio or another overlooking the sea, chatting by a flower bed, golfing, larking about.

I'd seen pictures of the men on fly-fishing trips to Canada, or gunning somewhere for duck, frozen by a photograph in their return over the crest of a hill, shotgun over a shoulder and game bag on belt, silhouetted by the sunset behind them. In those days they paid someone else to work on the boat.

I'd grown up differently. We heated the second, smaller house when we lived in it—my mother and I—with a woodstove in the kitchen. Winters were spent in three rooms, with the rest of the house shut down, pipes drained, rooms cold. The first trip in the morning was to the woodpile, the second a dash upstairs into the unheated section for clean clothes. I mowed the lawn and cut the hedges—badly at that—and we never had a boat we didn't maintain ourselves. Odd. Quite a difference there. And then it was time to go, sell that house, and move inland.

In the gale, which had eased a bit, I walked across the big lawn, leaning into the wind, down-climbed the bluff, and then picked my way back through the long boulder field with the surf at its edge until I regained the beach, where the receding waves chirred down through the gravel.

After a short walk back through the woods and then over the dark roads, I returned to the cottage, passing *Daphie* as I did. She sat off to the side of the driveway, her tarp pocketing softly in the wind. What did that old boat represent, that had me flinching? I wasn't scared of night, or of hiking into the desert alone for a week. But that old boat had a hold of me.

On my desk, as was my habit, I had a stack of clippings from newspapers and magazines that friends had recommended. Once I'd made a fire in the stove and a cup of tea, I pawed through the pile, seeing what was there. A memory of something in that stack was moving me to it. All I could remember was a tiger.

Then I found it: a magazine with a drawing of a tiger on the cover, and a sticky note directing me to two quotes from an ecologist named Paul Shepard. I'd copied them out longhand:

"As a species we are Pleistocene, owing nothing or very little to the millennia of urban life, or to rustification with cereals and goats. . . ." "Like foxes and crows, we are omnivorous, edge forms."

I read them over several times as I sat in the chair by the stove, which ticked a little as it warmed up.

"Pleistocene, owing . . . little to the millennia of urban life." That sounded right. I certainly felt more allegiance with crows and foxes than with most of my neighbors. Moreover, it was, it seemed to me, getting at what the boat represented.

In the 1700s there had been a proposal to build a wall across the center of the Cape to keep marauding wolves from the outer part. This proposal was defeated because those on the main part of the Cape feared the increased lupine pressure this would place on them. Clearly, I had not known the Cape in those times. Yet if when dreaming I were chased by wolves or bears through forest paths, or along a shoreline, it could only be along paths I know in the woods here, or along these shores, or through the meadow and dense thicket of the islands southwest of here. Once, indeed, this land *had* been wild. In a sense it still was.

Once you were three yards from shore the sea could be as wild as you wanted it. I'd lost a few friends out there, two close to shore, and one somewhere between Bermuda and the Bahamas. I also knew a man who, not long ago, stumbled off a houseboat in Great Harbor in the dark of an early morning, and was rescued by chance miles out to sea, having been swept out through the Hole in the night. He was found, still swimming, at midmorning, a small creature in the vast.

But it was something else, something molecular, that spoke to me in Shepard's words, the same thing perhaps that drives my friend Nick to hunt, and many of my friends to go into the backcountry—a need that city life has yet to press out of us.

And I *like* that Shepard, who is correct in his assessment, recognizes that our mechanism was refined to respond to the demands of life as hunter-gatherer, rather than as bean counter. Ah, but there is a wisp of the old life even in the description of the new.

I passed the night sleeping fitfully and then awakening at intervals to read *The Ascent of Nanda Devi,* by H. W. Tilman and to listen to the hail ticking onto the windowpanes.

8. *A Start*

THE NEXT MORNING, WHICH was Saturday, the weather had moderated, the ground was clear of snow, and the sun was shining. I was up early, pulled the yellow tarp off the boat and undid the screws that held together the hodgepodge of plywood scraps that covered the boat beneath the tarp. The first thing I noted was that the mast, lying fore and aft under the weight of the rough roof, had split the coaming—the mahogany rails that ran along both sides of the boat—where it met at the front of the cockpit. I had fixed this joint twenty years before, as a teenager, and I could see that the screws I'd put in had lost their grip to the weight of the mast, and that the bungs I had sunk to cover the screw heads had popped out as well. *Merde.*

I pulled off more of the temporary roof, and was then greeted with a difficult sight for those of us who love boats. *Daphie* was full of leaves, sticks, and trash to a depth of about two feet. The compost did look fairly dry. Nothing for it but to get it out of there.

A partial inventory of her stomach: a cubic yard of leaves and twigs, fourteen old paper coffee cups, and at the bottom, an inch of mud; five mouldering life jackets; one ten-pound Danforth anchor; one grappling hook; three old oars—serviceable; two good bronze oarlocks; one lobster pot buoy; fifty feet various line, half of it polypropylene—a dangerous and unforgiving sort of line which I chucked; one rotten sisal anchor warp—sixty feet; one empty Prell shampoo bottle; one green plastic army man (two inches tall) in the act of throwing a grenade; one dented can Budweiser beer—full.

Up forward, in the small fo'c'sle under the little plywood deck, a whole other universe greeted me: there was "flotation" up there—what had been a stack of Styrofoam blocks. These had been reduced to a slush of styrofoam beads, mouse dung, mouse urine, and whatever other scraps the critters had thought would brighten the place up. I put on my respirator, bagged most of the mess, and vacuumed out the rest.

So the boat was unpacked. It was noon on a Saturday. This was a huge accomplishment for one as overawed by symbolic acts as I. I had begun the rebuild. But what had to happen now was a shed, pronto, before the precipitation (always just over the horizon on the Cape) asserted itself. And I had not yet settled on a shed design, largely because the thought of the visual commitment to the project that this would represent scared the crap out of me. People would *see* that the project had commenced, and *ask* me about it. I knew I would put off this real indicator of a start as long as I could, and I knew I had to go ahead.

9. *January: Shed*

I THOUGHT ABOUT THE shed for a week. Then I put a new brown tarp over the boat and ruminated for another week. The holidays came and went.

During the day, I mulled the shed over as I ate my meals and drove around, went for a walk, went for a run. Lying in bed at night, I twitched through images of sheds: gabled roofs, Quonset huts, greenhouses. In my mind they all blew down and rolled into my neighbor's yard, caught fire after being ignited by an errant spark from the chimney. That was the end of the project, I was run out of town as a menace.

Finally, early in the New Year, I decided to break the spell and visit my friend Sean. He was in the midst of building a thirty-six-foot ketch of his own design but close to the lines of an L. Francis Herreshoff Diddikai, a double-ender (an exceedingly seaworthy type, designed to weather seas from bow or stern with equal aplomb) made to sail around the world. He'd been working on the boat for eight years, and I wasn't sure where it stood. I called him on Saturday morning, around ten, and he picked up.

"Hello."

"Sean, it's Dan Robb."

"Say, Dan. What's going on?"

"Not too much. Listen, I've got to build a shed for my boat, and I remember you telling me you were pleased with the one you built. Any chance I could come by and check it out?"

"Sure. I'll be here for a couple of hours. Why don't you come on over?"

"Now?" I said.

"Sure," he said.

Sean lived in a house two and a half miles north of me. His place was off the coast road on a low, wooded peninsula, most of which was conservation land. Along one side of this peninsula he owned a stripe of land vaguely above sea level. The only sign of his presence from the road was a narrow dirt drive that headed off at a slant to the west, into the woods.

He had inherited the place from his grandfather, who had built the house himself—a simple Cape with a room off one side that held a big kitchen. Sean's wife, Meghan, an emergency room nurse, lived with him. Sean built houses and additions once in a while when he needed money, and did some surveying, but he seemed to have six months of the year to do what he pleased. He made this possible by living simply, heating his place with wood, maintaining it himself, and perhaps by keeping himself out of trouble by working on the boat.

It had snowed a half-inch since breakfast, and the roads were lined with white as I drove along the coast until at the apex of a bend I saw Sean and Meghan's dirt drive, not driven on yet since the snow.

About a hundred yards into the woods, I pulled into a space next to Sean's truck. Meghan's car was not there—she'd left earlier for work.

The wind was light, coming through trees that stood between the house and a marsh fifty yards beyond. Sean was in the shed—I could hear him banging on something in *there*, in his version of my nemesis: in *The Shed*.

His shed, which was about twenty feet from the front bumper of the Saab, was an extended Norman arch covered with clear plastic. I'd never looked closely at it before, during my few visits. What else had I neglected to notice?

As I stood outside, I could see that he had built up the struts from two pieces of one-by-three strapping, bent into a slight curve, and separated by blocks of wood. He'd then stood these up in pairs on either side of a ridge beam. How simple. And then he'd covered the whole thing in clear plastic sheeting, through which I could see the hazy hulk of his boat. I rapped on the door he'd framed into the south wall.

"Hello!" I said.

"That you, Dan?" he said from within.

"Yep."

"Come on in. I'm just banging around. Not getting much done," said Sean.

Once in, I shook his hand. "What's goin' on?" he asked.

"Not too much," I said. "You?"

"I'm just trying to figure out a pattern for my chain plates, so I can have them forged by a guy in Wareham."

Chain plates are the fittings screwed, bolted or otherwise fastened to the hull of a boat, to which are secured the shrouds and stays which brace the masts. They are the anchors for the vertical spars, and like the pitons of a mountain climber, must not fail. Sean was banging a piece of copper flashing into a shape that he would then deliver along with measurements to the foundry.

The shed was impressive, but the boat that rose within was more so. The hull was done, as was the deck, and the doghouse (the cabin top). She was a powerful double-ender, with a classic Herreshoff form—high, fine entry, beautiful sheer, good deep keel, and a gracefully pointed stern that would make her exceedingly seaworthy.

"Man, Sean," I said. "She looks like she's about done!"

"Nope," he said, typically low-key. "She's half done. Maybe."

Sean stood about five ten, and was built like a halfback, which he had been in high school. He was about my age, but seemed somehow more settled in himself than I, perhaps because Meghan grounded him well, perhaps because he had a place that was paid off, and perhaps because he had a round-the-world boat taking shape in his backyard.

"Half done?" I said.

"Climb on up," he said, gesturing to the stepladder that leaned against the hull at the stern, "and take a look below. You'll see."

I did, and as I looked forward through the hatch into the doghouse and down the companionway, I saw a raw hull, ribs, floor timbers, and nothing else. He'd built the shell, but had yet to add a sole (the floor), bunks, bulkheads, cabinets, an engine, a sink, a reefer, a head—any of the interior.

"What about the rig?" I asked. "Have you done any of that?"

"Well, I built the mizzenmast, because I'd never built a mast and I wanted to see how that would go. I've still got to build the mainmast and the three booms. That'll go fast. It's the interior that's going to take time—figuring all of that out. But you've come for the shed. What's up—you got a new boat?"

"The old family twelve-and-a-half. I've got it in the driveway, under a tarp, and I'm going to rebuild her. But I need a shed first," I said.

"Cool," he said. And gesturing at the innards of his shed, he went on. "This thing has worked out well. I laid down four-by-four pressure-treated sills in a rectangle, pounded in some three-foot stakes to anchor them, and then I made up the struts—you can see how—and screwed them to the ridge beam, which is just a piece of pine one-by-five. Then I ran some bracing along the sides, wrapped the sucker in plastic, put in the door, left some gaps in the plastic at the ends for ventilation. And that's about it."

"How often do you have to redo the plastic?" I asked.

"Every three years, more or less. I've redone it twice, now,"

he said, "and it's been through some serious blows, no problem."

"Would you build the same shed again?" I asked.

"Nah," he said. "I'd get one of those aluminum-braced
Quonset-shaped jobs you cover with a big tarp. They're easier
to take down and put up, and they're reusable."

I was surprised by this last comment, but it didn't set me
back; I knew I could build a shed like this one, and that I *had*
to build a shed. I couldn't write a book about restoring a boat
if I didn't build the shed. But I was curious about a couple of
other things.

"So Sean," I said, "what have you framed *her* with?"

"White oak. And for the floor timbers, too, and deck knees,
and the stem and the deadwood. All white oak," he said.

"And what about the planks?" I asked.

"Philippine mahogany," he said. I could tell that being able
to say "Philippine mahogany" pleased him.

"Where'd you get that?"

"I got to talking to a guy whose wife works with Meghan,
and he said he had all this beautiful wood in his barn, all stick-
ered and set aside. He bought it at an estate sale, and it sat for
ten years, and he just looked at it, and then realized he was
never going to use it for anything. So he gave it to me."

"Wow," I said.

"Yeah," said Sean. "That's what I said."

And then we just stood there for a minute or two as I
looked the boat over. There is something about standing in the
shadow of a large boat under construction that is close to what
it must be like to stand next to a comatose elephant, or an
anesthetized whale. There is a life in there, but it is subdued,
hardly detectable. After all, the planks have yet to be caulked,
the decks are not yet paid, gaps between things pertain every-

where, and there is no question yet of seaworthiness. But the form has begun to coalesce. Nearly all of the elements that will make the boat capable of crossing an ocean have been assembled, even if the force that finally unifies a life and brings it rumbling to consciousness has not yet been activated. You can begin to see how she'll move, how she'll shrug off a sea, how the stern will finish the run over a wave, how the water will come together in the wake. You can begin to see.

"You want to come in for a cup of tea?" Sean asked after a bit, and I was quick to accept. Harry, his Scots terrier, met us at the door and barked hard in excitement. I took a seat in a large weathered armchair that sat in the northwest corner of the sitting room. Along the middle of the west wall was a fireplace. A small fire smoldered there, and I saw there was a bulldog lying half in the fireplace, snoring.

Sean came in the room with a pot of tea, and a box of cookies, and sat down in a rocking chair nearer the fire, and without looking at the dog, said, "Robbie, don't burn your nose."

The bulldog stirred, picked up his head, snuffled, and lay back down, a hot coal inches from his snout.

"Robbie likes the heat," said Sean.

"I didn't know you had a bulldog," I said.

"Yeah, got him a couple of years ago from the pound. My grandfather always had a bulldog, and he seemed like he'd fit in. Harry likes the company, and Robbie has a great personality, though he has odd habits." At the mention of his name, Harry came booming out of the entryway, where he'd been sniffing my boots, and skidded to a stop under Sean's chair, where he looked out at me from between Sean's legs.

"Hah," said Sean. And then, "Lie down, Pal," which Harry did.

There were a couple of questions that I'd wanted to ask Sean, and as he poured the tea, I peeled off the first one.

"So, why the Diddikai, Sean, if you don't mind my asking. I mean, it's not a big boat to sail a long way—you think you guys are going to have enough room?"

"Well, you're right," he said. "It's not huge, and I've wondered a lot if we'll want something bigger, but I was taken with the design—I looked at one a couple of years before I started, and there was something so strong and efficient about the boat that I felt, if nothing else, I'd enjoy building it a lot, getting to know the form of it. You know, we may sail this boat a long way, or perhaps we'll just wind up taking it across the pond, and dick around the Med for a summer, and call it good. Who knows. Maybe we'll sell it and buy some 'glass boat with a living room and a laundry. But I knew that this boat would keep me interested in the process."

He looked out the window toward the northwest for a moment, as Robbie groaned and stretched his front paws out into the ashes, and Harry looked for a crumb.

"I guess I also have a bit of the monk in me," he said, looking me in the eye. "I'm not sure I want to have space for a hell of a lot of stuff. Two good bunks, a table to write at, some way to bathe, a small galley, space to store provisions. You know, keep it lean. But all of that goes out the window if we have kids. Then this boat is too small. We might be able to fit a kid up in the fo'c'sle, but that's pretty tough duty in a blow.

"I don't know," he went on. "The older I get, the nuttier the whole project seems. Ten years ago, before my grandfather died and left me this place, I had my truck, my tool belt, my climbing boots, and my tele skis. That was all I needed."

The tea was a good black tea, and the fire and the dogs and the simple Cape house with its view of trees and marsh made me feel I might have landed anytime in Falmouth between 1700 and 1900. I remarked on this, and Sean said, "Yeah, my grandfather liked a hearth, and he built this house himself, over a few summers. He was a Scot, and I guess I carry on his pattern. I think he would have approved the boat. It's got the same efficiency he liked." He paused here, and scratched Harry's ears, which made the little black dog relax.

"He studied the marsh out here," he went on. "That was his work at the MBL [the Marine Biological Laboratory, in Woods Hole]: how the mussels benefited the crabs by holding the peat together with their byssal threads, how the crabs benefited the spartina grass by aerating its roots with their burrows, how the roots of the grass benefited the marsh by holding the peat together, and how the grass filtered the water, as did the crabs and the mussels, and everybody shat and pissed and fertilized everybody else—I think it appealed to his sense of the same kind of thing."

Suddenly there was commotion from the fireplace, and Robbie was up and barking at a coal that had rolled out of the fire and singed his nose.

"Calm down, Pal," said Sean. Robbie, however, was an animist, convinced that the fire had wronged him, and so spoke loudly his perturbation. When I left some time later, however, he was back to sprawling against the andirons. Sean walked me out, where I thanked him for showing me his shed. He was again banging on something in there as I pulled out, practicing his odd faith. So this was boatbuilding.

10. Building a Shelter

I WAS HOME BY 11:30 A.M. I pulled a measuring tape out of my tool belt (always inside the trunk of the Saab unless it was around my waist) and ran it up into the snow-laden sky above the boat. Small flakes fell down around the upstanding tape. Twelve feet looked like more than enough room. I'd buy a few bundles of twelve-foot strapping and get started.

The lumberyard (called "Wood Lumber" in one of the odder coincidences of name and trade I've run across) was four miles away to the north. It was 12:10 when I rolled through the gate and cranked down my window as Lenny the gate man approached in his plaid winter cap. He grimaced at me and said, "We're closed in five minutes back here, Pal."

"I know, Lenny. Sorry buddy. Last-minute plans."

"Yeah, yeah, yeah. Bah humbug, Pal," he said.

But I knew where I was going, and parked the car, and headed for the little workmen's room in the corner of the back shed, which housed two levels of wood stacked in a myriad of bays. Frank was there at the desk under the Makita-girl poster, sitting quietly, looking out the door. Above him, she stood brandishing two shiny blue Makita power drills. She had two massive and perfectly round silicone-implant breasts on her front side (thank god they'd installed them on the right side) covered by a Makita-blue bikini top with panels the size of butterfly wings. The office smelled of sun-baked wood and doughnuts.

"How you doin', Frank?" I asked.

There was a pause as he thought for a moment.

"Good."

Then there was another long pause as he stroked his mustache and considered me with a bemused look. Finally, he said, "You?"

"Good. I just need two bundles of twelve-foot strapping. Wood Lumber charge."

He wrote it up, tore the slip out of the machine, and handed it to me.

"What you building?"

"A shed."

"Ohhh. Hmmm."

He stroked his mustache again for a moment. Finally he looked at me and said, "Lightweight," with no rise of tone at the end to make it a question. It was a statement.

"You got it. Boat shed. Temporary."

At this he nodded. His eyes smiled. We were done.

So I went out and grabbed a couple of bundles of twelve-foot larch strapping from the back shed, threw them on the roof rack, tied them down, stapled a red plastic pennant on the end of one bundle, and drove out again. Lenny stood manning the gate, ready to shut it as I left. It was 12:15. I lowered my window as I pulled up to him, and handed him my receipt. He eyeballed it, looked at the wood on top of the car, and then punched the paper with a little machine that left the outline of a man holding a bunch of flowers. As he did this he held the paper inside the window, so that the little paper man landed on my shirt.

"Thanks, Lenny," I said.

"Bah humbug," he said, with a faint smile.

I had the idea that I would finish the shed during the remainder of the day, although that was wishful thinking, particularly because I'd forgotten to buy the plastic sheeting I needed to enclose it.

The real issue, of course, was getting past my intimidation about building the shed in the first place. Prior to visiting Sean, I had dilly-dallied for two weeks, often late at night, worrying about this goddamned shed. Before falling asleep I would stare at the ceiling in the little bedroom, and see there the simple light fixture, a bulb covered by a globe of frosted glass with a pattern of leaves in relief on its surface. A few bugs had gathered in its bilge, visible as black specks from below, and all was bathed in the faint green glow of the light-emitting diode on the transformer for my laptop, which sat on the bureau to my right. In this strange light I imagined all of the worst-case scenarios, and the headlines.

MAN'S POOR EXCUSE FOR SHED CARTWHEELS ABLAZE
OUT OF YARD, REDUCES NEIGHBORHOOD TO ASHES.

LOCAL FOLLY: MAN FOUND BURIED ALIVE IN
SHED AFTER DISAPPEARING FIVE WEEKS BEFORE.
SAYS HE "THOUGHT I'D JUST BUILD IT MYSELF."

Why did this loom so large? It didn't make sense. I'd built additions, porches, greenhouses, chimneys, whole houses, barns. A temporary shed shouldn't be a problem. I had to get to work.

I was home in fifteen minutes. First I arranged eight landscaping timbers—pressure-treated fence posts that were on my property when I bought it, and finally seemed to have a use—in a rectangle in the melting snow around the boat. These would serve as a foundation. I spiked them together with Five-inch galvanized nails toed in from the sides, and pounded three-foot spikes of pressure-treated two-by-four into the ground at each corner and at the midpoint of each of the longer sides. These spikes would serve as anchors. I nailed these to the sills with sixteen-penny galvanized framing nails.

Then I set up the jig I would use to bend the strapping. I found a twelve-foot two-by-four in the pile I kept along the back fence, and laid that down near the front of the boat. Then I screwed a three-foot two-by-four to it, so it jutted out at one end, forming a jig shaped like a big *L*. Then I screwed a block of two-by-four to each end of the L, and one in the middle of the long section, and I was ready. *If* all went well, I would be able to make the strapping bend from the top of the L gracefully across the block at the midpoint and then down to the block at the end of its foot. At this point a dim sun had begun to show itself through the low clouds.

I grabbed a piece of strapping, caught it behind the first block, bent it carefully across the fulcrum, and tucked it behind the block at the end of the L. It stayed! Didn't crack! I put another length of strapping alongside that first piece, forced blocks of two-by-four between them at five points, and screwed it all together with galvanized decking screws.

And when I popped it out of the jig, it held its shape. Eureka! I had an arching strut that felt strong, and was relatively light. I walked it over to the boat and stood it up amidships on one of the sill timbers. It reached well over the boat, curving up to my imaginary ridgepole. This would work. Eleven more of these and I would be home free.

So, I put another piece of strapping in the jig, bent it, and watched it snap at the fulcrum. Shit. I tried again. Same result. And again. *Snap snap snap snap snap.* By the time I'd run through my stock of twenty pieces of strapping I'd managed to build three more struts, and to break twelve pieces in half. What the hell? Toward the end of the carnage I noted that the sun had set behind the bungalow across the street. My yard was in shadow, and had cooled twenty degrees from its high point when I'd first come back from the lumberyard. That was the problem. I needed to keep the wood warm and limber.

I would have to continue on Monday, when the lumberyard reopened. I covered the boat with the tarp for the night, and went inside, chastened but resolved to continue.

11. Shed: Done

CONTINUE WITH THE SHED I did, rolling into the lumberyard at 9 A.M. or so on Monday. Lenny was there at the gate. I lowered my window.

"Hey Lenny, what're you doing up so early?"

"Bah humbug," he said.

"Lenny," I said, "There's only a hundred and eighty-two shopping days til Christmas. You aware of that?"

"Not if they drop the bomb on us, guy," he said, smiling at me.

He had me there. All I could do was drive on. I bought three more bundles of twelve-foot strapping. I had a whole bundle to break and still have enough to make the struts. On the way out Lenny checked my receipt and made sure the punchout (a little paper silhouette of Batman, this time) fell on my lap.

"Thanks, Lenny," I said.

"Bah humbug," he said.

It was about 9:30 when I got back home and began the process of making struts, again, being careful to keep the strapping in the mild sun as I did this. I broke just one piece, and soon had the twelve struts I figured I'd need for the shed.

The next step was to cobble together a twenty-foot ridgepole, which I did by laying down two ten-foot pieces of old two-by-four, end to end, and scarfing them together with a couple of four-foot two-by-four cheeks. This made a twenty-foot beam. Then I fished a couple of twelve-foot posts made up of doubled two-by-fours out of the lumber pile. I had used these in staging I'd built to shingle a house, and they had been lying around ever since. I stood these up plumb at either end of my rectangle of foundation timbers, and then held them there with a couple of two-by-four braces. This was rough carpentry at its finest.

Then I screwed the ridgepole to the upright posts, one end at a time, and I was ready to lay my prebent struts along the sides, bowed out, so they would come together along the ridge beam like the ribs of a whale along a backbone. Which I did, and screwed them on, and added horizontal bracing between

The Shed, with boat inside.

the struts. Then I spread an old tarp folded long and thin along the top of the ridgepole to take care of rough edges that might puncture the plastic wrap, and I began to wrap the shed.

It took three passes, beginning at the bottom. Each layer was held on by a few staples, with the final pass draped over the ridge. Then I stapled two-inch-wide strips of old shingle onto the outside of the struts to hold the plastic securely.

And it held, and seemed to work. Time to get Bill over for a look.

12. Consultation

I CALLED BILL AS soon as I was done with the shed, which was at about four in the afternoon. He answered, sounding weary.

"Hello," he said.

"That Bill?" I asked.

"Yup," he said.

"Dan here. Wondering if I can get you over to look at this boat when you have a chance."

"How about now?" he asked.

"You sure?"

"I gotta get the heck out of here," he said. "I've been waiting for some epoxy to go off so I can get at it with a grinder and it ain't. Think I must have let the can freeze this winter. I dunno. But I've cut as many bungs as I can stand to cut while I wait."

"Well, now would be great," I said.

"I'll see you in a few," he said, and hung up.

That was remarkable. Although it is good, if you're a trades-man, to get out and look at somebody else's problems. I suppose it's good if you're anybody. Ten minutes later he was in the drive in his pickup, which was a Japanese two-wheel-drive manual shift with a logo on the door, "Mayhew Boatbuilders, Senegansett, MA," in narrow gold letters.

He strode up to the shed in the same clothes he'd been wearing the other day, produced an awl in his right hand, walked through the opening I'd left in the plastic, and jammed the spike into the bow of the boat.

"Stem's solid there," he said.

"No time for hand shaking, huh?" I said.

"Oh, sorry," he said, sticking out his hand, which I shook. "Yeah, I needed to get out of the shop," he went on. "One of those days."

"Rafe driving you nuts?"

"No, not today. He's out on his own today, checking out a double-ender a guy in Woods Hole wants us to cold-mold for him."

He was referring here to a practice where one takes an older wooden boat, shores up the hull, and then encases it in two or more layers of thin strips of wood, the second layer running in direction counter to the first, with epoxy gluing it all together. This wood-epoxy shell is then finished off with gelcoat, which results in a wooden boat which feels like wood and looks like wood (on the inside, anyway) but which looks and acts like fiberglass on the outside. The hull is suddenly immaculate, maintenance free, and leak free. It also becomes a much stronger boat, all for the addition of a shell around the hull a half an inch thick.

"I didn't know you guys did a lot of that," I said.

"We don't do it much, but it isn't real hard, and it does seem to be a good way to go."

"What do you think of working with the glue?" I asked.

"It's not so bad, but talk to me in thirty years when I've grown my second head, then I'll tell you what I think," he said. "Both of us will. So let's see what we got here."

He walked all the way around the boat, stopping here and there to look at details and to poke his awl into the hull.

"The planks go all the way fore and aft on this side," he said. "That's good. And the stem is fine," he said, poking again into the piece of oak that formed the leading edge of the bow. "The planks are continuous on this side, too," he went on, as he completed his circle around the boat. "Good."

"Everything's a little dry, but that's okay," he said, continuing to walk around the boat, "and the planks aren't pulling away from the frames much. This piece here is just filler," he said, poking at a two-foot chunk of oak at the forward end of the keel that was clearly gonzo.

"That can come right off. Cut a new one, screw it right back on there, and fair it out," he said. "No problem."

"The deadwood," he went on, poking at the big slabs of oak that made up the keel between the hollow part of the hull and the lead at the very bottom, "looks good, too. You know, Dan, I've seen a lot worse. But I can see that some of these planks are coming away from the frames [Bill, like many boatbuilders, calls ribs "frames"], so I think you have at the very least a complete reframing and refastening project on your hands."

As he said this he poked his nose over the gunwale, and looked down into the bilge.

"Oh Lordy yes, look at that. Those frames are just about to dry up and blow away." He went on, "I tell you what, man. You're going to need to replace most of those frames, which means taking off this cap rail." As he said this he tapped the thin piece of mahogany that formed the "rail" of the boat, the rim around the edge of the cockpit. "You gotta do that so you can get at the tops of the frames. You're also going to have to cut the rivets which hold the bottoms of the frames to the floor timbers, and split those frames right out of there."

The floor timbers were trapezoids of oak held perpendicular to the top of the keel by long bronze bolts. At intervals of every ten inches or so along the spine of the boat down in the bilge there was a floor timber. A frame was riveted to each end of each timber (one on either side), and the frames then rose in graceful curves up to the gunwales of the boat, with the planks screwed to the frames and running horizontally. It was a simple, strong way to build a boat (sometimes called "carvel-built") and as Bill assessed the boat's structure it lost some of its mystery, and with that its ability to intimidate me.

"How do I get at the floor timbers?" I asked.

"Well, if I were you," he said, standing quiet now in a mote of sun with his arms crossed, "I'd take off her two bottom planks on both sides. They're going to need refastening anyway, and once they're off, you'll be able to get right in there and see what you need to do."

I took this in, seeing that taking off the bottom two planks on each side would indeed make things vastly easier, allowing me to reach into the bilge (where all the action was) from the outside of *Daphie.* But it was also going to be weird, because once those four planks were off, the whole upper part of the boat would be supported only by the frames, without the skin of planks holding it together at the waist. This would be like seeing a person reduced to skeleton through the lower part of her abdomen, while she retained her torso and the rest of her body. But I would adjust to it. This was, after all, the only way to health for *Daphie.*

"One last question, Bill," I said. I actually had three.

"Yup," he said, and looked back at me with his eyes open wide.

"Would you replace the keel bolts?" This was a question I dreaded asking, as replacing the keel bolts could mean a huge investment of time: I would need to get new ones made, and then install them somehow under the floor timbers. The keel bolts held the heavy oak and lead keel to the rest of the boat, so they were critical components. As I asked this I had visions of lying crushed on the sand under the lead keel after it had fallen off the boat.

See, I knew that to replace the bolts I'd probably have to remove that lead keel (somehow) and then recast it, which would mean making a mold from the original, setting that mold into the sand on the beach, cutting up the old keel and then melting it in a kettle over a fire, pouring the old molten lead into the mold for the new keel, and hoping all went well. If I were still upright and breathing after that whole scenario, I'd still have to tap new holes for the new bolts in the new lead keel, and then reinstall the new 750-pound behemoth—all of which process increased the possibility for disaster and mayhem.

RIVER OF MOLTEN LEAD ENGULFS COASTAL
COMMUNITY: AMATEUR BOATBUILDER IMMOLATED.

"No, I'd leave those bolts alone," he said. "You could take one out and have a look at it, but in my experience they're usually okay."

"Really?" I said.

"Yup."

Yahoo! This was hugely good news.

"What about the floor timbers?" I asked.

"They look okay," he said.

"Really?" That was two questions up, two down. I was very

surprised by his answers, and was now beginning to hope for the trifecta.

"Yep," he said. "As Confucius said, 'If keel bolt ain't broke, not to fix.' Let's take a look at the transom."

I felt like a condemned man who'd been pardoned. And then Bill addressed my third question, all on his own. He walked to the stern of the boat and stood for a moment eyeballing the transom's wineglass shape. It was made of broad mahogany planks running side to side, and held together by long iron drifts, which are rods that go down through the panels. He dug his awl into one of the four black stripes that ran vertically down the transom, showing where the drifts were corroding within. A chunk of dusty black wood the size of a small stone came out of the first place he probed.

"Yep," he said. "That's fugly. This is what happens to all the ones made like that. Earlier ones are oak, and not fastened with iron, but they have other problems. It all came down to this wide transom they had to have. It keeps the length of the boat down, and keeps the boat wide, and it looks pretty without any cleats holding it together, but those damned drifts always corrode. You're going to want to do something about this sometime."

"Can I put it off?" I asked.

"Sure you can. And I probably would if I were you, 'cause it's tough to replace. You've got to cut the edge of the new transom precisely to the angle at which the planks come back to meet it. But the angle of the planks changes constantly, so it's a bear to get it right.

"But," he went on, "your planks and transom are still solid along the outer edges. As long as you can keep the transom from decaying any further in the center, I'd leave it for now, 'cause the edges look good. It's still sturdy."

He probed a few more places, and then put his awl in the front pocket of his coat, and walked out of the shed.

"All right, enough boat. You got a cup of coffee?"

"Sure I do," I said. "Come on inside."

I gave him a cup of coffee, and he stretched out in the one decent chair in the house.

"This is an okay little place," he said. "When'd you pick this up?"

"Last year. Last place in town with a roof for less than a hundred grand."

"I don't doubt it," he said, looking around the one room. "Has it got a bathroom?"

"Yeah, and a loft and another little bedroom. But it didn't have much left in the way of a roof when I got it."

"You know, you've got a nice old boat out there," he said. "I hope you can find the time to bring her back."

"I'd like to," I said. "Though I'm not quite sure why, beyond the obvious goal of saving a good old boat. That's what I'm trying to figure out."

"I know what you mean," he said.

I waited for him to say more, and when he didn't, I asked, "You having second thoughts about the career?"

"Well, no, not really," he said. "At this point it's kind of like breathing. But it's beginning to bother me that I can't have a client who's a fireman or a clerk. When my dad was starting out, he worked on everyone's boats—lobstermen's, fishermen's, the fireman who kept a string of pots, the real estate guy who'd retired from the Coast Guard and had a catboat he'd take over to Tarps [Tarpaulin Cove]. You know, it was regular people along with wealthy folks. But it changed about five years after I got back from the service, around seventy-five. I still enjoy the boats, and the craft, you know, but the clientele has changed."

"That's a problem for me, too," I said.

"How so?"

"Well, I'm trying to write about this boat here, but it's not something most people will ever own. It's an MG, or an Austin Healey, not a common thing for people to have. It has a value now, but it's hard for me to define it. The why of the value."

"The why. Jesus H.," he said. "I guess I've stopped asking that question. Maybe I shouldn't have."

"And you've replaced it with?"

"I'm not sure. Maybe with the how, as in 'how to pay the kid's tuition' . . ." He trailed off here, seemed to be observing his boot, which he had propped on the little table that sat in front of the woodstove.

"So Rafey gave you an earful the other day, huh?" he said after a moment. "You got to him right after he'd read all about the bogs along the river in the paper, before he'd had a chance to let it out on anybody else."

"I didn't mind that from Rafe," I said. "I mean, why should he hold back if someone walks through the door and he's got something to say?"

"If you're Rafe," he said.

"If you're Rafe," I said. "Plus, he lives alone on a boat, no one to talk to out there."

"Not everyone feels the need to create personal sounding boards at every turn in the hall," said Bill.

"That's true," I said.

"I hope you didn't take it the wrong way," he said.

"Nah," I said. "Rafe's a friend."

"He's a good guy, all right," said Bill. "And he sure can cut a plank. Jesus, he cut a plank with the bevel right on it the other day. I only had to give it half a swipe with a plane and it tocked in there on the first try. Blew my mind for the hundredth time. He's a savant. I love him. Hey, I gotta get going. Thanks for the coffee. Let me know how it goes."

"Last two questions," I said, catching him as he sat up in the chair, prepared to stand.

"Okay," he said.

"What kind of wood am I getting for the frames?" I thought I knew the answer to this, but I wanted to see what he'd say.

"White oak, white oak, and only white oak," said Bill.

This was what I'd thought.

"But it's got to be *green* white oak," he went on. "Not seasoned. You've got to be able to bend it, and it's got to be quartersawn, with the grain running straight out both ends. If it's been seasoned you'll snap half as many as you bend, and it'll never be as good," he said.

"Quartersawn?" I asked.

"Sawn so the grain is perpendicular to two sides, parallel to the other two. You gotta get the grain to stack up like pages in a magazine, so you can bend the wood, just like you roll a magazine up. If the grain ain't quartersawn, when you bend that frame it'll just snap on you."

"Where do you find that wood?" I asked.

He sat there for a moment, looking kind of tired. Then he said, "Well, I mill most of my own, so I'm not sure where you're going to find it, but that will be one of your new adventures. How's that strike you?"

As soon as I'd asked the question, I'd felt a wall descend between us, as if I had exhausted his goodwill, or the number of hints he was willing to give to the novice. Like a good mentor, he was going to make me earn the rest of my understanding.

"That strikes me fine," I said. "What do I owe you?"

"Don't worry about it. Maybe I'll call you to bend a frame for me sometime. I've got your number."

"Thanks, Bill."

"No worries."

And so he left.

· · ·

And I felt better about the whole project. Bill had come and seen the boat, and felt it could be done. He had yanked the whole thing out of "pie in the sky" into something close to respectability. I, on the other hand, still needed to figure out why I was doing this, other than the obvious motives of a paycheck and another arrow in the quiver of my literary career, such as it was. I wasn't sure what I was trying to get at, through this pile of oak, lead, cedar, mahogany, bronze, iron, paint, varnish, and rot.

13. *Opiner*

I COULDN'T SLEEP THE other night, and found myself immersed in the following:

> There are a great many varieties of oak and most of them are very poor indeed for they soon rot. The true white oak is one of the best things that God gave us here in New England, and I will try to describe it because nearly every lumberman will attempt to palm something else off on you. He (for the white oak is very masculine) is not called white oak because the wood is white or light color, but because as you walk through the woods his bark has quite a light shade in contrast to the rest of the forest, and when the breeze lifts or turns the leaves, the undersides are quite light. . . . White oak is without doubt the best oak for the frames of small boats.

So wrote L. Francis Herreshoff, son of Nat, who like his father was a designer of boats. He drew the Rozinante that Bill and Rafe were hoping to build, and the *Prudence, H-28, Ticonderoga, Diddikai,* and *Marco Polo,* among others, and he knew his craft down to the dimension of the pintles. It was in his *Sensible Cruising Designs* that I found these words again. It lay beneath some other books—spine facing away—at the top of the shelf under the steep stairs that lead to the loft. I pulled it off the shelf at about 2 A.M., when I couldn't sleep, wondered what it was, lit a kerosene lantern, opened the beat-up tome and was reminded of the man's strength as a writer. I lay reading on the old green Edwardian couch, the lantern hissing softly on the table next to me. There was no wind, and occasionally the donk of the bell buoy at the western end of the Hole came to me, stretching across the water, crossing the fens and lowland, to bump up against the window. Only on still nights can I hear that bell. Another passage:

> If *H-28*'s design is only slightly changed, the whole balance may be thrown out. If you equip her with deadeyes, build her with sawn frames, or fill her virgin bilge with ballast, the birds will no longer carol over her, nor will the odors arising from the cabin make poetry, nor will your soul be fortified against a world of warlords, politicians, and fakers.

There we have L. Francis on the construction of his twenty-eight-foot ketch the *H-28*, which slept four and in a slightly scaled-up version is one of the more popular cruising boats ever drawn. In his words (perhaps) may be discerned some of his father's philosophy about boats, the why of his own boats, and so the why of the H-12½ Here is another of his thoughts:

. . . as I stumble along the beach, making the fiddler crabs scurry for shelter, or see the squirt of a clam on ahead, a sense of contentment fills me. My dog, too, feels the joy of living as he bounds on ahead, starting up a flight of killdees or rock snipe, which wheel overhead, making a delicate pattern on the sky, coasting downwind on curved pinions. As I sit on a rock and give thanks for these blessings which are freely given to all who will see them, the H-28 comes in view at her mooring, and as her white form is silhouetted against the opposite shore she seems beyond the realm of mere things—a mythical dream come true, the answer to a sailor's prayers.

Amen.

Donk. The bell buoy's bell reaches across the water, and Ted, my cat, jumps up on the couch, wonders why I'm up at 2:30 A.M., butts her head into my knee. Yes, Ted, why are we up?

14. Description

I SAT ON A stump in the shed last night, next to *Daphie.* After a while a half moon rose over the marsh. As I looked out the doorway, sighting along her starboard side, I could see some of the street, and the house across the way; the light from a television in the house reflected silver-blue on her white hull.

Daphie. How to describe her?

Many people, when asked to describe a boat, will begin by

saying, "She sails like a Laser," or, "She's a great heavy weather sailor," or, "She's got a weather helm. I've got to get the center of effort a little further forward." Or, "She's a dog in a seaway, and downwind she weaves around like a drunk," or, "She'll heel—yes—but once she puts her rail down, she just jumps—I mean in any breeze above eighteen knots she *goes!*"

And then they will give you a few dimensions—length overall (LOA), and width (beam), and length on the waterline (LWL), and draft—and they'll tell you how many sails she has, and something about the shape of her bow and the stern.

"She has a lot of sheer," someone might say, meaning she curves gracefully down from her bow to her waist, or, "She looks like an Alden," if her lines resemble those of the graceful designs of John Alden, who took fishing schooners in the 1920s and '30s as the models for his boats.

In short, it's tough to describe a boat. References to other boats presume foreknowledge, in the way that "She looks like Katherine Hepburn" does.

So.

Daphie is a small boat. But big enough that I can stretch out on the floorboards and fall asleep. Her cockpit, which is broad and commodious, has benches along each side, so she's big enough to seat four or five adults comfortably.

She is a lively boat, though she weighs fifteen hundred pounds. Half of her displacement is lead in her keel, three feet below the waterline, which is one thing that makes her so seaworthy.

Her bow is "fine," meaning it's narrow, and comes to a point, and there's a slight hollow behind the leading edge of her stem, as if she were sucking her cheeks in a bit.

This is known in the trade as a fine entry, and makes for a swift boat, able to sail well into a sea. That fine entry also tends to fling water back into the cockpit when she's beating into waves.

Daphie's bow begins fairly high in the air. From my seat here I can see the entire line of her keel, beginning with the stem as it moves down and back from the bow. When the stem reaches the waterline it loses some of its downward curve, but it continues to deepen as it moves underwater and aft, segueing into the lead keel, and then into the so-called "deadwood" of the bottom of the keel, which ends finally under the stern of the boat. It's there that the long, narrow rudder is attached.

Why is this important? Well, this underwater aspect of the boat, her full keel, is part of what separates *Daphie* from the dinghy that one flirts with for an afternoon on a lake. It makes her potentially ocean-worthy. A fellow roofed over much of the cockpit of a 12 ½ back in the '50s, and sailed it to Ireland. In the question of freedom, the 12 ½ boasts real possibility: She is practically impossible to capsize; stiff and strong in a gust of wind; steady on her course in a following sea; able to sail hard to weather in heavy winds. This is important, because in a sudden gale you might have to be able to "claw off a lee shore," or be wrecked. Ability to sail to weather is what separates excellent craft from the rest. Having a full keel also means she runs aground in anything less than three feet of water. Having a lead section of the keel means that when she does run aground, the landing is usually pretty soft (as the lead takes the blow). With slight modification, one could sail this boat anywhere.

Moving above water again, as we move aft from the bow: there is a foredeck, centered on which is a forecleat. Above this hovers a small jib [the smaller, forward sail] when *Daphie* is rigged.

Next aft of the foredeck is the point of the coaming—two broad mahogany planks, set on edge, that start at a point, and then curve out to run along the inside of the gunwale. Just behind their beginning is the stout spruce mast (when she's rigged) stepped down through a bronze ring at deck level, and then down another three feet into an oak frame on top of the keel. The mast rises about twelve feet above the foredeck. It is varnished, and if it were stepped now and were rising into the light, it would glow a light brown except for a few dark spots where over the years moisture has seeped under the varnish. It is a strong old mast, and those spots are just blemishes and don't affect its integrity.

We are now in the cockpit. It is a wide place, with two big benches, one on either side, and room in the center to stretch your legs. At the back of this cockpit is another short deck, and then the boat ends in that transom, shaped like the silhouette of a wine glass. The boat ends abruptly, on a slant, which is a good way to save boatbuilding money, and to make a wide cockpit in a small boat. Not everyone thinks a wide hind end looks good, but I do, when it's done right.

Underfoot there are mahogany floorboards, widely spaced to allow water to drain down between them, and if one pulls these away one sees the floor timbers—trapezoids of white oak—bolted down to the keel, with the frames curving down to meet them. The floor timbers are the vertebrae of the boat, and between them is the bilge, where one sticks the suck-end of a pump when the sea or rain has come in. This is also where one puts the beer to cool.

Now this boat did not come out of nowhere, and as I look around its dimensions in my mind I see *something* of what it is and what it's not. But I have to give credit where it is due, and it was Giff Hogarth who helped me see this more clearly one day a couple of weeks ago, when I dropped by his shop on a Saturday afternoon.

15. Giff

TO FIND GIFF'S PLACE I had to drive to the eastern edge of town, find a dirt road that wound through the woods on top of the moraine, and then take another dirt road that turned off that one. This last road was rutted, and strained the suspension of the Saab, wracking the chassis until it groaned. Finally I saw his place in a clearing. There was a rough-hewn house, and to its left a big boat shed. There was just one boat in sight, sitting under a tarp off to the side. It was a remarkably neat place for a boatyard.

Giff was in the big shed, looking over the new decking of Dynel (a tough synthetic fabric) and epoxy that he and his guys (he has two or three carpenters working with him most of the time) had laid down the day before on a cold-molded version of a Herreshoff S-class sloop. The shed, which was really two large metal sheds attached end to end, was clean, quite unlike Bill Mayhew's place.

It was also not a temporary structure, but a founded steel structure, with doors that closed tight, and real heat. All along the northern side, however, was the same sort of long bench with drawers underneath that Bill's shed had, and everything was neat and put away. I noted that in the far left corner of the shed was an air scrubber, a big filtration device that would have been running during a normal day. This is crucial to the boatbuilder's survival, as it has been estimated that the three most dangerous professions in the United States today are deep-sea fishing, mining, and small boatbuilding (because of the many toxins in the workplace—not to mention the coffee).

Giff was up on the foredeck of the boat, which was a long, narrow racer/weekender, a twenty-five-foot-LWL class boat designed in 1914 by Nat Herreshoff with enormous overhangs and a great spread of sail. He was on his hands and knees, inspecting the decking fabric for bubbles.

"This is good work, these guys did," he said. "I can't find a damn thing wrong. Not a bubble. And that's good because they're my guys."

"How ya doin', Giff?" I said, knowing that formality was not something he prized.

"I'm well. I'm feeling pretty good about this boat."

"You guys are almost done, huh?" I asked.

"Just about. We've got to install the rudder post and the rudder, get some of the interior in (the S-boat has a simple interior plan of long bench seats that also work as bunks), and finish it—bright work, paint—you know, build the hatches and put on the hardware, but the boat's done, for the most part. Then we've got to build the spars, get all of the rigging stuff sorted out, but we'll have her done in a month, I hope, and then it's on to the next one."

Giff was not a big man, but he had the presence of quite a large man. He bristled, with grey curly hair and a mustache out from under which words poured in quick bunches. He moved fast, in small rushes that caught one off guard, yet it was plain that he was also capable of long periods of quiet attention to detail, a turn of rail or the joinery of a hatch cover, that made his boats command sums beyond the reach of most mortals.

"So what can I help you with, Dan?" he said from his perch on the boat, looking into my right eye and focusing there. "What is it that you've got going?"

"I'm writing a book about rebuilding the old Herreshoff twelve-and-a-half that's been in the family forever, and I need a lead on the boats Herreshoff would have been influenced by in that design. I've got a thought or two . . .

"I bet you do," he weaved under my sentence.

" . . . but I figured I'd ask you what your thoughts were, and then I wanted to ask you what you'd do with the transom on a twelve and a half that was coming a little apart around the drifts."

"Ah, the old corroded-drifts scenario," he said, as he climbed down the stepladder that stood alongside the boat, and then leaned against the smooth white hull, almost narwhalesque in its curve and shade.

"Well, if I were you, if you don't mind coming over to the glue side of things, I'd cut the mahogany—you've got a mahogany transom there, don't you? Yeah," he said, seeing my nod, "I'd cut the wood away where the drifts are most corroded, scrape the rust off them real good, prime them with a rust inhibitor, and then epoxy a nice scarf in there of mahogany, which will look a little beat, but it'll hold things together, and then fair it out and varnish it, and live with it as long as you can. Unless you've got a shed full of dough and you're aiming for perfection, that'll get the boat sailing as well as anything."

"That's what I was thinking of doing," I said.

"Yeah, I mean there will always be purist guys—the kind of guy who commissioned this boat behind me, for example—who will give you shit about something like that, but I say to that what I say to all the neat-freak naysayers."

"What's that?" I asked.

" 'Fuck you, neat-freak naysayer. This'll work, get outta my face.' "

"Amen," I said.

"Amen," he said. "Of course," he went on, "I can play the neat-freak game, too."

"Of course," I replied.

"So, you're wondering what boats I see in the run-up to the twelve-and-a-half?" he asked.

"Yup."

"Hmmm. C'mere, Brody," he said, calling to a black Lab that was nosing around in some old wild asparagus still standing at the corner of the shed. At the sound of his voice the dog flopped down on the bush and began rolling around.

"That dog does what I'd like to do, most of the time, not what I'd like him to do," said Giff, smiling. He crossed his arms, and looked off out the door.

"I guess I'd have to say that the twelve-and-a-half, even though it's clearly built for pleasure, is a tough little boat. Underbuilt, in that you've gotta reframe every fifty years, but that's maybe not so true, because you'd really expect that in any wooden boat. I dunno. It's not quite a fisherman, but close, and it's got the rig for it, in some ways, if the boom rode a little higher, and the mast was a little further forward. But that's the kind of boat it's coming out of, the little cats they used to use for shellfishing and scupping and lobstering in Narragansett, and the spritsails out of Woods Hole that were the little trucks around there before they went to racing them, and to a lesser extent the No Mans Land boats, and the Block Island boats. That's what I'd say. Boats like that."

"Different than this boat here?" I asked, gesturing to the one he was building.

"Oh Christ yes," he said. "This was a goer, a real machine, using the same principles as the twelve-and-a-half maybe, but they were all extended, stretched way out, long overhangs and a cloud of sail, almost a fin keel, not a boat for anything but racing, really. The twelve-and-a-half was a Volvo, whereas this thing—" as he said this, he turned to look at the boat for a moment, and I could tell he was admiring her— "was an Aston Martin Lagonda."

16. *Origins*

AS A BOY ON the waterfront in Bristol, Rhode Island, in the 1850s Nat Herreshoff would have known many small sailboats.

There were the Block Island boats, named for the island he sailed to many times, several hours off the entrance to Narragansett Bay. These were open boats (sometimes called cowhorns because their ends rose so high in the air), designed to be fished from in any weather, and then to be pulled easily up on the rocky beaches of Block Island, which in those days lacked a good harbor.

They were shallow, double-ended (which meant they could be backed off the beach into a sea, or brought onto the beach in a heavy following sea), and had a good wet well at their center for fish. They were working boats, with two masts in a cat-ketch arrangement, and they were broad and stable. That boat surely influenced Nat's thought.

How? Well, the 12½ does have a shape to the cockpit—in the wide, stable middle—which is similar, and it does have a rig that is simple, low, easy to repair, easy to remove, easy to maneuver, and which interferes little with work.

Then there was the No Mans Land Boat, named for the small island just south of Martha's Vineyard where many fishing families once summered to be closer to the good fishing grounds.

Like Block Island, No Mans Land had no good anchorage, so the boats developed there were also double-enders, able to launch backward into a sea, and able to be hauled again easily onto the beach, sometimes by oxen who dragged them up greased wooden skids. They were often sloop-rigged, and were, again like the Block Island boats, broad, shallow, stable, and able to carry many fish in wet wells at their center. They had a lot of sheer, could take a sea, could be rowed well, and were all in all suited to their duty.

Of both types one could say that while Nat was not drawn entirely to them in designing the 12½, he would nonetheless have leaned on them as boats that could go offshore, carry a load, and sail well when laden.

Then there were the small working catboats of the Newport area, just down Narragansett Bay from Bristol, such as one designed and built by Button Swan in 1880. This was a twelve-foot-long catboat, full and deep enough to handle the offshore waters around Brenton's Reef, but small enough to poke into the shallows as well. She was a pickup truck: She could be used for lobstering, fishing, or any sea errand; could go to weather in a chop; had a generous wet well at her center for storage; and had a cat rig (one big sail, with the mast stepped far forward) that made her easy to handle and work. She was a stout little boat.

How did the 12½ differ? She was deeper, with higher sides which made it harder to haul lobster pots into her, and the 12½ had a more complicated bow which was harder to plank up. But her rig was similar in its simplicity, and in how it stayed out of the way of work in the cockpit. The H-12½ owed a great deal to this traditional Newport cat, especially in terms of overall concept.

Indeed, there was another old Newport catboat, the *Kingfisher II* (pictured in the book *Watercraft* by Maynard Bray), which to my eye is very reminiscent of the 12½. She is clearly a cousin.

And then there was the Woods Hole spritsail, a boat Nat knew intimately, for he had designed a spritsail, *Sappho*, to compete in the A division of the spritsails that raced at Woods Hole around 1900. These were working boats too, designed to fish the currents and shoal water around Woods Hole. They were shallower than the previous craft. They had a centerboard, and were light enough to be rowed easily when the wind died and the current ran foul.

They also had a simple rig, which could be lowered quickly in order to pass under the many low stone bridges in the area, and in particular under the bridge that spanned the channel into Eel Pond in Woods Hole. Their rig was remarkable for its simplicity and utility. It was the "slant six" of sailboats, consisting of a mast, a trapezoidal sail, and a stick (the sprit), which was tied to the lower mast and the top rear corner of the sail. It could be doused or raised in a long moment.

The Woods Hole spritsails, though not double-ended, were still exceptionally seaworthy, were able to carry a good load of fish or lobster in the bilge, and were fast enough under sail to best the strong currents of the Hole. Which is pretty fast.

When I look at a photo of a Woods Hole Spritsail (or when I go to the small boat shed at Mystic Seaport in Connecticut and look at their Spritsail) from the stern quarter, so that I can see both its transom and the line of its sheer, and then look quickly to the same view of the old 12½ in the same shed— *even though* the spritsail has less keel, and no foredeck—it is as if I am seeing *very* close relatives, staring into the face of siblings I know well, and seeing there a geometry that is closely shared on a genetic level. I recognize this, I feel, with the same part of my mind that recognizes the gait of a friend in a crowd at two hundred yards.

By the time he drew the 12½ Nat Herreshoff had seen a great many boats, and made a great many. The main characteristics of boats that did well in local waters were simplicity, breadth, speed, stability, and serving as a good working platform. The 12½ *differed* from these standards most in her greater depth, which gave her added speed in some conditions, as well as greater stability, but which would have been impractical in any of the aforementioned working craft because she really can't be hauled up on the beach. She is also lighter in her skeleton.

And her skeleton is key. One of Herreshoff's innovations was the extreme lightness of his structural design. The frames in a 12½, at thirteen-sixteenths of an inch square, are lighter by far than frames used in most contemporary boats her size. Is this good? Yes. Lightness and flexibility are among the chiefest of good qualities.

Most boats contemporary to the 12½ would have been framed more heavily, and less often. Heavier frames make for greater initial strength, and fewer frames mean less work hewing, bending, and fastening them.

But Herreshoff's boats relied on engineering for their strength, and you can see this in *Daphie*. Running down the inside of her cockpit is a web of frames, one or more every foot, each taking its part of the load, each of white oak with the grain running out the ends, each bent with steam. In short, *Daphie* relies on her sinew.

Another Herreshoff innovation was to screw planks to frames, rather than nailing or riveting them. By doing this he made refastening easier, but above all made it possible to use smaller frame stock. A nail requires some length of penetration to grip, while a screw, so long as the wood it grabs is sound, will grip hard in a shallow hole.

What he got for his trouble was a springy craft. In a collision Herreshoff's boats tend to bend and not break. I have seen a few hard collisions, which one often sees coming a long way off, and which are usually caused by stubbornness. One captain refuses to bear off on port tack, another refuses to give way on starboard tack, unto the truth of the crash.

This light, almost canoe like flexibility in the hull, combined with the cushioning effect of the soft lead in the massive keel (which dents nicely when it strikes a submerged rock), made the 12 ½ resilient. She wasn't built for a lot of heavy anchors and fish traps being dropped in her bilges—she wasn't double-hulled, and I would want sturdier frames down there if I were fishing hard from her—but for what she was designed to do (haul folks) she was more than strong.

17. February

THE DAY AFTER FINISHING the shed, I started in on *her.* I still had an outside chance of finishing before summer, of sailing her again in a few months. I pulled a toolbox out of the Saab, grabbed my tool belt—I feel naked doing carpentry without it on my hips—and headed into the shed.

Daphie sat there, impassive, quiet. I walked around her, touching her hull where a couple of planks were a bit proud, perhaps where someone had caulked them with something that had dried hard in her seams. Hard caulk doesn't give planks room to swell once they are submerged. Instead, they buckle outward. It looked like there were a few places where that had happened, one spot in particular right along her waterline on the port stern quarter.

But first, the garboards and the broad planks—the bottom-most and next-to-bottommost planks—had to come off. Bill had said so.

"Yep, just get a few screws out of the hind end of that garboard, get it started, and that thing'll peel off slicker than shit," he'd said. "Those screws are tired, and the frames down there are all burned out, so the screws'll pull right out." He'd also said, "Don't get me wrong. Those planks look good, but they're on there by habit. Flip those off, and you'll be able to see into the bilge, see what you're getting into."

Lighthearted words followed by ominous, I'd thought. What *would* I be getting into?

I began on the port garboard by digging out the caps of white lead paint that covered the heads of the screws that held it to the boat. The best tool for this is an awl—a hard steel point with a good handle on it—because once the paint is gone you can clear out the slot in the top of the screw with that point and then get a screwdriver in there—if there is a top of the screw. As I worked on the screws their tops mostly disintegrated in little clouds of green dust, and I was left looking at unturnable roots. Which meant move to the next screw.

When I *was* able to turn a screw all the way out, I held what was left of a bronze number eight one-inch flathead boat screw. Some of the thread would remain, but usually not much. Bronze is undoubtedly the best metal to use for this application. Monel is good, too, as is stainless steel. But silicone bronze is the best. It is, despite the previous description, very corrosion resistant, relatively cheap, and it is soft—harder than wood, but with some give, which is good in a wooden boat. You want an overall limberness rather than brute strength, which when pressed will break.

Once I had the first foot of the port garboard unfastened

and was able to get a small pry under its edge, it happened just as Bill had said it would: the whole plank peeled right off "with relative ease." A few screws did hold on and pulled their heads through the plank as I peeled it off the hull, but those small holes would be easily repaired with epoxy. And it was frighteningly easy to peel it off. I didn't like to consider that too much. One of my nightmares was to have a plank spring loose a mile offshore, to watch the boat go down fast under me, and be forced to swim for shore. In October or November, that would be hard to survive.

In the early 1990s two men sailing an old wooden sloop out of Padanaram (a village in Massachusetts) were reported overdue. It was late autumn. I was on Penikese, a small island near the end of the Elizabeth Islands, working at the little school for delinquent boys there. We'd heard on the ship-to-shore radio about the boat's being overdue, and we'd resolved to walk the island several times a day, looking for any sign of them.

We also decided to sit for a while each day in the little cemetery there, on a bluff above Buzzards Bay, looking for them. We had long views north, west, and south from there, and the boys were quiet as they sat among the headstones and scanned the horizon with the school's various beat-up binoculars. The seas were big, breaking hard on the rocky coast, remnants of a nor'easter that had come through several days before. It would have been hard to spot a person in them, but we tried. And it was something to see the boys, all from hard circumstances, tough, brash, often loud—how subdued they became as they looked for those guys.

On the third day we found a cooler on the beach that might have been theirs. One of them might have held on to it for a while. We heard the report on the radio a couple of weeks later: a fishermen had brought up both guys in his nets down toward Mattapoisett. I didn't know them, but I knew we had much in common. Habit and caulk. I want more than that holding these planks on.

The broad plank came off even more easily than the garboard. Once I'd taken out what screws I could, I was able to work a flat bar between the now-exposed frames and the plank, and pry it off in one motion. Voila! Suddenly the bottom ten inches of the port frames were exposed, as were the floor timbers and the bilge. I felt in that moment as if I too were strangely exposed. But that didn't prevent me from sticking my head into the innards of the boat and having a look around.

Everything in there looked *dry. Muy seco.* And the interior wood below the waterline had turned black with many years of salt exposure, almost like old firewood in the desert; the frames were wizened; the floor timbers looked brittle. When I gripped the floor timbers and tried to budge them, though, they felt solid, despite having big checks in them. Good old white oak. I knew I might have to replace some of the floor timbers, but I didn't want to if I didn't have to.

Each frame was fastened along its bottom ten inches to one of these floor timbers with three copper rivets, and the rivets seemed in fine shape. Copper rivets like these are another reason why bronze screws are such a good idea in a wooden boat: electrolysis.

Electrolysis occurs when dissimilar metals make contact through the conductive medium of water, and either lose or gain electrons, depending on the strength of the ionic bonds in their electron clouds. In practical terms this means that if your boat has both iron and bronze fastenings below the waterline, or bronze and aluminum (perish the thought), as Herreshoff's Cup defender *Columbia* did, your boat's gonna fall apart. Basically, you've set up a whole bunch of little batteries, and the ones that get drained (lose their electrons) eventually dissolve, which you hope happens after the race is done.

"Electrolysis is a bee-otch," my students at the Penikese School used to say as we refastened a boat. The copper rivets holding *Daphie*'s frames to her floor timbers, however, were similar enough to the bronze screws in her planks that electrolysis was not a problem with her. If someone had used, say, galvanized iron bolts instead of copper rivets, though, I would have been able to peel *Daphie* like an orange.

The first thing I did as I looked at these newly exposed frames and floor timbers was to stress out, as I wondered again if I would ever complete this project. And the second thing I did was demolish one frame, and see what that process consisted of.

The frames, as I have said, are white oak, thirteen-six-

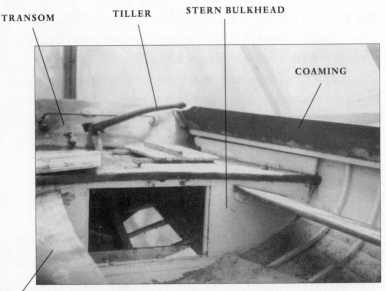

TRANSOM TILLER STERN BULKHEAD COAMING SEATS

The aft end of the cockpit, in some disrepair. (The opening or hatch in the stern bulkhead is called the "Lazarette.")

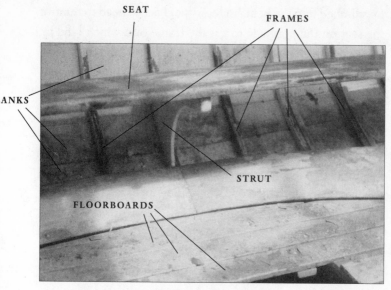

The port seat, with plywood strut beneath, and frames and planks beyond.

teenths of an inch square, and about five feet long, depending on where in the boat they are. Of course, toward the bow and toward the stern they are shorter. They are longest in the middle, where *Daphie* is widest. And they seem almost absurdly thin, until one becomes aquainted with white oak.

To remove a frame, first one cuts the three rivets holding it to the floor timber right down at the bottom of the bilge. Which is easy. Just put any old blade in the reciprocating saw, slip it between the floor timber and the frame, and pull the trigger. Copper is so soft that before you know it you are through and dropping down to put a nice unintended groove in the bent keel timber. Damn!

I cursed a couple of times, kneeling there on the dusty ground in the shed. Perfection was gone! But I knew that caulk would fill the groove I'd made. So I actively forgot my screw-up, climbed into the boat, and saw that I'd also need to remove the seat on the port side to get the frame out, which I did by taking out the nine bungs in the top of the seat, and the screws beneath them. Then I lifted the seat (a big mahogany plank) right out, and took out the floorboards (which came out in big panels), unscrewed one screw that held a little floorboard joist to the frame I was working on, and then it was just me and the frame.

It looked like an old bent stick, dirty white with old paint up high, black and dried out where it disappeared beneath the floorboards. All that remained was to free it from the boat. Before doing that, I decided to step back and take a breath, consider the big picture.

Below the waterline, it seemed to me the frames would probably just come away from the planks with relative ease— the disintegrating threads on the old screws wouldn't hold the old wood well anymore. But above the waterline, where everything was in relatively good shape, was another story. The screws there would be relatively intact, the wood relatively hard. I knew it would be a struggle to get those above-the-waterline screws out. How many screws? Well, nine hundred or so.

Every plank I worked on would have approximately forty-five screws that I would have to address. Eventually all of their little flat heads would have to be exposed on the outside of the hull. Then, once I had removed the frame that held them from the inside, I could just tap on the points of the screws where they came through the hull, and they would drop out onto the ground.

So, once I had thought about this a little, and as much as I wanted to just go ahead and rip that first frame out, I decided the next chore was to expose *all* of the heads of the screws fastening the planks to the frames. Only then would I proceed.

So for two days I did nothing but dig out the old white-lead paste that covered the screw heads. I did this on my knees, I did it sitting on the stump, I did it standing with a steaming cup of tea resting on the deck until I reached up to brace myself and dumped the tea on my boots. Eventually, after two full days, I was done. I would not have to do that again, I thought.

That is, until I took another look at the frames and realized that the cap rail, the thin strip of mahogany that runs along the top edge of the hull, had to come off. Bill had told me that. Which of course meant another sixty screw heads to be exposed, on each side.

This time I got out the radio and listened to NPR as I dug into the mahogany bungs glued with varnish that covered the screw heads. Until listening to accounts of partisan political idiocy started to stress me out even more, and I began to take big chunks out of the covering board with the awl.

It seemed to me that the Fourth, Fifth, Sixth, and Fourteenth Amendments (among others) were under assault—our fundamental rights to privacy and due process—and that there was little a man could say in their defense in these days without being branded unpatriotic. My head began to pound at the thought of the Bill of Rights having its teeth removed. So I turned off the radio and tried to tolerate being alone with myself.

Finally, I was done and could begin removing the first frame. Except I then found that in addition to forty screws going through the planks, a frame (and by extension, all of the frames) was also held in place by a copper rivet that passed through the sheer strake (the topmost plank in the hull, mahogany on *Daphie*), through the top of the frame, through the sheer clamp (a strong inner band of fir that runs around the top edge of the boat just inside the sheer strake), and then through the coaming. *Merde*.

So I cut *that* fuggin' rivet with the Sawzall, backed out all of the screws I could, and began to pull that' frame out of there. Bill had said, "Split that frame right down the center with an old chisel (I would do this gladly, I thought) and 'Y' it away from the screws, so it's almost like you're making a dousing rod, and then once you rip that thing outta there, just tap the screws backwards right out of the planks with a mallet."

That first frame came out just as he'd said it would, except that two of the screws held on to the frame when I'd thought they'd let go, and so ripped right through the plank, head and all, which meant that I would have to patch those holes with epoxy. No problem. One frame was out. I held what was left of it in my hands, shards of dry wood darkened by salt, an old piece of white oak in a rough Y, and thought, Now I need to replace it. I need new wood, and new fastenings. And I need to have my head examined. This is going to take forever!

But it was clear to me. It was still February, and it was time to take Bill up on his challenge. It was time to find some green white oak.

18. The Quest for Wood

THE QUEST FOR WOOD began the next day.

It was a Friday that began as winter days on the Cape do— with weak sun in early morning giving way to grey skies, and my getting in the Saab and driving four miles, out through the quiet streets of the village, past the seals floating on the surface of their pool at the little aquarium, past the calm waters of the harbor, over the drawbridge, onto the state highway, finally down Locust Street (named for the black locust trees that line it), and left into the Wood Lumber lot, where Lenny grimaced at me as I rolled slowly through the gates at 7:45.

"Hi ya, Lenny. How ya doin'?" I growled out the window.

"Bah humbug, guy," he grimaced back, working his one-liner hard even at this early hour.

I pulled past him, and parked, and headed for the little pine-paneled room in the corner of the big lumber shed, where I knew a guy or two would be sitting by the space heater with their morning coffee and their feet up on the desk, under the watchful gaze of the Makita girl.

Bernie and Frank were there. Bernie, the older man at sixty or so, was silent, wore a green ball cap, and let his belly rest against a set of green suspenders as he leaned back in an old wooden office chair. Frank sat opposite him, a forty-year-old with a cowlick standing up above his short brown hair, his eyes bright above a bushy mustache. He, too, was leaning back in one of the two tired, green-cushioned office chairs, waiting for the morning to move him. I was the morning, regrettably.

"Hey, Bernie, Frank," I said.

They both nodded. Bernie, who was from Maine, did not speak. Rather he looked at Frank, so I looked at Frank too.

"What's up?" he said.

"I need some white oak," I said.

"Ummmh," said Frank. Bernie looked the other way, out the window.

"Some green white oak," I said.

Frank looked at me for about four seconds. Sometimes it took him a while to warm to speech.

"You got any oak?" I broke the silence.

"Nope," he said.

"Nope?" I said, leaning on it with as much incredulity as I

could muster. I'd been buying lumber at least a couple of times a week, on and off, for ten years from Frank, so humor was part of the deal.

"Nope," he said again. "I said nope and I stand by that."

"No oak at all?"

"Well," he began, and then waited ten seconds, then said, "we can order some, and we might have some threshold stock, or some flooring . . ."

"No, I need it for frames for a boat. I've got to steam them so it's got to be green," I said.

"Oh," he said. There was a long pause. "Geez."

At this point two of Frank's colleagues at the yard, Larry and Garry, came out of the stacks of moldings and into the office, each followed by a jabbering customer. It was getting crowded, so I stepped out of the little room. Frank stepped into the doorway, having followed me.

"Yeah," he said, meaningfully, pausing to put a hand on the doorframe, as if it were the rail of a great ship, and to gaze across the parking lot toward two long metal sheds of roofing supplies and plywood. And then he paused some more. And then suddenly he looked me in the eye with an open expression on his face, and said, "I don't know where you'd get that. We don't have anything green." In those moments he'd been through the entire inventory of the lumberyard in his mind.

I waited to see if there was another thought coming. He was looking over at the piles of pressure-treated lumber now, as if there might be a thought surfacing over there.

"I seem to recall," he began, and then stopped, and kept staring out across the lot, and then began again. "I recall a place off-Cape, maybe in Rochester [near New Bedford], where some of the boatbuilders would go, but I can't remember." This memory seemed to flicker and then fade in his eyes.

"And you can't think of anyplace else?"

"No," he said, and looked a little sad.

"Back to your original refrain, huh?"

He paused again, looked toward the piles of shingles, which were grouped in their various grades. Then he looked back at me. "Yup," he said.

"All right, Frank, thanks for trying," I said, and waved as I walked away.

Part of me felt Frank had been a little cagey, as if someone had given him a phone call and said, "Hey, if that dilettante boatbuilder guy comes in looking for green white oak for frames, don't give him the goods. Make him work for it."

And the thing is that Frank, for all of his laconic replies, is smart as they come. Smarter. Aw hell. I'm pretty sure he wasn't holding out on me. But then again Bill had also seemed a little reticent to spill the goods, and Frank *had* had a trace of that Cheshire cat grin that said, "I'm not telling you all I know." Damn. I knew he was an excellent carpenter in his own right. Hmmm. Perhaps he was holding out on me.

My next stop was the phone book.

There was a place listed out in East Falmouth on Route 28, "The Hardwood Guy," that said it had all kinds of woods, hardwoods and softwoods, ready to go. I would try there.

I found it at the back of a small strip mall across the road from the weed-strewn lot of the defunct drive-in theater. A tall, harried-looking man stood in an office that smelled of stale cigarette smoke. Outsized signs on the walls blared "We Have Hardwoods," and "We Know Your Wood." There were no chairs or Makita gals in sight.

After saying hello, and inquiring about the quality of his day, I said to the guy, "I need some white oak. Do you have any?"

"Yeah," he said. "There's a stack out there somewhere to the left," pointing to the warehouse beyond the wall of the office. "Go on out there and see if you find what you need. If you do, we'll haul it out of there for you."

Okay, I thought. At least there's some oak around. Let's see what they've got.

It was good stuff, twelve feet long and longer, lacking knots for the most part, all nicely seasoned, dry, stacked with little dividers between the layers, ready to be turned into furniture. And it all looked like it would just *crack* as soon as it saw steam. It was useless to me.

I went back into the office and told him what I was looking for, and why. He shook his head.

"Can't help you there," he said, nicely enough. But the damnable thing was that he wore one of those little grins, too. A half grin, like he was pulling something over on me. I didn't trust that half grin. Clearly, a conspiracy was afoot.

So I beat it out of there, pulled onto the state highway leading back toward home, passing as I did a couple of small car dealerships, and then several small frame houses, each of which used to mark a small farm. They were plain little gabled houses on improbably big lots, their utility outmoded by split-level ranches and deck houses with expanses of glass. But god they looked sound. The small-time truck farmers who'd lived there fifty years ago would have known where to get some green white oak.

So I headed to Woods Hole to get the mail, right through the gauntlet of fast food and discount footware on the edge of the town center. The best lumberyard in town had no green wood, and if the only specialty lumber shop around didn't know where to get it, if Bill Mayhew hadn't felt able to tell me where to get suitable white oak, I was going to have to get serious, go underground. Nothing to do but head to the post office, get the mail, get a coffee, see who I ran into.

The route home, once I had passed safely through the

town's commercial district, took me along the northern edge of Vineyard Sound, and eventually along the long barrier beach that fronts the ponds and marshes of central Falmouth.

Looking seaward, I could see the wind was at eighteen knots or so out of the southwest, the whitecaps plain; oddly, a forty-foot sloop was reaching across toward Vineyard Haven under a big mainsail and genoa, which were pulling strongly. They were having a hell of a good winter sail.

Once I'd driven two miles along the barrier beach, with the big salt ponds stretching inland to my right, the road climbed up again into the rolling hills of the moraine that made up most of the rest of the coast down to Woods Hole. We serpentined along, the Saab and I, passed through a white cedar swamp, dove under the railroad tracks, and then emerged into clear air just east of Nobska Point, where the lighthouse sits high above Vineyard Sound.

I knew that as we swept through the high curve by the lighthouse we'd be looking west straight through the long main channel of the Hole. The water between the islands and the mainland there would be dark blue. The nuns and cans [buoys marking the channel] would stand above the water, like figures striding down a long aisle, and I could imagine the obstacles near each buoy—the dark pile of rocks near the first nun, and the spindle to the left of the third green can, with the current booming past on a flood tide.

Then I was beyond the lighthouse, winding down again to the barrier beach. A dune ran along the back of the beach, reinforced by grass and snow fence and old Christmas trees half buried upside down. And then I was climbing again, back onto the moraine, curving into the village of Woods Hole, pulling over to the right, and stopping with a squeak opposite the post office, which was a square, two-story brick building with flower boxes outside its two front windows.

I went in and there was Roger, the short-haired, bagpipe-playing postmaster. He leaned his forearms on the sill of the service window and peered out into the lobby. It was a fair-sized room, with banks of combination boxes on three sides, all framed by wood paneling darkened by eighty years of conversation.

"Hey," I said.

"Hey yourself," he said.

I turned right, to look into the window of my three-by-five-inch postbox. Nothing but the gas bill. I turned back to Roger.

"How you doin' today back there in heaven, Roger?" I said.

"Oh it ain't heaven all the time, pal. Not all the time. But I'm all right. You?"

"Good. Boat in the water yet?" I asked. This was an unfair question. Roger had a big old catboat, a twenty-four-foot Marshall with a broad cockpit and lovely big cabin.

"It's only March!" he said. "Are you nuts? I'm still comin' out of hibernation."

"It's February, Rog," I said.

"Whatever!" he said. "See what I'm saying? It's February! Quit it! I'm waiting for John Weaver to fix the rudder. You know down at the bottom? I hung it up on something last summer, and he's supposed to get to it, but he hasn't yet, and I can't do a thing till he does."

"You like that boat, huh?"

"Oh yeah. Does everything I need, goes anywhere. Heck of a boat," he said.

"I'm looking for some green white oak," I said. "I gotta steam it up for some new frames in my boat. Got any ideas?" I asked.

"Nope," he said, rubbing his chin with his right hand. "None at Wood Lumber, huh?"

"None," I said.

"I don't know, then," he said, and then, "But you know me. I'm a fiberglass man all the way."

"C'est la vie," I said.

"Pulling out the French on me, huh?" he said.

"How's the pipe-band?" I asked. "You guys still headed to Ireland?"

"Yup," he said. "Two weeks and we go tear the place up. Hoping for a ribbon, but you never know."

"Okay, Rog. Thanks for nothin'," I said.

"Use your zip code, Pal," he said, and then, "Hey, I got a book at home you ought to see. I'll bring it in. Remind me next time you see me."

"Thanks, Roger," I said, and I walked out after receiving his nod. I then decided to grab a cup of coffee at Pie in the Sky next door.

I entered the little cafe, which was built flat-roofed and crisp of line in the '50s, and now had hardwood counters and tables, shade-grown coffees (promoting triple-canopy ecosystems, birdlife, and general ecological health), and whole-grain pastries. It is, of course, a vital part of the process of "boatbuilding" to visit such places often, and sitting there at a varnished hardwood table was Ben Travis, local hydrology engineer—a wiry, grey-haired forty-five-year-old who seemed always to have a glint in his eye, and (more to the point) was building a thirty-six-foot schooner in his backyard, which he intended to sail around the world with his family.

I asked him the green white oak question, and suddenly the glint vanished, replaced by the blank look of one who knows he has valuable and arcane knowledge.

"Geez, I haven't bought any wood for four or five years now. I usually go out to western Mass., buy a tree, mill it up myself," he said.

Ah, I thought (not for the first time), here was one of the local men who will, until the last, put me to shame. I knew he had all kinds of gear on the family lot, back in the trees along a quiet street in Woods Hole: mills, planers, presses, lathes, even a mammoth old Bucyrus-Erie self-propelled bucket excavator that he kept in running order, because, well, what kind of person are you if you don't have a self-propelled bucket excavator?

"I do remember a place in Fairhaven I went to a couple of times," he finally said, slowly. "Or—wait. Maybe it was beyond New Bedford . . . Some old mill. Don't know if it's still there."

But there was a hint of possibility. Frank at Wood Lumber might have been thinking of the same place.

"No name, huh?"

"No. I don't have a name for you. What do you need it for?"

"Frames for a twelve-and-a-half. An inch square by four or five feet."

"Umm," he said, and thought for a moment. The best local welder, sitting across from Ben, dressed in many-times-patched coveralls and a flowery painter's cap, surrounded his coffee cup with his big hands and said nothing.

"Yeah, I'd go find a tree and mill it myself if I was you, but there's got to be someplace around that'll do it for you."

We finished up the conversation with small talk about family, and then I headed out the door, brought Roger the postmaster a small Ahab's Revenge coffee, crossed the street, and was getting into the car when I heard a shout behind me.

"Hey, man!"

A white BMW 325i had stopped, and in the driver's seat sat a mountain of a man—John Weaver. He beamed, his red face redder for the effort of beaming. His nephew Jess sat next to him. They were both old friends. John had a superb 1920s forty-six-foot cutter called *Wren*, which he had restored, replacing floors and frames and planks. She often won awards at classic boat shows, and was sailed as hard as possible.

"What are you doing walking down the middle of the road?" John barked out the window at me.

"Just trying to get to the other side alive. What are you guys up to?"

"Going to see Ma."

I'd grown up going to John's mother's old frame house for potlucks and contra dances in the living room. I continued to do so whenever I could. Something interesting was always afoot there. I considered tagging along. But then it occurred to me to ask John the question. His answer was instantaneous.

"Delano's! You go to Delano's! That's where I got all my frame stock, for Chrissake! Every damned bit of it, and then I threw it all in the pond down the road from me tied to a rock to keep it wet till we were ready, which worked pretty damned well!"

His eyes bugged out slightly as he hurled this information at me, and then he paused to see if it had sunk in.

"Delano's," I said.

"Delano's!" he barked back.

"You know where they are?"

"Do I know where they are? I just told you to go there!"

"Right," I said. "Where are they?"

"South Dartmouth. Go down Six, and when you're past the mall and all that crap, past Home Despot, soon as you see Wal-Mart, whack a right, and they are right down there. Like walkin' into a Currier and Ives Norman Rockwell deal without all the pretty people. Just like it was a hundred years ago. Except all the pretty people are lumberjacks with food in their beards. Call 'em up. That's the only place you're going to find it unless you're going to go cut down your own goddam tree, but only nuts do that anymore."

And then they were gone. The BMW's tires chirped on the

pavement as John shifted to second, and just like that I had one of the sacred keys, and headed straight home, to the phone. I needed wood, and I could smell it over the phone.

Thank you, John.

But before I get too far into the world of the lumber hunt, I ought to explain something more about the frames I was seeking to replace.

I had known, even before my talk with Bill Mayhew, that the wood I needed was white oak. I'd absorbed this detail in part from my experience working on *Daphie* twenty years before, when I had added a few sister frames alongside several frames that were cracked. Back then those sisters had come from a friend who had put a few sisters in her old boat and had a few remaining, and was willing to let me have them.

That had been a stopgap kind of repair, like putting a splint on a broken leg with duct tape. It works for a while, and then the patient returns with worse problems.

And I had known too that the wood had to be green. Bill had told me that, but I had picked that up somewhere else too, maybe from my time working on schooners in my twenties—this knowledge had settled into me. But what I hadn't realized was how the wood needed to be cut.

This business of "quartersawn" that Bill had mentioned—I understood it—the wood had to have the grain running parallel to two sides, and perpendicular to the other two—but I wasn't sure how I would select the wood for that. Wasn't sure what condition I'd find the wood in, either, or how much it would need to be milled.

So I called Delano's up.

"Hello," answered a male voice.

"Hello. Is this Delano's Sawmill?"

"Yeah," the voice said.

I imagined a guy sitting in an old swiveling steel chair in an office paneled with rough-sawn wood, with old lumberyard calendars on the walls, in a building at least a hundred years old.

"I'm looking for some white oak, green white oak, to use for frames in a boat," I said.

"Got some," he came back.

"You do?" I said.

"Yup. Got some red and I got some white, all mixed in. You know your dimension?" he asked.

I wondered for a moment if he meant my galactic coordinates, and then I caught on.

"I need to mill it down to one inch by one inch or so," I said, finally.

"Four quarters. Yeah we got that. All the white and red oak that's piled out there is four quarters."

"Four quarters?"

"That means it's four actual quarter inches thick, not three quarters posing as four, you get me?"

"Ten-four, I said."

"We'll see you," he said.

"You still just before the Wal-Mart there?"

"Still and since 1964, open till five, closed twelve to one for dinner."

"Thank you."

"We'll see you."

19. The Source

ABOUT TWO HOURS LATER I pulled into the old sawmill, having driven north to the bridge, and then southwest, to Dartmouth, where I rolled past the malls and big-boxes, until I saw Wal-Mart, and turned right and then right again at a big millstone standing on its side and half buried, hung with a sign that said "Delano Sawmill."

I was immediately in a copse of old elms and beeches and white oaks, which stood among a museum-like collection of wood-frame buildings covered with ancient shingles, some of which had disintegrated, leaving the walls covered with just as ancient tar paper, which came off in strips.

The eccentric buildings were often missing a wall or a door and sheltered old milling equipment—giant rip saws, buzz saws, and planers—each with its own massive pile of sawdust. Farther back on the lot I could see great piles of lumber—tree trunks three and four feet thick awaiting the blades.

I parked in the shade of one massive pile of reddish sawdust, and walked through a doorway in the building closest to the street, which had a National Wildlife Federation sticker above it, and found the proprietor within. He was about forty-five, with round wire-rim glasses, a soft-spoken manner, and was sitting in an old green swiveling steel chair in an office paneled with rough-sawn wood, with old lumberyard calendars on the walls.

"Hello," I said. "I called a couple of hours ago about some white oak for frames for a boat."

"Oh yeah," he said. "Follow me," and walked out the door past me, saying as we walked, "It's a pretty fresh pile of wood, and there's red and white oak in there, so you'll have to sort through and take what you need."

"So," I said, my list of queries in the front of my mind, "how do you tell the difference between white and red oak?"

I knew some of this from working on an old herring lighter called the *Sylvina Beal*, an eighty-four-foot staysail schooner built in 1911. I'd spent a couple of months on her fifteen years before. We'd had to replace the top five feet of her stem because some knucklehead had put a piece of red oak in there as a repair a few years before, and it had rotted to a custard by the time we got to it. We'd dug it out of there with an old spoon, and I was told that the red oak rotted so well because the wood had very large and straight vessels in it—vesicles—through which it brought water to its leaves. These vesicles were like straws in a drink. Even after the wood was cut and dried, if you stuck one end in water, the water rose to the other end, and rotted the wood along the way. This was the miracle of transpiration.

We walked toward the back of the yard, and then to a fence line, where a jumbled pile of planks lay under an inch of old snow. He bent down and picked up the end of a plank, brushed the snow off it, pointed to the sawn end and said, "This is red oak. It's the pores in the end you can tell it by. In red oak, they're relatively big. Look at the end of the board, and you can see them right there."

I looked. He was right. Where the board had been sawn in half, the pores looked like dots made by the touch of a wood-colored ballpoint pen, scattered through the grain at the cut. These dots were the vesicles in cross section.

"With white oak," he went on, "the pores are much smaller. In fact you can hardly see them. And white oak looks whitish, and so does its bark. Red oak, well, looks kind of red, but it's hard to tell them apart sometimes. Some guys say they can smell the difference."

He dropped the plank he was holding, and gestured to the pile of twelve- and sixteen-foot planks, all about an inch thick and six to twelve inches wide, lying in a jumbled pile.

"There you go. Pick through the heap and see what you come up with."

"Thank you," I said, "I will." And that was the last I thought of him for some time, for the wood was before me.

I kneeled down and began to look at the planks. In some, the grain was arrayed diagonally across one end like this [////////////////////////], and was even more diagonally skewed at the other end. Those were not for me. In most planks, however, once I'd cleared the snow away, I could see that some part of the grain was favorable. An example might look like this: [/////////|||||||||||||||||||\\\\\\\\\]. This plank was usable for my purposes in its center. I'd have to rip it down and get as many frames as I could out of the center section, and use the rest for something else that didn't require bending.

I spent forty-five minutes sorting planks. I'd settle on one, then check its pores again and find that it was red oak, *not* white, then move on to another one, disappointed. Finally I settled on five planks, all rough-sawn, all usable only in parts, and hauled them out to the car, laid them on the rack, and tied them down.

I drove the Saab back to the office. The proprietor came out and measured what I had, and then said (once he was done with his calculations, which took him only several seconds to do in his head), "I wish you luck. That's twenty-five dollars of wood there, and it sounds like you're going to do ten thousand dollars of work with it, so I hope it holds up all right."

"I'm sure it will," I said, and then went on, as the momentous quality of the occasion (in my mind alone) overcame me: "One time around 1990 I was working on a schooner in Vineyard Haven, the *Sylvina Beal*, built in 1911. It was late spring, and we had to replace a couple of lower frames. They were white oak and original, and they were spent. They'd been good for seventy-nine years and that impressed us, but what really got our attention was the locust trunnels [tree-nails] that connected the lower frames to the upper frames. The trunnels were still so hard you couldn't dent them with your fingernail."

"That's good to know," he said, seeming not to mind listening to a customer. "I like to hear wood stories. Locust. In a fence post, they say it's the only thing that'll last longer than granite."

About locust we had an understanding.

I thanked him, and climbed into the Saab, and started it, and then jumped out and walked back into the sunny, beat-up office.

"I wanted to ask you another question if that's okay," I said.

"What's up?" he said, taking his attention from a legal pad on the desk which he was writing in. His eyes were clear behind the round lenses of wire-rim glasses.

"Where does the wood I bought come from? Do you know where was it cut?"

He stood up.

"I don't know precisely," he said, "but I can tell you this." As he said this he moved to the middle of the room and raised his arms into a sideways V.

"My right arm is pointing at Williamstown, and my left arm is pointing at Becket," he said, referring roughly to the northwest and southwest corners of the state.

"That lumber comes from somewhere out there, between my arms, west of center. Beyond that, I don't know."

"Thanks," I said, shook his hand again and headed out. When I was home, after supper, I brought the old circular saw and the table saw out into the yard under the moon, rigged a work light hanging out the doorway of the shed, lopped one of the planks in half, and then ripped that half down on the table saw into four-quarter by four-quarter strips, five in all. I had five potential frames.

Then I narrowed the gap between the fence and the blade and ripped a sixteenth of an inch off two adjacent sides of each piece. Next I narrowed the gap by another sixteenth, and took a sixteenth off the two other adjacent sides of each piece, which brought each piece down to a width of fourteen-sixteenths of an inch square. Then I left all of the wood in a neat pile by the boat shed. I put away the saws, and the cord, and smelled the moist sawdust in the air, its scent sharp, nutlike, almost like burnt acorn, and not as sweet as I knew red oak would smell, but sweeter for what it stood for.

20. *To Build a Steam Box*

I FINALLY HAD SOME white oak on my hands. I was now in serious trouble. I needed to get that oak into the boat in the form of new frames, and I was lacking basic equipment. I had saws—I could mill the stock down to the right dimensions—and I had drills, bits, and screws—I could fasten the wood to the boat. But I didn't have a steam box yet. That was the next thing: to build a steam box. Which I didn't know how to do.

I had some idea, of course. I knew I needed a vessel into which I could put a frame and let it sit in steam. Steam was also a problem; I didn't know how I would generate it. A kettle I supposed, but . . . I needed to consult. I needed to go see Bill and Rafe again, see how they did it. So I got in the Saab, and went.

It was a typical late winter Cape Cod day, grey, with the temperature hovering at about the temperature of the sea—thirty-five damp degrees. I took the shore road, along Vineyard Sound, before cutting across the moraine, as I wanted to look for a grebe that I'd heard had been seen in one of the salt ponds, but I saw no sign.

When I got to Bill's, smoke was curling out of the stovepipe that rose at the far end of the main shed. I let myself in, and as I turned to close the door I felt a nudge in the back of my knee. I looked down, and there was Roland, Bill's bull terrier. He looked up at me with a gleam in his right eye, and I stared back with what I hoped was the same, and gave him a scratch as he capsized and, four legs in the air, presented his belly. Which I rubbed for thirty seconds while he grunted with his eyes closed.

And then I walked back toward the scene I imagined Rafe and Bill were making in the back shed. "Hello," I said.

"Who goes there?" yelled back Rafe once he heard me.

"Hello, Rafe. Dan here, come to ask about steam boxes."

"You're going ahead with it, huh?" he asked.

"Yeah. I can't turn back," I said.

"Well, I hope I stiffened your resolve and didn't annoy you when I told you not to fix her up," he said.

"I understood you were just being helpful, Rafe," I said.

"Good. What's up?" he asked.

He stood holding a block plane, and looked like he was heading into the innards of the big Concordia. Bill was nowhere to be seen, and Roland had flopped down in the sawdust near the potbellied stove that stood in the corner. It ticked as it heated up. I could see my breath as I spoke.

"I've gotta steam these new frames, and I'm not sure what to use for a steam box."

"Okay," said Rafe, putting down the plane on its side on a table. "We use that length of six-inch stovepipe, just tin stovepipe," he said, pointing to an eight-foot length of pipe that leaned against the wall of the shed in the corner.

"Stovepipe is easy to adjust to length," he went on, "and it lets enough steam out so you get new steam comin' in, if you know what I mean. The gaps keep things moving along."

"You don't want it airtight?" I asked.

"No, no," he said. "Then the whole piece you got in there wouldn't get steamed. The box would just blow up. You've gotta keep the steam moving right through there. Just like your gut—you should see steam coming out the end."

"What do you use for steam?" I then asked.

He looked at me oddly when I asked this, wondering if he'd have to start at the beginning with fire. I clarified.

"I mean what do you use for a kettle?"

"Oh," he said, relieved. "Our rig's right there." He pointed to a big one-ring propane burner that sat under the bench along the wall on the far side of the shed. I'd seen similar burners at clambakes and cookouts, and I knew it would attach to a propane tank somewhere. I could see a hose ran from it and through the wall—that had to be it. On the burner sat a big kettle with one end of a big rubber radiator hose clamped to its snout.

"We heat water here in the kettle, the steam goes through the hose, into a hole in the stovepipe, and we've got steam in a box," he said.

It was simple. Simpler than I thought.

"I'm going to let you get back to work, Rafe," I said. "Thanks for the lowdown."

"No worries, mate," he said, already turning back to his work in the bowels of the Concordia.

"Say hi to Bill," I said, and found my way out. They were busy, and I had what I needed.

Except that I didn't quite, because I'd been talking to a guy who worked at a place called Valentine's, a highly regarded boatyard, and he said they used a piece of old aluminum mast for the same job. They welded a cap on one end, put it on a slant, filled it with water, put the wood they wanted to steam inside, put a loose cap on the high end of the steam box, made a fire under the low end, and *boiled* their wood, never mind steaming it. That sounded good, except I wasn't going to do that. I could screw, rivet, nail, solder, caulk, weld, and braise iron and steel, but welding aluminum was beyond me.

So I decided to drive back to Woods Hole to see how my boatbuilder friend Todd Johonowats did it. I called him up from home (where I'd stopped for coffee) a little while later, and got him. He said I could come down right away, as he was working in the basement. And why didn't we meet at Pie in the Sky first?

So I drove into Woods Hole, past the site of the old guano works, and the yacht club, and the squat lab buildings, and over the drawbridge, and met him at the cafe, next to the post office. He was standing on the gravel patio, blond and about my height, in overalls and a heavy, coarse wool sweater. We had coffee and talked about many things having little to do with boatbuilding, like whether it was better to have a wife who made a lot of money so we just had to work for relatively less money (and throw in a lot of child care), or to have a wife who was happy to take care of the kids and would leave one alone to make the money. We both came down in the former camp, and then in an informal survey in the coffee shop found that 90 percent of the people inside (five men, four women, and a malamute-Lab mix) shared our view. Then I followed him home, down into the hollow where he and his wife had their place.

He'd been working in his shop there, shaping drogues for experimental naval sonar devices out of a Kevlar carbon fiber material. He showed me those while I quizzed him about them until I realized he wouldn't tell me any more because their use was classified. So I moved on to questions about the steam box, which apparently was not classified yet.

"Well," he said, "I used some fir planks I had around. I thought they'd be good because they resist rot pretty well, and I made a big box out of them. Then I got a hose, and drilled a hole in the box for it, and then I hooked the other end of the hose up to that water kettle thing under that table (he motioned to a kettle just like Bill and Rafe's), and then heated the kettle on this burner thing (he motioned to a propane stove identical to Bill and Rafe's that was under a workbench) and it worked!"

He showed me his steam box, and it was a thing of rough beauty, nearly a small coffin made out of grey fir boards, big enough to steam two eight-foot four-by-fours side by side. Too big for my purposes, so when he offered it to me, I turned him down, but with many thanks.

By then it was really time for another cup of coffee so we agreed it would be a good idea to stop again at Pie in the Sky on the way out, since he had to go pick up his kids anyway. It was there that we figured out that Pedro Martinez was likely the best pitcher the Red Sox had had since Luis Tiant in his prime, with a nod to Roger Clemens too, and that the best hitting duo in our lives had been Jim Rice and Fred Lynn in 1975, although Manny Ramirez and David Ortiz were a close second. And then we drained our cups and were out the door. This boatbuilding with its coffee and conversation, was a rough deal, I reflected inwardly, as I thanked Todd for his help.

Then I headed out to ponder. I drove to the yacht club, at the head of Great Harbor, and looked out on the broad anchorage there, with the Hole flowing past it on its southern edge, and the nearest of the Elizabeth Islands—Nonamessett and Uncatena—looking like the Scottish Highlands in winter on the far shore. The sun was bright on the water, which was the dark cold blue of the winter sea.

I had spoken a few weeks before with one of the other local boatbuilders about steam boxes. He was an older fellow, the father of a guy I grew up with. I had gone by his house one evening, a Cape tucked back in the trees just up the road from my place, and found him finishing up a heavy skiff in the basement. He'd built it almost entirely out of plywood, except for the stem and the squarish posts at the corners of the stern. It was sixteen feet long, with a plain, square console for steering, a heavily built transom, a sharp bow, and enough rocker to the bottom that it would likely take waves well. He planned to put a thirty-five-horsepower four-stroke outboard motor on the back, and fish for bass and blues from it, he said, and said he hadn't needed a steam box in building it because it had "hard chines," meaning a sharp corner at the joint between its sides and bottom. "There ain't a bend that needs steam in this boat, which is a little strange to me," he said. "But they liked the design in *WoodenBoat*, so I thought I'd give it a try."

He was about seventy-five, and had been a boatbuilder before he'd gone to work as a merchant seaman, after which career he'd returned to boatbuilding. The boat was overturned on two large sawhorses, and he'd been planing the side of a plank that he'd fastened to the bottom along the port chine. He was making it fair with the hull, and I could see his hands were still strong. They were large, mottled brown with sun, and thick with muscle. They searched along the plank's edge for high spots, fingertips running back and forth over the wood, and then gripped the plane again, and gave the board a few licks, and then ran back over the wood, as if he could see with them. As he did this he didn't speak, and then after a minute or so he paused, leaned against the boat, and said, "Yup, this boat is marine ply, bronze screws, and epoxy. I gooped it up good, every joint, and believe me, that stuff has got the grip of God. I also used some 5200 here and there, and that stuff is grippy as hell, too, and it lasts. I used to build boats the old ways just like everyone else, but the snot has something goin' for it. But as for the steam box, last time I just used a piece of PVC pipe, the heavy plastic plumbing stuff, a little longer than I needed, and I ran a hose into it from a big kettle, and I plugged the end with a rag, and it worked fine."

Man. I had to decide. Wood? Aluminum? Tin? PVC? I started the Saab, threaded my way back to my cottage, went in and said hello to Ted under the stove, got yet another cup of coffee, and went and sat on a cinder block by the boat. *Daphie's* bottom planks were off, and her frames were ready for replacing, and here I was thinking, They all do it differently! All this time I thought there was one way, and now I see there are at least four ways to build a steam box. I wonder if there are four ways to do *everything* that I'm trying to do the *one* right way?

It was late afternoon by now. A couple of kids walking home from school ambled by the drive, and Ted went out and followed them at a safe distance to see if they'd flush anything from the underbrush as they walked.

And then saws began coming out of the truck and wood began to splinter, and pretty soon I had a box, made out of a five-and-a-half-foot two-by-four ripped right down the middle. I turned the two halves on their narrow sides, separated them by three inches, and then joined them top and bottom with six-inch strips of half-inch plywood. That gave me a box one and three-quarters inches high, and three inches wide. Which meant I could (barely) fit four frames in there at one time.

I screwed the whole thing together with galvanized inch-long decking screws, using my 9.6-volt Japanese cordless drill, circa 1987, and caulked every seam with clear silicone window caulk. The next thing was to put a cap of plywood over one end, which I did, screwed down, and caulked.

Then I cut a plate of plywood to cover the other end, and put one screw through it into the end grain of one side of the box, so that it could be turned open or closed. I had my box. Now I needed a pot to boil water in, a hose to carry the steam, and a heat source. The hose I would buy to fit the pot spout, so I had to find the pot first. The hospital thrift shop seemed the logical place. A light rain began to fall.

21. Kettle

IT IS ABOUT A fifteen-minute drive to the hospital thrift shop from my place. First I drove up the hill onto the moraine, and then north for a mile and a half through a beech forest to a four-corner intersection. To the left (northwest) the road went down to Quissett Harbor, where during the Revolution our privateers tied tree branches to their masts as camouflage and eluded their British pursuers. Sixty-seven years ago *Daphie* first sailed there.

But I turned right, and then left onto the state highway, and headed north through town, along the rutted stretch past the ice rink and the package store, and the VFW hall, and through the hospital lights, and then took a left into the parking lot of the white house that is the thrift.

There is a good smell in the hospital thrift—of attics, cedar chests, old books, potpourri. Immediately to the left of the door is a desk, which this day was manned by a woman who wore blue rayon pants and a white rayon blouse with ruffles down the front under a lavender-grey wig. She was tanned and thin, her face deeply lined. She sat with her hands on either side of an open cash box, which had a few bills in it, and her eyes were fixed on an item across the hall in the kitchen section. I said hello, and she didn't waver, just stared steadily for several more seconds, and then shifted her eyes to mine, bright with life, and said, "Howdy."

I often need to gather myself before addressing people much older than myself, for I know they might see through me to the core and then announce what they have seen to anyone within earshot, so I carried on, right past the desk and into the shoe section and then up the stairs to the old button-down and flannel shirt section.

I browsed there for a few minutes, seeing if I could feel from the texture of a few shirts whether the former owned had died violently within those sleeves, and finding no shirts that seemed to announce that they should leave with me, I walked back downstairs to the kitchen section.

There was a phalanx of polished chrome—waffle makers, blenders, toasters, and coffee urns. Frying pans, bread pans, cookie cutters, and whisks. And there on the bottom shelf at the left, looking to me it had been made to be part of the rebuild of a Herreshoff 12 ½, was one squat stainless-steel teapot with a big round snout. "I could clamp a radiator hose to that snout," I intoned internally, as I stooped to grab the pot.

I brought it slowly over to the desk, and placed it there in front of her. She looked at it for a moment, and then raised her eyes to me, tilting her head to one side and back to accomplish this, and squinted a little at me, as if I might match an image of someone in her memory of wherever she was from—Oklahoma by the sound of her greeting—if she just squinted hard enough. I looked back at her.

"I'd like to buy this teapot," I said, and then, "if I might, please."

She looked at me for another moment, and then back at the pot, and then up to me again, and leaned back in her chair, and made her right hand into a fist, which she left by the cash box.

"Young man, I can't let you do that," she said, not unkindly, but with finality. I wondered if she knew something about me, from how I walked or bore myself, could see my true lack of focus, the hours spent reading aimlessly when I could have been writing, the time lost spent scanning the Internet for cheaper brake rotors.

"You can't sell me this teapot? Really?" I said. "Is there perhaps another one I could buy?"

"No, there is not," she said, and straightened up in her chair, and looked right at me, and continued, in an even voice, "I cannot sell you that teapot, because that is not a teapot. That is a tea*kettle*. I would be happy to sell you that teakettle, as long as you understand the difference."

Here she waited for a moment, until I said, "And that is?"

"A kettle is for heating water, and a pot is what you make the tea in."

As she said these words she seemed to direct them the way

a conductor would, moving her hands through the air. She was smiling with her joke, and then was writing out a bill of sale: "1 Tea Kettle—$2.50," and then she figured the tax, and I handed her the money, and she put my receipt and the kettle in a big plastic bag that said "Benny's" on it.

"Thank you," I said, "for setting me straight."

"Oh, that's all right, young man. You just remember where you learned to tell the difference, and you'll do fine."

"Yes, ma'am," I said, and left, wishing I'd known her when she was sixty years younger.

So I had the kettle. So this was boatbuilding. I sat in the truck and measured the opening of the kettle spout. One and a half inches. I needed a hose one and a half inches in diameter, and what, two feet long? Time to go to the auto parts store.

22. The Auto Zone

AT THE "AUTOZONE," ABOUT a mile across town on Jones Road, there were plenty of hoses to choose from. I could see them there, hanging in the stacks behind the orange counter, but when I asked the young mustachioed clerk if he had one that was one and a half inches at one end, which was the diameter of the teakettle spout, he shook his head, and said he couldn't do it that way.

"Give me a car model, make, and year, and I'll find your hose. Otherwise I can't help you" were his words, as he folded his arms on his chest and rocked back on his heels. Unfortunately for him, his supervisor was walking past him at that moment.

"Excuse me, sir," I began. "Maybe you can help me. I'm wondering if you guys might be able to help me find a hose to fit on the end of this kettle," which I held up.

The supervisor, a man in his fifties with short grey hair and a potbelly, didn't care to play the manipulation game, and said, "Sure thing. Why don't you just hop back there into the hose section and find what you need. Lionel here will be glad to ring it up when you've got it."

Lionel glared at the supervisor as I walked around the counter.

In about thirty seconds, I found a hose that would work hanging among the others in the domestic section. I chose one with an internal coiled wire that helped it hold its shape, so I could put a bend in it, and found a couple of hose clamps to go along with it. Unfortunately, by the time I was ready to purchase, Lionel had been called away to the battery section.

Another clerk was manning the register.

"What kind of car is that going in?" he asked as I paid him.

"Herreshoff," I said. He nodded as he took my money, and said, "Never heard of it," and turned and walked away.

23. Nine Miles by Water

As I WORK NEAR the shore of Buzzards Bay, I think about others who have done so, do so. Much of the work done hereabout has been anonymous, has escaped attention. But not all.

Frederick Douglass was seen by Lincoln as "the most meritorious man in the United States," given his rise from slave to writer, editor, philosopher. Douglass lived for a while in New Bedford, nine miles west-northwest of my cottage by water, and the center of American whaling in his time. I can see New Bedford if I walk a hundred yards up the lane, cross the road, and go down to the rocky beach there. I bring up Douglass because I often wonder how important bending in a frame is. It's a rib in a boat, not one in a man.

Perhaps he comes to mind because a boat can bear one across an ocean, to a new land, to freedom (or to slavery, if we're honest). Even this small boat. One guy (as I said before, and it's worth saying it twice) covered the cockpit of an H-12 ½ to make more storage space, and sailed it to Ireland.

There is something of freedom in any boat, I suppose. What better man on the subject of freedom than Lincoln? What greater person than the one he saw as "most meritorious"?

And where does that leave me, here on this far shore, thinking primarily about oak, and steam boxes?

24. March

IT WAS TIME TO bend in some frames. I was ready. I had the wood. I had the steam box. I had some focus. And I'd reconciled myself to the task of milling the wood into frames, steaming them like the large tough vegetables they were, and putting them—new bones—into the boat.

And then life intervened. I was given an article to write, and then another, and then a barn was offered to me to build, and I couldn't refuse. And then there was a summer job high in the mountains of Vermont, where I would play a major role in an Equity production of *Much Ado About Nothing*. Life came at me like an out-of-control semitruck and drove me off the road. I stood the precious wood up in a moist corner on the north side of the cottage, hoping it would grow moss and keep until fall. I put the hose and kettle inside the shed. I rented the cottage to friends. And I put everything on hold.

25. September

THE COTTAGE: THE DOOR is open, a breeze blows through, and my luggage sits open on the floor of the bedroom. I am home recently enough still to be pulling my garb out of the bags each morning. But I am finally getting back down to it. I have been home a week, after a summer of much work, little of it connected to the boat. I have thought a lot about the boat every day this week, and haven't done anything toward her. She sits in the shed, reproachful, silent. I've got to break the inertia.

At least Ted and I are friends again. She ignored me for several days, after putting up with a summer of strange caretakers. I would be angry, too, if I were she. Yet she looks healthy, and seems to be settling in. And I find myself wandering to the boat shed, sitting on the stump out there, wondering when the lassitude will pass and I will open up (as my friend Kyle says) a can of whoop-ass on her, on *Daphie*. There is much to do. I feel I have barely begun, and I wonder if there is enough out there in the shed to hang a life on.

Bits of lines keep rising from the play we staged, high in the hills of Vermont, like this one:

> *"I had rather be a canker in a hedge than a*
> *rose in his grace,*
> *and it better fits my blood to be disdained of*
> *all than to fashion a carriage to rob love*
> *from any. . . ."*

and

> *"In this, though it cannot be said I am a*
> *flattering honest man, it cannot be denied*
> *but I am a plain-dealing villain. . . ."*

This fragment is from one of my speeches as Don John in *Much Ado About Nothing*, and it rumbles around in my head. A plain-dealing villain? A Herreshoff-rebuilding villain? I have played this misanthrope twice now, and he stays with me darkly, an opaquely troubled fellow who is above all committed to his own integrity. Why have I been cast as him twice, this guy who will be himself at all costs?

26. *Walden*

I WAS FEELING PRETTY tense about the rebuild, until yesterday. Six years ago I was asked to lead a group of Harvard freshmen on an orientation trip, one of many the school offered to help them acclimate to Massachusetts. The assignment was to take them around Walden Pond, in Concord, about two hours north and west of here, and about twenty miles due west of Boston.

I was a writer who wrote sometimes about nature. Couldn't I lead the trip? Their regular guide had abandoned them, and the dean's office was desperate. In the end I didn't refuse the chance to ruminate on Henry David Thoreau. The day was set. Since the topic never arose, I knew I would be paid in pine needles and oak leaves.

I have now led the trip five times, most recently yesterday. Twice it has been cancelled by rain. But it has become part of my autumn, to walk and think about how to present Henry, and then to visit Walden for a day. I am no expert in Thoreau, I hasten to add, but will I apologize for being a generalist? No. Thoreau was arguably the greatest of American jacks-of-all-trades: writer, lecturer, teacher, carpenter, plasterer, chimney builder, apple tree grafter, surveyor, botanist, long-distance walker, and self-appointed inspector of snowstorms. He offered no apology.

Each year I arrange for twelve or fifteen students to catch an early train from Cambridge to Concord, one of the most influential towns in American history. Early Revolutionary War battles were fought there (the "shot heard round the world" was fired at the Old North Bridge, which spans the Concord River, on April 19, 1775), but just as important was the role Concord played in the development of the new nation's conscience.

Ralph Waldo Emerson, minister, philosopher, writer of important essays (*Nature* and *Self-Reliance* among them), and mentor to Thoreau lived there in the 1800s, along with Thoreau himself, Bronson Alcott, Louisa May Alcott, Nathaniel Hawthorne, and many other luminous but less well-known citizens.

Once disembarked from the train, my charges faced a mile-long walk up Thoreau Street to its junction with Route 2. Along the way they passed old frame houses, a bean field, the high school, and a Starbucks Cafe. Once they crossed the highway, I was there, at the corner of Walden Woods, waiting to take them into the trees.

Thoreau is one of America's most original thinkers, which sets us apart, but I do feel some kinship to him, and admire his ways. Were three hours enough to convey his exuberant life during a saunter around the pond? Not a chance. Not any more than this book can convey the essence of that damned old boat.

But I did have allies: the Pond (61 acres, a half mile long, and lined in fall with trees whose leaves were turning red and yellow); the site of his cabin, now marked by eight square granite columns; a replica of the same cabin built near the far end of the pond; and the day.

It was a cool morning as the column of students approached

Route 2. They paused at the light, then crossed. There were seven freshmen and one chaperone, a junior named Marielle. She was of medium height, and had a silver bar piercing the upper lobe of her right ear.

"Here we are," she said, and I invited them into the grove of white pines—tall, straight trees with a rough, dark brown bark—where we could talk more easily, away from the hiss of traffic.

"You're only eight," I said.

"Yeah," said Marielle. "We had fifteen, but when we met this morning, only seven showed."

"No matter," I said. "By the way, you came on a route Thoreau walked hundreds of times." Everyone looked a little less tired.

It was good, it seemed to me, that there were so few. Eight was an easy number to connect with in a short time. I had divided my talk into seven sections, which I'd sketched out a few days before:

1. Cabin site: Thoreau on economics/recycled building Materials/Farming/The true cost of things in terms of time/effort

2. Thoreau as scientist, his theory of the succession of trees/ The scaffold for plant samples inside his hat/Identifying the white pine

3. Transcendentalism—having a personal relationship with the sacred

4. Harvard education

5. Thoreau's essay "Civil Disobedience" and his opposition to the war with Mexico, his night in jail/Why are you here?/ Thoreau's other works (on hiking Cape Cod and the Maine Woods/etc.)

6. Concord as community/Emerson—his teaching of Thoreau at Harvard and mentoring him subsequently in Concord/ Thoreau's traveling "a good deal in Concord"

7. "We are constantly invited to be what we are."/Thoreau's defense of John Brown—his opposition to slavery in 1859

Each number was keyed to a different site around the pond. I had a plan. As a veteran of many teaching assignments, I knew that I might have to chuck it all.

As we stood in the trees, I said a couple of words about myself by way of introduction: "I'm Dan Robb. I'm a minor American writer. I have a couple of books. Suffice it to say we are here to study his writing, not mine. I've worked as a teacher, a carpenter, political consultant, and editor, and this beats the heck out of any of that. I'm here today because I like to be, there is no pay involved but your company, and you are free to escape at any time." They smiled at this, but no one budged.

"I want you to know," I went on, "that your walking up here, and walking around the pond with me, and back to Concord, was something Thoreau considered holy in life. He was a saunterer, to use a word he liked, from the French *sainte* and *terre*, together meaning holy or sacred land. To Europeans of the Middle Ages and of the Renaissance, it was common to go on pilgrimage, to walk toward some holy land, like what Chaucer wrote of in *The Canterbury Tales*.

"For Thoreau, walking was a holy act in much the way it was for those European pilgrims. But for him there was no need to go away—he felt the woods and rivers and swamps of Concord were as sacred as anywhere, and he didn't need to visit a church or reliquary on the way. He wasn't odious about all this, though. He really just loved to ramble around in nature. So let's go, about two hundred yards downhill to where he built his cabin, and just consider as we go whether you are a *sainte-terrer,* or not, and where a holy land might be for you, if anywhere." This we did, the nine of us, walking easily down the broad, wooded lane, wide enough for a Jeep, carpeted in needles, descending toward the northeast corner of the pond.

When we were near the pond, and had climbed up the little rise to the cabin site, I asked, "How many of you, when you decided to come on this trip, felt like you knew something about Thoreau?"

Two hands went up. "I wrote a paper on him last year in English," said Kip, a tall blond kid from Iowa, who had one arm in a cast. The other who had raised a hand, a young woman, said, "I did, too, and I was wondering the whole way up here if he had walked that route." Her name was Mary, she was from Kansas, and wore work boots and a dungaree jacket.

"Okay," I said. "You two guys are going to help me today where you can, but I want the others to chip in too, and ask me questions. What was your paper on, Mary?"

"Uh, it was about his attitude toward John Brown and slavery. Brown spent time in Kansas, working to make it a free state, so I was interested in, like, what others said about it."

"When was Thoreau lecturing about John Brown?" I asked.

"That was 1859 I guess," said Mary, "and he only lived until 1862."

"What'd he die of?" asked Adia, who was tall, from Mississippi, and whose short hair was in cornrows.

"Tuberculosis," said Kip. "I wrote my paper on 'Civil Disobedience,' about how we owe our allegiance to what we feel is right, not the law, and how if there's a law we consider unjust, then it's our responsibility to get the law changed. He went to jail for not paying his taxes to protest the war with Mexico, which he thought was a sham, but then this guy Emerson paid his taxes for him, so he was out the next day, which made him mad. But Gandhi read all about that, and used it in his campaigns, and Martin Luther King learned some things from Gandhi, so he had his effect down the line, I guess."

"That's right," I said, a little alarmed at how quickly things had taken off. I hadn't intended to talk about Brown or "Civil Disobedience" until later, and I decided to delay our discussion of them, which in retrospect was dumb, as we were on a roll.

"Thoreau." I began again, "just to back up a little, was born in 1817, and died in 1862. His parents weren't rich—they had a small pencil factory—but they sent Henry to Harvard on its proceeds. He was young when he died, and one of his lines I like a lot was one he said on his deathbed, when a minister asked if he had made his peace with God. Thoreau said 'We've never quarreled.' He was a spiritual man, and saw God's works everywhere in nature. Nor did he see conflict there with Mr. Darwin's work."

"So this is where he built his cabin, huh?" said Sean, who was on his own course. "How big, like, tall was it?" Sean was short, with spiky brown hair, and was from South Boston.

"Just one story, with a gable—a pointed roof," I said.

"No way, huh?" said Sean.

"So was he a hermit?" asked Rebecca. She was tall, from Connecticut, with long brown hair.

"That's a great question," I said. "No. He liked people. His motivation for the cabin was economic and philosophical. He wanted to know exactly what it would take, in time and money, to live simply in New England, and said, 'The cost of a thing is the amount of what I call life which is required to be exchanged for it, immediately or in the long run.'

"His mission," I went on, "was to live wide awake, and to get others to wake up to a life fully witnessed. 'Only that day dawns to which we are awake' is something he said. A large part of that, to him, was creating a consciousness of what things actually cost. So he wasn't a hermit as much as an experimenter, and a philosopher. The cabin was his laboratory. He did say, 'Fire is the most tolerable third party,' though, by which he meant he'd rather hang out with just one friend and a woodstove, so he wasn't necessarily a party animal."

"How long did he live here?" asked Ralph, a big guy from Brooklyn with a flattop haircut.

"Well, two years, basically—age twenty-eight to thirty, but he liked to walk four hours a day, so he was in town all the time for the newspaper or to visit a friend, and he was very close to his family. I've got this by heart: 'I think that I cannot preserve my health and spirits, unless I spend four hours a day at least—and it is commonly more than that—sauntering through the woods and over the hills and fields, absolutely free from all worldly engagements.' That's from *Walking*.

"What I'd like you to do now," I went on, "is to imagine him, college graduate, twenty-eight years old, already taught some school, been a carpenter, plasterer, laborer, surveyor, decides to come out here, a mile from his nearest neighbor, and build a cabin to live in and write in. His friend Ralph Waldo Emerson owned the land, and lent it to him. So he cobbled together his cabin for twenty-eight dollars and twelve and a half cents—well-built—he hewed the timbers right here out of white pine with an axe, and then bought the boards to sheath it from an Irishman who lived with his family by the railroad." I pointed to the tracks running by the pond on the heights two hundred yards away. "He brought the lime and the horsehair for plaster and the lathes on his back, and the shingles, too. He built his chimney himself out of a thousand used bricks—did everything on his own."

I stopped there, conscious that I was going on too long. Jason, a tall guy from Boston wearing an Islanders hockey jersey, raised his hand.

"Did he write *Walden* here?"

"Largely he did," I said.

"And how did he feel about John Brown?" asked Adia.

"He thought he was a great man," said Mary. "And I kinda agree."

"Tell us a little about Brown, Mary," I said.

"He was the guy who took over the arsenal at Harper's Ferry, hoping a lot of slaves and free blacks would join him and start a rebellion. Thoreau hated slavery. Brown failed, got caught, and they hung him."

"Who did?" asked Adia.

"Federal government did, after they tried him," said Mary.

"That's right," I said. "Thoreau said they'd found the best man they could to hang. But that was 1859 when he said that. He was here in 1845, and he also grew crops—corn and beans—in a field nearby, to know what the cost of that was, too."

We walked down to the pond, which stretched out before us, about half a mile long and three or four hundred yards across. I remember feeling frustration in that moment, along with the elation of being there. Walden! I was upset that in the few hours we had, I couldn't impart all I wanted to these eight.

So we began to walk around the pond, which was lined by trees of various autumn hues. The leaves of the red maples were particularly bright. When we'd strolled for five minutes or so along the narrow path that rings the pond, I stopped at a clearing. On the hillside behind us were bear oaks, hardy little trees that grow in mean soil, and a couple of gnarled pitch pines.

"Thoreau," I said, "was something of a scientist, too. He carried in the crown of his hat what he called a scaffold, a little framework where he'd put plants that he wanted to take home to identify. He knew literally every plant in Concord, and he's credited with the theory of succession, which says that a given forest ecosystem will evolve until it reaches its climax—around here maybe a beech forest, or white pine forest—and will hold there until fire or storm or age knocks it down, when it begins the process again."

Just then a *pop!* came from beneath Rebecca's foot. She jumped back, and then leaned forward to see what it was. "I stepped on something and it exploded!" she said.

She came up with an oak leaf with a golf-ball sized protruberance attached, now somewhat crushed.

"What is it?" she asked.

"Anyone know?" I asked. No one did.

"It's an oak gall, made when a wasp lays her egg," I said. "She injects the leaf with chemicals that interact with the leaf's growth hormones, and the leaf grows the gall, inside of which the little wasps grow. Let's spread out a little and see if we can find more."

Within minutes Jason, Ralph, and Adia had found leaves with galls, and we saw in each the small hole where a young wasp had escaped.

"That's how it left?" asked Jason. "Amazing."

We pressed on along the trail, and soon came out on a crescent beach at the northwest corner of the pond.

"I want to talk a little about Transcendentalism," I said. "Anyone know what that was?" We went down that road some, talking of whether one could find divine inspiration within oneself, rather than in church or temple, and then I repeated a few bits of Emerson that I had in my head, letting silence grow between the short phrases. "Give all to love. Obey thy heart," and "God enters by a private door into every individual" (from "Intellect") and then "The foregoing generations beheld God and nature face to face; we, through their eyes. Why should not we also enjoy an original relation to the universe?" (from

Nature). They heard each of these, blinking, and all remained silent when I asked for comments. So we walked some more.

Soon we were back where we had begun, at the little crescent beach where Thoreau often swam, just below his cabin. We ate lunch there, and had a dip, tied up a few loose ends. And then I offered what I feel is one of Thoreau's most important lessons for college students who would soon be thrown into the world of work.

"He was a hardworking man," I said, "but his work was not typical. He felt that many people marked time in service to business or farm, and didn't ever get down to real work, considering why we're here, how to move humanity toward freedom and happiness. He felt that his contemplations, travels, and writings, his experiments into simplicity and attention, with four hours a day for walking, was his real work. So when they're driving you hard at Harvard, remember how Henry responded to that. Consider building your own cabin."

Not long after that I walked them back up the Jeep road, paved with white pine needles, to the corner of the wood, where Thoreau Street meets Route 2. Along the way, I asked Ralph if he liked the white pine needles we were walking on.

"How do you know they're white pine?" he asked.

"I know that the tall pines around here are white, because of their stature, which is unique in this area among pines, because of their bark, which is as you see, and because their needles come in bundles of five, same as the letters in *white*." We pulled a branch down and he saw.

"Five," said Ralph. "Same as in *white*. Cool." He pulled the bundle of needles off, put it in his hat, a retro Dodgers cap, and put the cap back on.

And I'll tell you: As I drove back from the day in Concord (after stopping to walk out to the Old North Bridge, and be reminded how gracefully it rises over the Concord River), I felt much calmer about the boat. Rebuilding it made better sense, having taken the saunter around the pond.

27. November: Bending In a Frame with George

IT WAS THIRTY-ONE DEGREES Fahrenheit at dawn, and the sky was a mix of cloud and sun, with snow showers in the forecast. Though the year was waning, it was still far enough from the solstice that it seemed there was a long way to go. And rather than looking back at a summer of sailing a boat I had so beautifully restored, I was back in the cottage having left the deconstructed boat in the shed all summer as other things happened. What I'd thought might take six months was now in its eleventh month. Ted was again lying on the foredeck of *Daphie*, in a mote of sun, her paws hanging off the side. How had this happened?

I had a fellow named George arriving at 11 A.M. to try to bend in the first frame with me, and I needed to be ready for him.

Last night I finally made a run at bending a piece of oak. Around 8 P.M. I got out the hot plate I'd bought at the local hardware store, deployed it on a milk crate in the shed, plugged it into an extension cord, put the kettle on the left burner, propped the steam box on a sawhorse above it, ran the hose from the snout of the kettle into the hole I'd cut for it in the butt of the steam box, and waited.

After five minutes the kettle was boiling, and steam wafted from the end of the hose when I removed it from the box. But the box remained cool. Impassive.

Then, after ten minutes, wisps of steam seeped fom the hatch at the far end of the box. After twenty minutes the box itself was hot, and steam had leaked from several of its seams and rose in a solid column when the hatch was opened. So, among other things, I found out last night that it took twenty minutes to reach full steam.

Earlier I'd milled a piece of oak down to fourteen-six-teenths of an inch square, with the grain running out both ends in parallel, so that on each end the grain made a pattern like a striped shirt. When I had ripped the wood down (wood that had been leaning against the north side of the house all summer) I found that it was still moist inside after its summer in the shade—still "green." So far, so good. So, last night, as the stars grew brighter in the sky, I stuffed that piece of oak in the steam box, and waited.

I sat on another milk crate and watched the steam rise. Then I looked up at the port side of the hull, which rose above me, green with old bottom paint below the waterline, white with old topside paint above. Seventeen rows of screw holes, three to a plank, rose like zippers from the keel to the gunwale. For two days last spring I had dug the white lead and caulk out of them, exposing the heads of those old bronze screws. The roughly four hundred and fifty screws that I'd uncovered were still in the planks, each screw requiring removal and replace-ment. And that was the port side. Four hundred and fifty more lurked to starboard!

I'd also removed the covering boards back in the spring, the thin five-eighths-by-two-inch mahogany strips that formed the narrow "deck" between the gunwale and the coaming on each side of the boat. Once these were off you could look down between the sheer strake (the uppermost plank) and the sheer clamp (the tough two-by-three-inch fir timber that forms the inner band of the hull, to which in effect everything else is "clamped"). Looking down between the two you could see how the frames rose up from the bilge to end there, right under where the covering boards usually sat.

The tough question (the answer to which I did not yet have) was how to slide a hot wet frame up from the bilge, get it to follow the curve of the hull as it slid upward, get its top end to slip right up between the sheer clamp and the sheer strake, and then, when it was in position, screw it into place while the steam rose off it, before it cooled and stiffened.

I had already removed one frame, amidships, back in the spring, splitting it down the middle with an old chisel, and then y-ing it away from the screws at its center. It was sinewy at its top, but had cracked easily down near the bilge, where it had been soaked so often. I had half of that old frame in my hand now, and drew lines in the duff on the floor of the shed with its blunt end, and waited.

At ten minutes of steam a vole scritched in the leaves just outside the shed, tossing them around carelessly in the night as it barreled down its subterranean route, rhinoceros-like. And then it was gone, and for some time the only sound was the ticking of the kettle. I looked at my watch. The wood had steamed for twenty minutes. I was trying not to stew, as I sat there watching the box heat up, about one thing in particular.

I had gone the week before to C. E. Beckman's in New Bedford, the only place around here to find real marine hardware. I had driven around the head of the bay on the highway, and then off at Route 18 (toward downtown New Bedford) and past the fish docks (which are largely idle) and then turned right at the Whaling Museum exit and then left along ancient cobblestone streets (which jounce the suspension and froth the stomach) past the Seamen's Bethel and several old chandleries, now closed, and finally to the jumbled buildings of C. E. Beckmans.

I like very much the truth that "if they don't have it you probably don't need it" that applies to Beckman's; but the thing I like best of all there is that the buildings are knit together by a web of brass pneumatic tubes which whoosh reassuringly with each purchase, as a pod is sucked skyward with money inside, and then returns momentarily from heaven with a receipt and change.

I bought three hundred silicone-bronze number eight one-inch wood screws there, on Friday. These are the only thing to use in such a boat. But I was stewing about them because I'd chosen screws with a Phillips head, rather than the traditional slotted screws that were original to *Daphie.* I felt that Phillips would be easier to drive with a power driver, and were less likely to be damaged in the process. The downside was that their slots might be harder to clean for the next fellow refastening the boat, as he tried to take them out. Since that fellow was likely to be me (in forty years), I agreed to this possibility, and made the purchase. But this is the sort of thing that hangs over your head as you rebuild a boat—the thought that the purists, the boatbuilding gods, might denounce you for such a departure from the gospel of, in this case, the slotted head.

Then I reflected on the fact that it was screws occupying my thoughts, and not some of the larger issues of the day—the current fight over the Fourth and Sixth Amendments, the halting of the full counting of votes in Florida by the Supreme Court, or the missing weapons of mass destruction. The screws retreated a little in my thoughts, and then, somehow, ice cream wedged its way in there, and I contemplated a bowl of mint chip for a while. I wondered if mint chip would some-day go the way of the dinosaur and the Constitution.

At twenty-five minutes of steam I looked out at the night sky and thought more of Beckman's, which is, as I said, one of those businesses which stays with you. To get there you have to go to the very heart of the old seafaring district in New Bedford, where the streets date easily to Melville's time and before.

I feel, as I walk the crooked cobblestone streets there, lined with stout old wood-frame storefronts and houses, that there must be a whaleship nearby needing men before the mast (perhaps even a harpooner, if that is your trade, dear reader). Everything in that small district works on one to create the impression of a different age, until one's gaze falls on the wa-terfront, where the modern blue and red and green steel fish-ing vessels lie idle. Melville's time, it seems, is truly gone, as are Queequeg, Ahab, and the whale.

Beckman's, however, which lies on the edge of this district, is a world unto itself and is perhaps the link to that past time. It is a jumble of buildings housing paint, electronics, cordage, hard-ware, canvas, and fastenings, among other things, with those pneumatic tubes knitting it all together, disappearing into the ceilings, emitting wheezes and occasional thunks as cylinders arrive. This is the place where you can get any marine thing you need, in rooms where people have been getting these same things for a hundred years or more. Everything that can't be sold is bolted down and painted battleship grey, including the commode in the bathroom upstairs, where, like everywhere else, it smells of marlin and jute and tar and salt. I appreciate the ambience there very much, even though I am a yacht-boy at the moment, not a fisherman or even a schooner guy, as I once was. At least I wield a chisel and mallet on occasion.

But we were at thirty minutes of steam, finally. I opened the little hatch in the box, pulled out the trial rib, and dropped it in the duff on the floor of the shed. Was it hot! At it again with work gloves, I found I could bend it with the grain pretty easily to about fifty degrees from straight. Then it cracked. But that would do. My friend Hugh had said, "Don't overcook 'em. You don't wanna toast 'em dry. They wanna be just right."

So half an hour it was. And the thing would bend! Like a pretzel, practically. And I could feel the strength in the wood, too, as I leaned on either end with the edge of a block of twelve-by-twelve as a fulcrum. It would bend, but I really had to lean on it.

Well, that was last night. Today George was due at eleven, and I needed to be ready. I'd taken that first frame out of the boat ages ago now, and removed its screws from the hull by tapping them out from within. This morning I'd milled a new frame to the correct length, and I'd readied the steam box. And I was nervous as a cat.

George didn't unnerve me. It was the task that unnerved me, this first act of *re*construction I would undertake, and so the first act that could be judged by peers and boatbuilders and family and ghosts, as inadequate. I could hear Bill Mayhew saying it now: "Well, I guess you coulda done it that way."

Shit. So I waited for George on the porch, as the morning lengthened, and then when he didn't arrive right on time, I went to the shed, put the frame in the steam box, and plugged in the kettle. An occasional flake of snow fell, and a gull descended out of the sky and flew the length of the little road in front of the cottage.

After a couple of minutes George arrived, pulling up in a silver Toyota sedan. A lean, broad-shouldered, seventy year-old, about six feet tall, George had neatly cut white hair and a solid handshake. I offered him a cup of coffee or tea, which he declined, so we went into the shed and I offered him a milk crate, which he accepted, and we waited for the steam to build.

I didn't know him well. He and his wife had moved to town only recently, and were befriended by my mother, who learned he was an avid sailor and would love to lend a hand with the boat. He'd read my book about the island school and liked it—what better recommendation could one want? So we sat, and talked, our heels on the dirt floor of the shed. I asked him how he'd come to sailing.

"Well, I was a flyer in the fifties, and that's where it came from."

"A flyer? What were you flying?" I asked.

"Early jets for the air force. Like the Starfire, and other fighters," he said.

"Really. Where?"

"First in Florida, and then later in Greenland, which was a pretty tough deal."

"How so?" I asked.

"Well, it was tough weather up there a lot, and you had to go when they said so, had to scramble. There was no 'I'm having a bad day,' or 'Geez, I'd really rather not.' They'd get a bogey and you had to intercept, whether it was a Soviet bomber or a flock of brant. There wasn't any waiting for nice weather to find out. And it's a tough thing when you have to take off in heavy snow at night. Can't see a thing. You leave the runway, flying when anyone in their right mind is on the ground, and you have to . . . just go." He made a whooshing sound like a jet taking off. "Into the blackness. Get thrust, hit takeoff speed . . . ease the stick back . . . up. Can't see anything but snow and blackness. Just go up. Trust the instruments. You're up and you're way beyond alone."

"That got you into boats?" I asked.

"When I got out of the service, eventually I went for a sail, and that seemed like it had a lot of the same feel to it, having to get things right, the discipline of navigating, dead reckoning, having a tight ship—all of that. You had to work with the elements to get where you wanted. It's similar, although not usually as much adrenaline is involved. You never find that again, after jets. But there's no orders from someone else on your boat, none but yours. You sail or race on your own time. Even on the Bermuda run, if the weather's too much, you tack, take in sail, moderate the situation."

We talked some more, as snow fell slightly on the clear plastic roof of the shed, making a subtle and numerous percussion, the frisson of salt shaken lightly on an oilcloth. And then it was time. The steam had been at the new frame for thirty minutes. George ascended the stepladder, hoisted himself into the boat, and put on some cotton work gloves I'd given him. I talked him through how I thought the task would go: I would take the new frame out of the steam box, hand it up to him, he would put it in place on the outline the old frame had left when I took it out, and somewhere in there he would figure out how to slide the new frame up between the sheer clamp and the sheer strake.

That all made sense to him, so when he was ready (He said, "Okay, let's give it a shot.") I slid the steaming rib out of the box, and handed it up to him, and then kneeled down and picked up the first of the two cordless drills I had set up outside the hull. One had a countersink on a drill bit in it, to make a few holes in the new frame by going through old holes in the planks from the outside; the other drill had a Phillips bit in it ready to sink the new screws.

As I knelt, George grunted, strained, groaned, and gnashed his teeth from within the boat.

"You all right?" I asked.

"Yeah. [Groan] It's gonna go. It's just a little stiff, but it's gonna go."

"You sure?"

"Yep. [Groan]."

"How are we, George?" I asked soon.

"Good. [Groan]. All right, put a couple of gee-dee screws in her for Pete's sake."

I did, at the middle, bottom, and top of the frame, per his instructions as to which plank. ("First. Okay now fourth. Right. [Groan.] Now eighth.")

Afterward, he had some thoughts.

"That was tough. The frame bent for me, but it was a struggle all the way. I think maybe they're gonna need more steam."

After we got that one frame in, George and I retreated to the cottage for a cup of tea, sitting by the woodstove as he unwound his legs.

"That thing went right in there," said George. "It fit right in there. And that was the biggest bend of them all, right amidships."

He was right. I put my stocking feet up on the coffee table, wiggled my toes to warm them.

"You think it needed more steam?" I asked.

"I'd like to try it with a little more steam," said George. "It just seemed a little too hard. I'm no moose, but I still have some shove, and it went with a protest all the way. *Barely* went."

"Next time we'll give it another thirty minutes anyway," I said.

"Sounds good," he said.

•   •   •

Over the next month he and I put in fifteen more frames, two or three at a whack, and once we had hit upon an *hour* of steam, things went easier.

When George was gone after a session, I'd have a few days to catch up on other projects, mill a few more frames, remove a few old ones, plan for the next assault, and of course insert the remainder of the thirty or so screws that held each frame in place.

Then, when all was ready, I'd call George, and he'd come over for a couple of hours of carpentry and mayhem followed by tea. It all worked out very well. The New Year came and went. Then mid-February arrived, a small writing project landed on my desk, and all progress halted.

28. *One Frame*

THAT WAS THE STORY of framing to that point, except for one frame I put in by myself on February. I felt I had to see if I could handle installing one alone. But I had another concurrent thought.

I had been to a meeting several evenings before at a Quaker meetinghouse in a different town. A group of us had come together to discuss how the Bill of Rights was impacted by provisions of the "Patriot Act," which of course had been occasioned by the terrorism visited on the nation on September 11, 2001.

We were concerned, each of us, that while much of the

act was useful and necessary, its provisions 213, 215, and 218 undercut several lines in the Bill of Rights, among them the Fourth, Fifth, Sixth, and Fourteenth Amendments, and the writ of habeas corpus.

We sat in the old shingled, high-gabled building, built on a granite foundation next to a cemetery where slate headstones leaned with age. We were Republicans, Democrats, Libertarians, independents.

In the old pews we sat quietly and discussed our options. "Make your thoughts heard" was where we all stood by the end of the meeting. We agreed to meet again soon. I drove home in a light snow, which brightened everything, gathering the light from the winter sky and reflecting it back up.

I began the day of the solo frame installation with a walk down the road to the beach, where I sat on a rock for twenty minutes or so, looking northwest in the general direction of New Bedford. Then I came back and made a pot of Earl Grey, and got down to it.

By cutting a stout scrap of oak to a precise length, I was able to prop it against the starboard coaming so that it would span the cockpit and hold something—a steamed frame, say— hard against the opposite side.

Then I cut the frame to be installed and sanded it so it was particularly smooth. Then I copied the words of the Fourth and Sixth Amendments, and the Writ of Habeas Corpus, onto the underside of the frame with a fine-point indelible marker, and then I steamed that frame for an hour.

When the hour was nearly up, I prepared my drills, put them on the ground outside the boat, pulled the frame out of the box, and looked. The texts remained. I swarmed into the boat, jammed the frame up under the sheer clamp, pinned it against

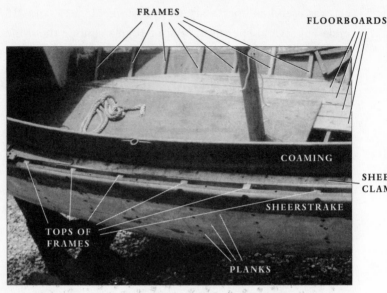

FRAMES

FLOORBOARDS

COAMING

SHEER
CLAMP

SHEERSTRAKE

TOPS OF
FRAMES

PLANKS

A view of the port side, with new frame ends visible between
sheer strake and sheer clamp on the near side, and new frames
visible on the starboard side.

the inside of the hull with the scrap of oak that ran up to the opposite coaming, jumped out of the boat, put five screws through
planks at intervals to hold the frame, and relaxed.

The boat had something in its gut now, beyond just being a
boat, which is a considerable thing to have in your gut to begin
with. I put the rest of the screws in when I'd caught my breath,
and went for another walk.

29. Harbor Ice

FEBRUARY 12. YESTERDAY AT 3 P.M. there was an inch of fine snow on the car. It was twenty-six degrees out, and I rolled out the dead-end lane with the window open, the tires crunching on the fresh snow. I saw no one until I reached Water Street, where a few people crossed. They made no noise. I saw no moving cars. My tires hummed suddenly on the steel deck of the drawbridge, and then were quiet again. I passed the post office, and the Coast Guard station, and wound out the shore road to the lighthouse.

The beach below the lighthouse was white with snow and salt ice until the dark line where the waves broke. The sea itself was grey, and darker in the troughs of the small waves. Once I had passed the lighthouse and was back in the trees, the landscape seemed of an earlier era—with the white of the road reaching out into the white that covered the forest floor, bringing the two together.

I was heading east, toward Falmouth, and soon I came out of the trees and rolled down off the moraine and out onto the great barrier beach, and drifted down the empty road at twenty miles an hour. Vineyard Sound was to my right, with small grey waves lapping at the snowy beach along a dark line, and the dark waters beyond absorbing the snow as it fell.

If it were a little colder still, I thought, there would be ice forming up on this water, with a layer of heavy rime along the wrack line, as there was when English raiders came over from Naushon Island one day in 1775 to burn the town.

They had said to a Tory they were visiting on Naushon that because the people of Woods Hole had refused to give them food, they were going to burn the town. The Tory, loyalist though he was, couldn't stomach the thought of a surprise attack on Woods Hole, so he sent his son to warn the town. The boy ran down the island at night, and then rowed across the channel and spread the word.

The British tried to land at this beach and were confronted in their long boats by several determined companies of locals, who raked them with musket fire from the beach. I can see them now, the line of twenty or thirty men at the back of the beach, forming up, kneeling, firing, the puffs of smoke from their barrels rounding up into the air and then swept off by the wind.

The English replied with cannon fire from their landing craft, and with fire from the ships as they lay offshore. The technique was to fire low, so that the shot would skip across the water and then bound up from the water's edge to mangle. The cannon of the English failed, however; the balls buried themselves harmlessly in the slush that gathered in a thick band along the beach. The oppressors were repulsed.

What must that have been like? The English were approaching in small boats with one-pounders mounted on the bow, perhaps, and the locals—fit to be hung by the king if caught—were formed up in ragged lines, taking cover behind low dunes, their horses held back a ways by younger men and boys, ready to be brought up if the British tried to land farther down the coast. The war was not close to won, the Constitution still in the distance, Daniel Shays not having forced the hand of Congress to put our founding principles into writing. And they fought, and the victors were defended by slush. And here I drove along their battlefield.

I coasted down to the end of this stretch of road, two and four-tenths miles I had run a thousand times, and turned around in a parking lot where the road headed inland. I had just wanted to see the beach. I hadn't seen anyone else since clearing the village.

After I turned around I drove west, retracing my steps. I could see that the big salt ponds just inland of the barrier beach were frozen. The first pond was milky white, colored by its high salt content (it being called Salt Pond). The second pond—less salty—was a dark lambent gray where the snow hadn't gathered.

This second pond was Oyster Pond, and its ice was harder and more reliable than that of Salt Pond for skating. Along the edges of these ponds—between the ponds and the road— were low dunes, with beach grass and bear oak and *Rosa rugosa* growing there, and when you walked into these scrublands, and then sat on a rock to lace on your skates, you disappeared among the low trees. This is what I'd done a few days before.

Once I was sitting down on the rock, the road was suddenly gone and the houses on the far shore were gone, and there was only the small world of the little trees and the grass, and the pathways the animals had made through them, and the next edge was the edge of the pond, where the ice was whorled around rocks that rested in shallow water. When my skates were tight I pushed off, crossed over where the sand ended, and glided out onto the dark frozen pond water.

Today I had gone for a drive again in the snow, and the Saab chugged softly as we drifted down the road. I was less interested in the ice of the ponds than in the ice on the bay three-quarters of a mile distant, due north across the waist of Woods Hole, so once I cleared Oyster Pond I bore right, turned the car dead downwind, and let her ease through the curves of Oyster Pond Road and then across the state highway, across the spine of the moraine, and down the other side steeply to Quissett Harbor.

Ten thousand years ago, I liked to think, I would still have had three or four miles to drive to the ocean here, descending three hundred feet more as I did so, but now, conveniently, the sea had risen, and Quissett was right there where I knew it would be, where I had it calibrated in my bones.

The inner harbor there was still frozen. We had had a long stretch of fourteen days averaging twenty degrees, with the nights dipping to eight or ten degrees. And the sea ice in particular held my attention, particularly out near where I moored the boat in summer, because sea ice changes from moment to moment.

But it was set up good, for now. Michael Casso, with whom I had skated on Oyster Pond on Tuesday, said that on Sunday he and a friend had walked a mile out onto the sea ice at Gunning Point, a mile north of the harbor here. He said they were roped up and were wearing dry suits, and that once they got away from shore the ice was solid. It sounds like a foolhardy thing to do. I wished I'd been along.

Today, though, I wanted just to see the sea ice and assess it, and of course to imagine what setting out across it would be like.

I left the car in a space at the back of the harbor, and strolled along the seawall there, and then past the dock, where I observed the silent sheet of ice that lay over the harbor, covered by the inch of new snow, except right along the shore, where a tinge of green shone through as the tide came on, and seawater rose through the splintered margins.

The late afternoon light was low and tinted red, nearly horizontal, and lent objects a subtle integrity. The edges of things became sharp in this light—and the few boats left afloat in the harbor were crisp against the white ice.

A crow cawed from the trees to my right, and then the ice thumped ominously, as it cracked with a distant report. Across

the harbor lay a long black sloop. Only a small doghouse inter-
rupted her stiletto-like lines. A plump little catboat was moored
nearby, an old boat by the looks of her backward-leaning bow.
I'd watched two men tromp around the cat the evening before,
no doubt plotting her release.

I took the path that threaded through the woods on the
north side of the harbor, and headed toward the beach and
open water, moving quietly under the low trees, their branches sheltering me a bit from the snowfall. They were mostly pin
oak and white oak, sassafrass and eastern red cedar: small trees
in this windblown, sandy soil.

I soon broke out of the woods, and saw the white sea ice
of the bay stretching away. I kept on along the path, and then
out along a narrow isthmus with the sea on either side, and
climbed quickly to the summit of a sharp little hill known lo-
cally as the "Knob."

This small promontory overlooks the outer harbor of Quissett, and beyond that, Buzzards Bay, which gathers on all sides.
From here I could see two pressure ridges curving out from
the beach to my right, curving out into the grey-white haze of
the sea ice and the falling snow. I could also see, two hundred
yards to my left, in the shelter of Gansett Cove, *Daphie's* mooring site, where she would float in the warmth of the coming
summer.

But the snow kept on, slanting in from the east at about
eight miles an hour. I looked out for several minutes at the
ice stretching away and disappearing into a horizon of snow
and sky intermingled. Then I retraced my steps off the little
hill and along the narrow isthmus, back to the main body of
the peninsula, and took a side path off to the right and down
through low trees—bear oak and black cherry here—and then
down the side of a little ridge, descending again toward the
harbor, until I came out on a beach. I stood there, at the back

of the beach under a small oak, its brown buds crowding its twig ends.

The snow came on, more heavily, and began to gather on me. I stood there for thirty minutes looking out at the harbor, at the dark line of eelgrass along the beach, the irregular plates of white ice along the shore, and far across the ice to the cove where *Daphie* would float. Occasionally a pool along the beach would gurgle as water flowed into it, or a piece of ice would slump into open water, and I would hear the water cover it.

My shoulders became white, as did the tops of the tree limbs; the creases of my clothes held small drifts. And there was the sound from the light brown leaves on the ground as the snow landed on them—a chirr.

The muted hues of the day worked back into my eyes—the white curve of the shore strewn with dark granite boulders capped with snow, the green light of the rising tide, a white oak fallen on the beach twenty feet from me, its grey trunk horizontal and reaching out over the ice, its dark roots thrown up in a fan above the edge of the peninsula. The sea had eroded the bank here until it had given way. It was carrying the land away, gradually. And this, somehow, was boatbuilding: To watch the ice as it moved, know the place that way too.

30. Talisker

ON AN EVENING NOT long after that walk, after the wind shifted and blew the ice out to sea, I drove again to Quissett, down the steep approach road. If the harbor is shaped like a comma, then this road brings one to the dot of the comma, with the tail being the channel reaching out toward Buzzards Bay.

It is an intimate cove, just a quarter mile across, with a lane along its back edge. A heavily wooded peninsula separates it from the sea. As evening comes on in winter, the hills around the cove darken and take on mass, and the water seems somehow more cold, the wind moving above less friendly, as the sun fades in the distance.

I parked where the road met the harbor's edge, and began to walk along the back of the cove. The light was just going from the western sky, and the harbor was nearly empty. A few boats still swung on moorings. I had walked a hundred yards, looking down at the dark water, when I saw a person moving toward me, a dark shape against darker trees, moving fast along the same side of the road.

"Hello," I said, and after a moment back came "Hello." It was Rafe, I could see now, with his arms swinging loose as he moved easily along.

"Who goes there?" he said.

"Dan Robb here, Rafe. Nice night for a walk."

"Fine evening," he said, and then "What're you up to?"

"Coming back from the A&P. I thought I'd take a ramble, see how the harbor looked. You?"

"Out for a walk," he said, sniffing at the wind as a gust moved past.

"How far'd you go?" I asked.

"Couple of miles," he said. "I'd be all crippled up if I didn't walk every day."

"Yeah," I said, "I need to get out and move, too. Harder to hit a moving target."

"That's it," he said, and then we were silent for a moment

as we both looked out over the dark harbor. Then, squinting at me, he said, "You have time for a dram on *Altair*?"

This was an unexpected offer, to be asked onto Rafe's boat. He lived on her, one of two liveaboards in the harbor, and he was famously retiring, sometimes not asking anyone aboard for months at time.

"Sure," I said. "I'd like to see her."

"Come on," he said, and sparked off down the road back the way I'd come. I caught up to him as he got to the low dock where three or four dinghies swung, and we shoved off in his pram, which he'd built himself out of half-inch marine ply. He propelled it by sculling a single oar, swaying it back and forth in a leather-lined notch in the top edge of the transom. Quickly we were in the lee of *Altair*, his forty-five-foot steel ketch, which lay on the far side of the inner lagoon.

She was painted dark blue, with the lines of an old wooden boat, and had a dark wood deck and cabin top. As we clambered through the cockpit, and then down the companionway into the cabin, I experienced for the many-hundredth time the feeling of going from the raw and inhospitable deck of a boat in winter to the sheltered and welcoming space of a well-kept cabin. Get belowdecks, out of the wind, and suddenly all is well, you feel warm, and when the hatch is shut and the air is stilled within, you have entered another world, safe, calm, replete.

Rafe took off his jacket and hung it on a hook behind the companionway ladder, and then took mine and hung it there, too, and then in the semidarkness struck a match and lit three kerosene lanterns, two mounted on the bulkhead at the forward end of the salon—the main cabin—and one on the starboard side of the cabin above a chart table.

We were in a classic salon. There was a long, comfortable bench on each side of the cabin, with a pipe berth folded up above each, tucked up under the deck. To starboard forward against the midships bulkhead there was a small coal stove on a tile hearth. At the back of the cabin (to port of the companionway ladder) was a simple but efficient galley, with alcohol stove, a small oven, a generous sink. To starboard of the companionway ladder was a large desk, facing forward, where there was a GPS, a radar monitor, and a ship-to-shore radio, all folded out of the way. A small pile of mail lay there, unopened. Astern of this nav station was a small door, which was ajar, that led into an after cabin with a double berth.

Forward, beyond the bulkhead by the stove, I could see there was a large head to port, and then a generous forward cabin with two more large berths. All was finished below in bright mahogany, the bulkhead was painted white, and booklined shelves were fit here and there. On the sole, which was painted a russet red, was a thick runner of Oriental pattern. All was snug, clean, and looked ready to go.

"What'll it be?" asked Rafe. "A friend of mine from Aberdeen just brought me a bottle of single malt. Talisker," he said reading from the bottle, which he'd pulled out of a cabinet. "Will you join me?"

"I'll have a finger or two," I said.

He produced a couple of tumblers, poured the ration, handed me mine, said "L'Chaim" as he held up his glass, and then commenced building a fire in the little stove, which was soon ticking quietly and warming up.

"I don't often have visitors out here, as it ain't too big, but once in a while it's good to get another voice on the boat, or I begin to take both sides of the conversation," he said.

"Mind if I take a look up forward?" I asked.

"Not at all," he said.

I went through the doorway in the bulkhead, past the little head with its tile shower, and into the forward cabin. The port berth was made up—clearly this was Rafe's bunk—and there were several canvas bins of clothes on the opposite bunk, and a few books in a pile, one of them the great French mountaineer Lionel Terray's *Les Conquérants de l'inutile,* which had a bookmark in it about halfway through.

Above each bunk a small kerosene lamp was mounted, and there were several small bookshelves here and there. The hull was ceiled with mahogany up forward as well, with the bulkhead into the chain locker in the bow painted white. The sound of the wind was more muted forward, with the sounds mainly water lapping at the waterline, and the slapping of halyards on the painted aluminum mainmast that came down through the cabin just across from the head. It was snug, an ideal place to read or rest, away from the sprawling concerns of the land.

"When was she built?" I asked as I came back into the salon.

"Well, I welded the hull up in the late '70s in my backyard," he began, "But she's an old design, drawn by a guy named Fenger back in '38. He called it a dhow wishbone ketch, but I just liked the way she looked. She's got a reverse drag to her keel like the Arab dhows, which I think is why she's so good in a seaway. Looks odd to the old-timers below the waterline, but heave to in her sometime in a good blow—bow on or stern on, it don't matter—and it feels like you're sitting in church."

"How did you manage to match a wooden form with steel? I mean, I'm assuming it was drawn originally to be built in wood," I asked as I settled onto the starboard bench, and took a sip of the single malt, which was dark, dense with flavors of peat and charred wood.

"Well, I matched it *pretty* closely," he said. "*Altair* does have hard chines, below the waterline, and the lines are not a perfect match, but they're close in terms of the overall effect. This boat handles like the one Fenger drew, I'm convinced, and she's round enough that if she were in ice, she'd just get squeezed up on top of the pack like a lemon seed, and ride it out."

"You ever taken her north?" I asked. I knew that he and Bill had worked together for some years, since the early '90s, but I didn't know much about Rafe other than that.

"I sailed her up into Hudson Bay one year, nearly got frozen in. I was toying with the ice. I had enough food to last the winter, thought it might do me good to just find a cove and watch the polar bears for a few months, but in the end I decided I'd rather spend the winter in Saint John's. More ladies around." And then he looked me in the eye and changed the subject. "So how's that boat of yours coming along?"

"It's coming along all right," I said. "I got about fifteen new frames in her this fall and winter, with the help of a friend, until I lost steam about a month ago. I was assigned a piece to write, and decided to let the boat go until the weather moderated."

"Whole thing treating you well?" he asked.

"It's going right along, but there's something strange about it, as if the boat had a life of its own, and keeps turning my mind back to it, even when I'm out for a walk on the Knob, or a run in the woods. It's like she's working on my mind, trying to keep my life centering on her, rather than anything else."

"Hah!" said Rafe, slapping his thigh with his left hand and jumping up. "That's what my ex-wife used to say. She'd say, 'Why is that boat on your mind more than me?' And I'd say, 'It's not, but if we're ever going to sail her around the world, I better build her right.' And she'd say something like, 'Well it's not so hard to take a plane to Paris,' and finally I realized about the time our kids were through college that she never had wanted to go sailing. I guess it was three months later I was living aboard *Altair,* and she was selling the house and moving to North Carolina. There you have it. Fourteen years later, I'm still living on her, plotting my escape."

"Where you headed?" I asked.

"Wait and see," he said, and his eyes twinkled a little. Then he said, "So look at this damned bilge, would you," and we spent about twenty minutes looking at the bilge, admiring the steel floor timbers, and the dryness of it, and how everything was painted well, and how all of the plumbing down there was color-coded—engine coolant pipes, freshwater pipes, and fuel lines. He showed me how, by moving a valve handle on a pipe by the companionway, he could switch from running seawater through the engine as coolant to pumping the bilge through the same circuit in case there were ever a catastrophic leak that the pumps couldn't handle. The boat was simple, well thought out, and tough, far as I could tell.

After he'd shown me the engine, which was painted yellow and was clean as a whistle—a big old Perkins diesel that looked as if it might have begun life hauling dry goods in a truck—I asked him what he thought of Herreshoff.

"You mean Nat?" he said.

"Yeah," I said.

"Well, he was a genius," he said. "Or if he wasn't a genius, he was close. Whatever he lacked he made up for with terrifically hard work, put it that way. I mean the guy worked all the time. I've thought a lot about him, over the years, as I've worked on his boats. You know, what was he thinking when he did that, why did he cut away the forefoot here and not there, etcetera, and there's six or seven things that I come up with. But I gotta pee. Give me a minute, and I'll tell you. You want a little more?" he said, gesturing to the bottle.

"Sure, a little more. Not much—I've got to drive home."

He poured me another couple of fingers, and then disappeared into the head. I took my drink, slid back the hatch, and climbed up on deck to look at the weather. It was dark out, and it took a few moments for my eyes to adjust. The boat was swinging lightly at her mooring, the breeze was light and cold out of the west, about eight knots, and the stars had come out hard in the sky. They seemed particularly close. I walked up toward the bow, beyond the mast, and leaned against the first forestay where it came down at the base of the bowsprit. It was easy to imagine her moving forward through this breeze, outbound, and it reminded me of the many nights I'd stood at the bow of one vessel or another, on watch, as the stem moved through the sea below me, the sound of the water parting rhythmically there, the wind moving through the rig, and the quiet thumping of reef points and rope against taut canvas sails as they pulled us along.

I went below again after a couple of minutes (after I heard Rafe pumping the head into the holding tank), returned to the warmly lit cabin, out of the wind, and Rafe was sitting on the port bench.

"Herreshoff was remarkable," he said. "I think the first thing that comes to mind is that he sailed small boats when they were used to haul things. The first boats he knew were designed for speed, but they were like pickup trucks that are meant to go faster than the other guy's pickup truck. They were catboats and cutters—this would have been 1850 or so—with the mast forward to give space to work, and a broad, deep hull so you could haul something, and they had to be able to survive any kind of weather. They were working craft, so he came out of a very practical side of things, even though he's known for his racers.

"Second," he said, and I realized that I'd opened a can of worms by asking this question, and that a few were going to get out and crawl around before the conversation was done, "the guy was a highly trained engineer, went to MIT, worked for Corliss designing steam engines, so he was always looking for better engineering, the efficient solution, so he had these things going for him in terms of design. Third, everyone is always saying that the whole world shifted with *Gloriana,* when he drew that cutaway forefoot, and lessened the wetted area and cut the drag, and got the mass lower in the keel, and grew the rig taller for more leverage up there, but if you look at his own writings, you hear him say that the shift away from the deep forefoot and more toward a cut-away spoon bow, and a higher-aspect rig—all of that happened *gradually,* through quite a few designs, and that people finally just noticed it in *Gloriana.*"

Rafe had pulled one foot up onto the bench, and was hugging his right knee into his chest as he talked, looking up and off into space, and I could tell that these were thoughts about the great designer that he had been pulling together for quite some time, as he puzzled while he was shaping a horn timber, or thought about the particulars of one of Nat's designs. Like a lot of people, Rafe was quite happy to harangue me with his ponderings, as long as he thought I was interested.

"He was also eccentric," he went on. "He built catamarans before anyone else in the country, and said they were his favorite boats to sail, which you might not guess when you're looking at all the work that went into *Reliance* or *Constitution.*" Here he was referring to two of Herreshoff's great America's Cup defenders.

"Another thing that you can't forget about him is his family. Like when he went to Europe when he was twenty-six. You know about that trip?" he asked, looking at me. I took another sip of the single malt. I had read of the trip, but I wanted to hear how he would tell it.

"A little," I said.

"Well, Nat was twenty-six, and was working for Corliss, designing steam engines, plus he was drawing all of the boats for his brother John's boatbuilding company in Bristol, which was going great guns, and John was blind—glaucoma—but he still ran the whole deal, and Nat just got tuckered out, so they sent him over to the south of France for a break. This would have been 1874 or so. His brother Lewis was also over there. And the two of them built a boat together, of course, and sailed that around the Med for a while, and then they built another one, and sailed that one all around the coast there, and then took it up all kinds of rivers and canals and up the Rhine, and had all kinds of adventures on waterways that led them eventually to the English Channel.

"Then they put the boat on a steamer, took it over to England, sailed it around over there for a while on all kinds of rivers and canals, then put it on another steamer in Liverpool for New York City. When they got there they threw their boat in the East River with a customs agent chasing after them for a while, 'til they lost him, and they just sailed right up Long Island Sound most of the way to Narragansett Bay, where their brothers John and James met them in a steam launch John had built with a boiler in it designed by James.

"Shortly after that their father showed up in his sailboat *Julia* that he'd built some years before, and they all sailed and steamed home together. And what I didn't mention was that Lewis, the brother he'd been traveling with in Europe, was blind, too. See," he looked at me here, "they had this family that was indefatigable. They did everything they wanted with boats. They had no 'impossible' filter between them and the world. Or at least a very thin one."

We both took a drink here, and he stared at the stove for half a minute, and then he went on.

"There's a couple of other things there, too. Nat designed

all of these great boats, Cup defenders, and steam-driven tor-pedo boats for the navy, designed every part, right down to the propeller, and he was the best at it, but it's interesting to me that his favorite boats were that second little boat from the Med which was named *Riviera,* and another he had built later, which was very close to *Riviera,* called *Coquina.* They were both lightly built, shallow, with a good piece of sail. They were monohulls, easily rigged, rowed easy too, and he liked to say that he could shove off from his boathouse and have one rigged and sailing before the wind could push him back in. He could just go.

"He said he liked sailing his catamaran best, and he said that *Constitution* was his favorite design among the defenders, but his favorite all-around boats, out of all of them, were those two little light daysailers, because you could sail them at the drop of a hat. No 'Do I have enough muscle with me to get the main up?' None of that. Just go. And that seems right to me. He was a sailor, and a practical man, and he knew that the point of it all, in the end, is to sail."

At about this point, I realized that the tea I'd drunk before going to the grocery store had worked its way through me, and that I had better offload it, but I felt bad about filling up Rafe's holding tank.

"Rafe," I said, "I need to have a slash. Any chance I can just go on deck, go off the stern."

"Sure," he said. "As long as it's dark out. I can't afford to have the local ladies angry at me for indecent peeing."

"It's dark," I said to reassure him, and headed up on deck again. Soon the tea was pattering into the harbor as I braced myself against the stanchions at the stern, careful not to soak the painter on the dinghy, which hung out behind. I had about a half hour left before I knew I ought to go. I noted, as I crossed the cockpit to go below again, that there were a few Tibetan prayer flags flying, strung from the mizzen sheet to the end of the mizzen boom. They were ragged, blown almost completely away. I hadn't noticed them in my trips past the boat before.

"I see you've got some prayer flags flying out there," I said as I came down again.

"Yeah," said Rafe. "I picked those up years ago, a bunch of them. I fly a few at a time, let 'em get ragged and then blown away."

"Do you know what the text on them means?" I asked as I took the next-to-last sip of the whiskey.

"I've got an idea, yeah," he said. Then he changed the subject, and I felt it was time to go.

"Rafe," I said, "this has been great, but I've got to go home in time to make a couple of phone calls."

"Right," he said, and quickly we were in the dinghy, and he was sculling it into the float, I was jumping ashore, and he was bound outward again, hunched in the stern.

"Thanks for the drink, Rafe!" I yelled out to him.

"We'll do it again," he bellowed back, and I drove home, after sitting in the truck for twenty minutes to be sure that I was clearheaded enough to drive.

31. *March*

IN MARCH I SURRENDERED again on the boat for a while, contenting myself to feed the woodstove and finish an article I'd been assigned. It was the time of limitless grey on the Cape, time to watch the weather, ponder the end of things, wonder if the forecasters could say something other than "sleet," "hail," "slush," "fog."

Toward the end of the month, a friend had a weekend, and wondered if he might come down to the Cape and see how one bent in a frame. I was quick to say yes.

Bart arrived in snow on a Friday night, and by the time we got out to the shed, around nine the next morning, the snow had drifted neatly up its sides to a height of four feet. I had fired up the steam box at 8:15, made him a breakfast of eggs and buckwheat cakes—his wages—and presented him to the interior of the boat at nine sharp.

"How many are we shootin' for?" he asked, and I replied, "As many as we're comfortable doing."

That day we managed five, and seven more on Sunday, and I didn't put the drill into the palm of his hand until the twelfth. The bit did not bite deep. But some of his questions did. On the first day he asked, from his perch in the cockpit, as we waited for a rib to steam, "Why white oak?"

To which I replied, "Well, it's what's used around here, in my experience, because it's here, for one thing, and because it's rot resistant, hard, strong, can be found with straight grain . . . When we were replacing frames in an old schooner I worked on, the *Sylvina Beal*, she'd been built with white oak frames, back in 1911, and we were just then in 1990 replacing those seventy-nine-year-old frames. The thing was, to replace the frames we had to take out the trunnels that held them, and the trunnels were locust, and they were still so hard you couldn't dent them with your thumbnail."

"Man," he said. I pondered that I had heard myself tell that story before, maybe liked telling it a little too much.

He also asked, soon after we'd begun on the first day, "So, how precise do we have to be with lengths here, and with milling in general?"

I was intimidated by this question because Bart is a furniture builder, a man of fine tolerances, one who would err on the side of microns rather than mere sixteenths. I on the other hand was a competent carpenter. I could do finish work and cabinetry if pressed (and pressed hard) but tended to build something sturdily and then be distracted by a bird. Or a conversation.

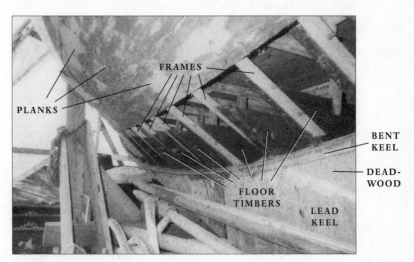

A view of the port side of the bottom of the boat, with two bottom planks (the garboard and the broad plank) removed, showing new frames.

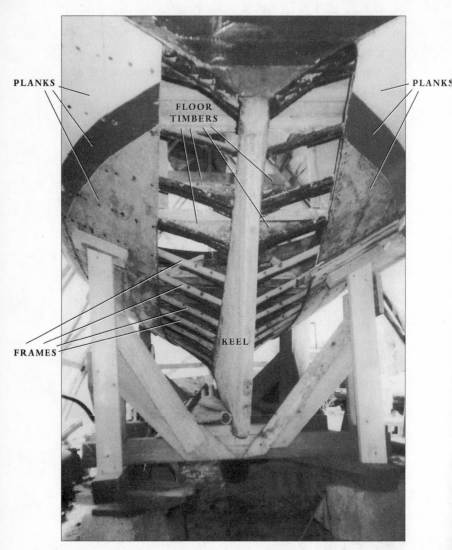

A view from astern and beneath with two bottom-most planks (garboard and broad plank) removed on each side, showing new frames.

"Well," I began to answer, "I've been milling them to thirteen-sixteenths of an inch *fat,* maybe as much as fourteen-sixteenths, because they're going to dry out some and lose that extra sixteenth. L. Francis Herreshoff, Nat's son, said you never want to leave the wood rough, because that will encourage rot, so I run them by the saw blade on all faces, and then sand them with the random orbital. Then I cut them to the right length, with an angle cut in the bottom where the new frame comes down right near the bent keel, and a few chamfers at the top to take the edge off and let it slide easy up between the sheer strake and the sheer clamp."

Bart grunted. This seemed to sit all right with him, although you never can tell with fussy craftsmen. They all have ways they like to do things. But I was glad rehabbing this boat was not particularly fine work. It was grueling, snowy, steamy, dusty, cramped work, with the risk (if you were my helper) of puncture wounds, but it wasn't particularly fine work. Thank heavens for that. And for friends like Bart, who helped me so much.

32. April

I HAD ANOTHER ARTICLE to bang out, and the light was returning. I had agreed that once the article was done, I would sign on with my friend Sean for a few months, working on a house he was building for a rich fellow over in North Falmouth. All of this would take care of itself. I had sharpened my chisels and planes, dug the debris out of the pockets of my tool belt, and hung the belt on the wall near the door in anticipation of the day, soon, when I would carry it out the door to the car at 7 A.M., again a house carpenter. Hammer, pencil, speed square, chisel, knife, cat's-paw, tape, nailsets—the standard kit. Show up with those eight items in a belt with some pouches for nails, a ring for your hammer, and your brain set to "go," and you can work in any of these fifty states. The boat would have to wait for a few months, until the coffers were full again. But Bart's visit had spurred a question in me.

This question kept redounding as I sat on the toilet and looked at the imperfectly finished light switch (I needed to get in there with some spackle and paint), and as I sat by the woodstove and noted it was not perfectly blacked, and showed some rust. I'd caulked it, and put screws in the stovepipe, and lined the old brick chimney with a stainless-steel pipe. That thing was bulletproof. But the collar around the pipe where it disappeared into the chimney looked a little rough. It was dented. Did I care? The system was safe, effective, installed to code. But the collar was dented . . . the stove a little rusty. Would the boat reflect the same standard? How perfectly would I refinish the boat? To what level of gloss and shine? To what level of finish in *all* things did I aspire, and what did that portend for the whole project?

This morning, as I made a fire to take the chill off the cottage, the answer came. I was not a stellar craftsman. I was a competent carpenter. I would make *Daphie* strong and sound, and make her look as good as I could; I would not insist on perfection of finish; I would shoot for making her Bristol—neat, clean, protected, pleasing to the eye—but I would remember always that I was not a god, but rather a mere man, with a boat that would look like it had been painted by a man. That was good enough.

33. May

I AM SITTING IN the shed, on the stump, in the evening. I spend forty-five hours a week these days framing, siding, building stairs, installing hardwood floors, and hanging cabinets. *Daphie* was built in 1939 by men like those I work with now. Most of them were good men, strong, eager to lend their energy.

Most of them were also friendly, interesting, sociable. (A few were quiet, angry, alcoholic, stifled. Those few didn't last long at the Herreshoff plant, no doubt. That type can survive around some house construction sites somewhat longer, especially if they can produce while grumping.) The bottom line is there was *something* to what these men did. They had pride enough to show up and not back down, to build boats, even when they'd never own the boat themselves. Perhaps theirs was a blind pride, attached to a product that might or might not have uplifted humankind. Yet there *is* a positive energy in any well-built dwelling, and in any well-built boat.

She is a thing of quality, this boat. She does have characteristics which make her *good,* somehow, not the least of which is the work that went into her—the hours men spent cutting, bending, fastening, making her with care. (I don't know if there were any woman carpenters at the Herreshoff plant. I haven't seen any pictures of women working there. If there were, then all of this goes for them, too.) From these actions they won bread, bought homes, raised families. Their work is in her.

She holds several people comfortably, and so is a vehicle for conversation and camaraderie.

She is simple, can be handled easily by one competent sailor, and so can also be a way to solitude and reflection.

And she is pleasing to the eye, in the way anything well proportioned and sweetly arranged is.

She is relatively economical to run. If you can sand, paint, and caulk, you can take care of your own boat like this one, for the investment of several long weekends of labor each year. It is a small price.

And she has something to her, an arrangement in space—where her mast rises, how her gunwales curve forward, defining the cockpit—that seems near perfect to me, as if a geometric/aesthetic law were followed in her creation. Like any room in which one feels comfortable, or forest clearing that seems right for a nap, she has this quality of security and peace.

But the question of the worth of the boat dogs me. Why am I either at work on the boat (occasionally, when weather, light, time, and inclination correspond) or pounding nails and feeling bad about not being at work on her?

Did a fifteen-foot boat merit this odd devotion? Yep.

34. June

THE LEAVES ARE OUT. It is Friday evening, the light is fading, and today we cut, hoisted, and nailed in place forty twenty-four-foot Douglas fir rafters. I am tired the way one is tired when every muscle has been tested and found somewhat wanting. As I lie here on the old green couch, inert, I observe that the calluses on my right hand, which swings the hammer are thick, and that my left hand is still tinged red from a small tear in the palm, torn as I slid it up a piece of plywood and caught a large splinter. Another month of this, of rock and roll on the radio, doughnuts and coffee at ten o'clock, nail guns, joists, mildly obscene humor, compressors, and the like, and it will be time to turn again to the boat. Which never really leaves my mind those days. However, I've been thinking about this exchange:

One evening three months ago, after a winter Saturday spent "wooding" brightwork (sanding down the varnished bits, including the seats and coaming, to bare wood), I went to a potluck dinner given by an old family friend. Soon enough I was cornered by a couple of guys, Mark and Fritz, who between them had spent close to a hundred years sailing and racing around Woods Hole.

At first I was talking by the stairs to Fritz, who had a glass of pinot noir in his hand, as did I. He was a big man who had spent many years dealing with the daily operations of the local yacht club, which sat about a hundred yards away on Great Harbor.

It was a workaday club, with inexpensive dues. It had a small cottage as home base on the shore, and a couple of simple piers at which one could land. Dinghies swung at lanyards along one pier; a small tug and whoever showed up used the other. Small sailboats and dories and pulling boats lined the beaches on either side, and the place had the feel of welcome and lack of pretense that was entirely right, in my mind. Fritz was looking for another good thing to say about his ancient Toyota pickup, when Mark backed up against the stairs and cut his engines. He was also drinking a glass of wine, and his hair stood up in a jumbled mass on his head, giving him the aspect of a sixty-year-old punker. In fact he was a marine biologist, but that didn't matter. They were old friends.

"Hey, pirate man," growled Fritz.

"How you doin', bandito?" scowled Mark back at him.

"You got your boat in yet?" asked Fritz.

"Which one?" asked Mark.

"I dunno," said Fritz.

"It's February!"

"So?" said Fritz. "Are they ready or not?"

"Well," said Mark, "the Thistle is ready to go, but the H-twenty-eight, I don't know what I'm gonna do with her."

"Now that Thistle," Fritz said, pointing his forefinger at me gently, with the rest of his big hand wrapped around the wineglass, and the other arm wrapped around the newel post. He was referring here to a class of canoe hulled, plumb bowed, eighteen-foot sloops that roared through races in Woods Hole. "That Thistle is a *hell* of a boat. Fast and lively, and draws about nothin'. I mean, there isn't a faster monohull boat around here, in the hands of someone who can handle her."

"That's right," said Mark. "And the key there is 'around here,' because that's the challenge!—knowing where you can go, where there's water, where there's wind, and where the current is. That's right. But I don't know what I'm going to do with my H-twenty-eight."

"That boat's a pig," said Fritz, not unkindly.

Mark looked at Fritz for a long moment, considered feeling hurt, then nodded, and said, looking at his feet, "That's right. She's underpowered. Not enough sail."

"And Dan," began Fritz, "your boat—Dan's restoring a twelve-and-a-half," he explained to Mark with a gesture of his wineglass toward me, "That boat of yours hobby-horses all day long. They don't go worth a fig. It's a lousy design, and useless around here."

"In the shallows," I said.

"That's right," agreed Fritz.

"But," I said. "I don't know if I agree that the H-twenty-eight is a pig. I mean, that's a boat that's designed to be sailed around the world, and plenty have, so her rig's designed not to be overpowered. I think it's a wonderful design, and you can sail the snot out of one in a gale if you know how. I think she ghosts pretty well, too, for that matter."

Mark looked at me for a long moment.

"I got one," he said. "You want it?"

"Well," I said, "maybe. But you've got to moderate your view on the hobby-horsing a little, Fritz."

"No sir," he said. "Those sons of guns hobby-horse to a fare-thee-well. You can't *make* 'em go in a seaway. But the Thistle, now there's a boat for all places."

This last bit of strong opinion got Mark laughing. I began to angle away toward the kitchen, and left as Fritz was saying, "There was a windward leg where I could see that—*if* I could split the boulder and spindle, and in so doing risk the skeg, I might win by a lot, or I could bear off and lose to that windbag again . . ."

"He can sail," said Mark.

"Ahhhh, but he's a son of a gun and you know it," said Fritz.

"Yup," said Mark.

"But," continued Fritz, "I saw this enormous trawler coming through Broadway *might* give me a propitious wake that I could surf right down through the gap there, and by gosh if he didn't. I went through there like stink, bumped the board lightly, tacked under the farmhouse, rounded the windward mark first, and lived on winning that race for at least six months. By gosh, that was a day I liked!"

Their advice, received later in the evening, was to "Let her rot. Get a Thistle, or a Knockabout [Cape Cod Knockabout, a Phil Rhodes design], and start for Pete's sake living!"

Odd. Barely a mile away the boat that I was restoring was wildly popular. But then there were deeper waters in Quissett, and over there the people knew how to sail them in a seaway, where they are the best small boat I've ever encountered. But you have to get the boat inside you to sail it in more than twenty knots of wind.

35. *June 21*

IT WAS EARLY SUMMER in the second year of the rebuild, and I had done enough house carpentry to coast for a couple of months. The boat sat on its cradle in the yard, next to the cottage, with tall grass, greenbriar, hairy vetch, and wild rose all vying for the light on its far side. It was time to get back to work on her.

I knew two things:

I had done the hardest single chore in the catalog of what the boat needed: I had replaced most of her ribs.

What remained was a lot of grinding, sanding, mucking out, bunging, priming, painting, caulking, varnishing, and painting some more. It would be a slog, like refinishing . . . a fifteen-foot-long violin.

The short list of the chores that remained:

• Repair and refasten floorboards, and the slender joists
  that support them.

- Recondition the four lower planks; refasten them to boat.
- Build five new mast hoops.
- Reattach covering boards along gunwales (rebung each screw hole, so eighty bungs).
- Reinstall seats.
- Recanvas decks.
- Epoxy, scarf, and fair transom.
- Fill all screw holes, above and below waterline.
- Recaulk all seams with appropriate caulk.
- Refinish interior, including eight layers (at least) of varnish on seats, covering boards, toe rail, and transom.
- Repaint the exterior.
- Refinish all spars (eight layers varnish).
- Rebuild bulkhead between cockpit and forepeak. Install new flotation.
- Launch.

As I looked from June out over July and August, this was my charge.

I don't have much to say about the skill set needed to accomplish these tasks. You do have to be somewhat dogged and willing to put up with repetitive work (a positive spin on this might be "meditative work"), but there are no special skills needed here. Well, happiness with drills in hand might be one (when drilling and countersinking new holes, cutting bungs, and driving screws), and with chisels (for trimming bungs once glued in). Patience might be another. And perhaps most important: an understanding that the work can be done effectively and in a manner salutary to the boat even if there is a bubble or two in the varnish, or a streak or two in the paint. In other words, my cars are seldom polished, but the belts are new(ish), the oil changed, the tires sound, the brakes in good shape. A couple of other thoughts:

1. When buying bung cutters for making the little wooden bungs one fills screw holes with, buy the best you can get, which are expensive, and which actually work in hardwoods like oak and mahogany. Fuller makes good ones, and these, being expensive, are usually kept like jewels behind the counter at the lumberyard, as in "with this bung cutter I thee wed."

2. When mixing two-part epoxy, budget your time wisely, and don't use a fast hardener unless you really can get it done in ten minutes. Better to use the slow hardener 99 percent of the time, and budget a glass of iced tea and a phone call to your bookie while it hardens, than to have it go to immovable snot before the piece is really in place. Or use that time to copy a Constitutional amendment and hide it somewhere to be found in a time of national crisis.

3. Always have a couple of good countersinking bits on hand. And consider buying a right-angle drill, as they can simplify life greatly, and can be hard to find when you don't have one.

4. And in doing all of this, I would defer to Joshua Slocum, the first man to sail around the world alone (1895–98), who said,

> It is only right to say, though, that to insure a reasonable measure of success, experience should sail with the ship. But in order to be a successful navigator or sailor, it is not necessary to hang a tar bucket about one's neck. On the other hand, much thought concerning the brass buttons one should wear adds nothing to the safety of the ship.

Amen. This little ship has no brass, nor do I, and though I have worn a tar bucket around my neck in the past, I'd rather stick to flat white paint and a rig of bronze and stainless steel now.

So my task lay before me. I had two months to finish the boat before other callings began to draw me down again. I began with the planks.

36. The Planks

ON THE FIRST MONDAY in July I began on the four planks I'd removed from *Daphie* long before. It was a crisp day, with a forecast for a high of seventy-five degrees; in the shed it was cool when I got out there around nine with a cup of tea.

Daphie's planks were original (as far as I could tell) and whole, meaning they ran stem to stern with no breaks (which would have meant blocks at the butt ends and possible rot). They were cedar, which meant they were relatively soft, strong, and rot resistant. For the same reason a cedar chest keeps off the moths, cedar planks give up only slowly to organisms of any kind. It is a resinously toxic wood, and apt for boats trying to survive.

These planks were three and a half inches wide, although they tapered some toward their ends, and five-eighths of an inch thick. Also, they were beveled along their edges, so they were wider along the inside of the hull, and narrower by an eighth of an inch or so on the outside of the hull.

This meant that wherever two planks met, they met only

along their inner edges, and that a one-eighth-inch gap pertained all along their outer edges, and this is *the* thing I like about planks (in plank-on-frame construction): they must have caulking in that gap, and it is in having to caulk a boat that I have avoided many hazards in life. For it must be done to the finish of the last iota, or the boat leaks.

The principle of it is this: when the boat is launched (hopefully like a swan but we'll settle for merganser so long as she floats) the planks swell, and as they do the gap between them is largely erased. The caulking (rolled raw cotton fiber pressed into the seam, followed by a layer of underwater seam compound) is the stuffing which seals the gap and renders things actually watertight.

It is a wonder to feel a boat finally tighten up, after several days of leak. She is suddenly no longer a collection of planks loosely affiliated—she is one hull in tension.

Looking at the four bottom planks I had to reaffix, as I stood in the little shed, with a thicket of wild rose beyond, I could see that they would still work. They lay at length on sawhorses, and they were cracked here and there—scarred from rough use over the years, or from a screw head pulling through. But they would hunt.

So I got to work sanding, and then epoxying the planks, clamping them where a crack needed mending, and then letting them rest as the epoxy set up. They didn't lie flat, of course, but bellied down into the space below the tops of the horses. And though the outside edges of some of the planks were somewhat scarred, the important edges, the inside edges, were perfect along every plank. I knew she'd float with those planks, and I knew I'd be able to make the hull look fair enough, and I wasn't concerned about the damned brass buttons.

"Now it is a law in Lloyd's that the Jane repaired all out of the old until she is entirely new is still the Jane." That is Slocum again, regarding his gradual rebuilding of the *Spray* (the rotten thirty-six-foot sloop given to him by an old friend) in the 1890s.

I thought about him as I put those bottom planks back on, once the epoxy had set and I'd given them a final sanding. I reattached them, a screw at a time, taking my time. This was a relatively easy job—like replacing books in a row of books. But as I did it, as the early afternoon sun came down outside the shed and shone bright on the sandy road, I knew something good was happening.

I clamped the first plank on, and put a few new screws into new frames to hold it, and then clamped the second one on, and put in a few more new screws, and then the third and fourth planks went on, and suddenly the boat was whole again. Wow.

If I was putting the lower planks back on, this meant the major structural work on the boat was done . . . by god! I kept putting screws through the old planks into the new frames, gradually filling the last of the old screw holes until there were no empty ones left, and I kept thinking about Slocum.

He'd lost his beloved first wife at sea to illness, and then a couple of years later near the same place off the coast of Brazil he lost the sweet little bark the *Aquidneck* he had worked so hard to buy. He had a new wife by then, and got her and his three children back to Massachusetts by building a boat on the Brazilian beach out of scraps and sailing it home. That boat was the *Liberdade*. Ten years later, after more hard times, he'd been reduced to rebuilding the *Spray* ten miles from my cottage.

He took the *Spray* completely apart, and replaced her entirely, piece by piece, oak keel and stem and hard pine plank, no electricity involved, and then starting in 1898 he sailed her around the world *alone*—the first human to do so—with his wits, simple tools, some charts, a couple of guns, some thumbtacks, and a tin clock. I was no Slocum.

But I was done replacing the planks and was feeling the need to commune with someone who'd been engaged in similar work (albeit on a different level). So I decided to drive to the place where he rebuilt *Spray*, about ten miles north by water from where *Daphie* lay.

It was late afternoon, it was cool out, and I let my arm rest on the open windowsill as I drove, and watched the pines that grew in the poor soil along the highway. I had an uneventful drive around the bay, got off Route 195 in Fairhaven, and took the Saab down the main drag past a doughnut shop and and a package store, several small car dealerships, and finally down small lanes past ancient wood-frame houses, down to the quiet of the waterfront.

The place where Slocum restored *Spray* is a small grassy park now, with a boulder in a corner with a plaque on it. The tract looks out, as it did in Slocum's day, on a cove of Fairhaven harbor. Across the Acushnet River in the near distance is New Bedford and the remnants of her fishing fleet, sixty- and seventy-foot steel boats streaked with rust.

It's a residential part of town now, as it was when Slocum resurrected himself. Time had taken his profession—he was a captain of sail when sail was fading—but he was defiant: he banged away on his old Delaware oyster sloop, and planned his epic sail. Of course he'd already been around the world. The *sailing* part would not be a problem. It was the *alone* part that was the new challenge. He began by replacing *Spray*'s keel.

It felt great to get those planks back on.

37. Mast Hoops

ON THE FIRST TUESDAY in July, I started on the mast hoops, because they represented a problem with no easy solution. I wanted those problems out of the way, although it also occurred to me that perhaps those problems were the point.

Mast hoops are simple wooden rings that attach to the luff of the mainsail at intervals, and slide up and down the mast, allowing the sail to be hauled up and down freely.

The hoops on *Daphie* were strips of white oak, half an inch wide and three-sixteenths of an inch thick, forty-one inches long, steamed, wound around a form, clamped, and riveted with copper. I needed three new ones—two to use alongside three old ones, and a third as a spare. It was a mild July day, and I had the whole of it to make hoops.

The first thing to do was to drive to New Bedford for copper rivets. (In the 1800s there was a cheap, fast ferry from Woods Hole to New Bedford, when that was the nearest city, but now I had to drive there. Again.)

Once there, standing in the little lobby in Beckman's chandlery, I found myself next to a bunch of premade mast hoops, roped together and hanging from a hook on a post. They were marked forty dollars apiece. Way too much for me, and they were too large anyway, but that wasn't the point. I had to make what I needed myself, at least to the extent that the old-timers would have.

So I procrastinated, and asked for a can of underwater seam compound and one last box of number eight one-inch silicon bronze slotted-head screws. I was using slotted screws, not Phillips head, for the last twenty or thirty screws in the rebuild, trying to restore my reputation with the boatbuilding gods.)

While I waited for the order to be filled I contemplated the making of the hoops. I knew I would have to ask the guys behind the counter if they had any copper rivets back there. Which would be seen by everyone in the room as my confession of ignorance about copper rivets. I would be confessing my weakness; they would immediately judge me unworthy as a man and as a workman in particular, because I didn't already know all about copper rivets. (How could I have gotten this far in life without knowing more about copper rivets?)

This ignorance stood directly between me and the rest of the day. Or rather my fear of the exposure of my ignorance did.

We were standing, a few of us, in front of the main gunmetal-grey counter, in the hardware/paint section, with the brass pneumatic tubes snaking around, hissing and sucking. The various counter guys said "hmmmm," as they held old fittings handed to them by customers in the hope that they could be matched, and after this initial moment the counter guys would stump off into the aisles between the seven rows of shelves (piled with screws, nuts, bolts, washers, and brackets) that ran way back until one entered, I imagined, a sort of marine storehouse twilit heaven.

Then suddenly it was my turn again. I was standing in front of the counter on which sat my pint can of seam compound and a box of screws. A thin man in a grey/green jumpsuit was leaning on the other side of the counter, his hair slicked back, his glasses grey plastic, his eyes pale blue. He was watching me carefully.

"So," I said, and paused, and looked him in the eye. He

looked back neutrally. "I also need some copper rivets for riveting through wood."

As soon as I was done asking the rivet question, a guy in the next line over became agitated. He was about my height, but built like a rhinoceros, and dressed in ragged paint-spattered blue shorts and a sweatshirt with the sleeves torn off. His belly bulged out under his crossed arms. A painter's cap turned backward sat on his head like a bottle cap, and his brown hair jutted from under the cap in a thick ruff.

Upon my initial inspection of him several minutes before, I had decided that if he opened his mouth it would be to curse me, or someone nearby, or to bite a doughnut to death.

"You know," he said, speaking in a clear voice, "my brother rivets all the time, and he just uses copper nails and copper washers, cuts the nails to length, peens them so they spread over the washer—it just works very well for him."

He was talking to me as if we were swapping recipes. Not that I've ever done that, or would do that.

"No special deal, huh?" I said.

"Simple as that," he said.

"That's what I was going to suggest," said the man in the jumpsuit behind the counter, where he leaned on his elbows, his face grey from cigarettes and lack of sun. "This guy said exactly what I was going to say, but better than I would have."

"Can you sell me some copper nails and washers?" I asked him.

"Sure I can. How many, what diameter, how long, and do you mind me asking what for?"

"I'm putting an old Herreshoff twelve-and-a-half back together, and I've got to build a few mast hoops like these," I said, pulling on one of the hoops hanging from the post.

"That's great, that you're putting the effort in," he said.

"That's a lot of work. Not many guys come in here doing that if they ain't from a yard. They're nice old boats. I'd say an inch long, eighth-inch shaft. How many'd you say?"

I thought to myself for a moment. Three rings are going to need three rivets each, plus mistakes. I pondered for a moment more while he pursed his lips and leaned his jaw on his hand.

"Twenty-five of each I guess, please," I said. He grunted and disappeared back into the shadows, and a minute later two little plastic sacks of copper landed on the counter with a satisfying th-thud.

"Any idea where the copper comes from?" I asked him. "Maybe the Anaconda mine in Canada?"

"I couldn't tell you," he said. "We just sell it. Anything else?"

"I also need a few of the bronze fittings which join the fitting on the sail to the mast hoop on a twelve-and-a-half." I showed him the fitting on the old hoop that I'd brought along and said, "Got any of those?"

"Nope. Those are gonna be tougher," he said, not unkindly.

"I'd go down to Carey Sails on the bridge over to Fairhaven if I was you," spoke up the burly paint-covered guy again. "They're a good loft, and they do a lot of small boat sails. I bet they'd have them."

"That's what I'd recommend too," said the guy behind the counter. Then he said to the rhino, "Maybe you should come and work back here, young fella, though you'd hafta get rid of the jungly togs."

I spend a lot of time being skeptical of human nature. But here were a couple of tough-looking characters giving me friendly advice. They were going beyond helpful. They were making my task easier. It was an odd feeling.

I paid the man for the rivets and seam compound and the screws—a little less than forty dollars, which entailed my bills being sucked skyward in the brass tube, and then three quarters and a receipt returning, all within less than a minute. So far, I had crossed this Rubicon without harm.

"Thanks for your help," I said to the fellow behind the counter.

"Sure thing. Anytime."

I turned to the rhinoceros. "Thank you, sir, for your help. I didn't get your name."

"Roland," he said, extending a paint-splattered hand, which I shook. If I am not mistaken, he bowed slightly as he did this, a thoroughly disguised saint of marine fastenings.

I headed out, into the sunshine, loaded the new gunk and the new metal into the car, and headed for Fairhaven.

To get there I had to follow Route 18 through the waterfront district, then turn right onto the causeway to Fairhaven, cross the Acushnet River, and then turn left into the lot of Carey Sails. It was a low-slung, prefab metal building, and when I entered I was impressed immediately by the floor.

It was a glistening expanse of hardwood, made for sails to be spread upon, stretched, rested, repaired. It smelled clean in there, and there was an intriguing simplicity to the place—there were bolts of Dacron and fabric and many sails bundled neatly and tied with strips of canvas on the shelves, along with spools of heavy thread and twine. In several places around the periphery of the room and at its center there were deep wells cut into the floor, with mountings for sewing machines, so that sailmakers could stand down in there and work comfortably on the sail at floor level. In short, everything in sight pertained to the construction of sails. It was a building and place devoted entirely to this.

A pleasant-looking woman of forty-five with a brown braid down her back approached me.

"Can I help?" she said.

I held out one of my three good hoops, tapped the fitting

which sat on the top rim of the hoop like a miniature bench on a little wall, and said, "I need three of these."

She took the hoop, and walked away, saying, "Just a minute, let me see what we've got." She returned a minute later with a fitting that locked precisely into mine, its other half, like those already on my sail, which I didn't need. "I've got these, lots of these," she said, holding the piece that mounted to the sail, "but I don't have their counterparts that mount on the hoop."

"No, huh?" I said.

"No, but let me call the other loft. They might. What boat's this for? A twelve-and-a-half?"

"Yeah," I said, nodding, but I was marveling at how well the *new* fitting she'd brought me, of fresh new bronze, clasped the *old* fitting I'd brought in. Both were drawn by Nat more than ninety years ago, and mine was forged at least sixty-eight years before, yet it fit the new sail fitting as well as a thing can. Someone, sixty-odd years later, had reproduced the pattern perfectly. How had all of the chaos in the world resulted in this—that a drawing done in Bristol in 1914 by Nat could then be passed down through the years, through two world wars, the '60s, the Vietnam War, Watergate, evenings with Sonny and Cher, and all the rest and be produced in bronze more than eighty years later to a tolerance of, say, a hundredth of an inch? This had been one of my concerns—the marriage of new fittings to the old ones I had. At least in this case, there would be no problem.

But there could have been. My grandfather could have been struck by a ricocheting bullet at the aid station near the lines when he was a surgeon in France in 1916, which would have ended this particular family's sailing right then, a mere two years after the fitting was drawn. Or the West might have responded to Ho Chi Minh's overtures for support and alliance in 1945, which would have obviated the French fortifying Dien

Bien Phu in 1954 and being wiped out there, not having cal-
culated that the North Vietnamese could supply their isolated
positions there by bringing bicycles overland laden with rice,
and so Kennedy might have avoided the beginnings of American involvement, and Johnson the escalation thereof, and my
two cousins, who both sailed *Daphie* in the early 1960s, might
not have served in Vietnam, and might have lived very different lives, might (being twenty years my senior) still want the
boat, and have constructed lives that would admit her to them.
How different things might have been.

But no. Somehow, down through all of those decisions to
turn one way, rather than another, I had come to this counter,
where she said, "Let me just give them a call over in Marion."

She made the call, and the other loft, in Marion, two towns
closer to home, said they had the pieces I needed. I thanked
her and headed for Marion.

In Marion I found, off of Route 6, a similar building, low
and long, abutting a salt marsh, the spartina grass and spar-
kling water visible beyond the back of the lot. I entered, and
saw the hardwood floor of another sail loft stretching away.
The crew there was working on a big white mainsail.

A man with a conspicuous gut approached the front desk.
"How can I help?" he asked, looking me in the eye, and allowing himself to bounce against the counter on the pad of his
stomach.

"I need three of these," I said, showing him one of my
good hoops with the old bronze fitting.

"Oh yeah, you're the guy they just called about," he said.
"I think I've got a few of those. Hang on." He padded in moc-
casins along a strip of carpet that ran around the periphery of
the room, and disappeared through a door that was parallel to
my field of vision; it looked to me like he'd walked through
the wall.

The sailmakers, a man and two women in their thirties, all of whom wore smocks, worked away. They had muscular hands from manipulating the heavy fabric, and each worked on a separate section of a large white sail, which seemed to be getting a rebuild. One woman drove a heavy needle threaded with white twine down into the peak, around a big aluminum grommet, and the other woman did the same along the luff, resecuring a slide to the boltrope there. The man in the pit worked a heavy-duty sewing machine, moving a section of the foot past it repeatedly, perhaps where a slide had let go. They took no notice of me, although I bet they felt caged, on display, and ready to attack if cornered.

Soon the counterman reappeared, smiling, with three fittings in his hand. He showed them to me, unlocking his pudgy fingers, and then dropped them carefully on the countertop, where they chattered lightly with the impact, and were still.

I had brought *Daphie*'s mainsail in, and now checked each new fitting. Each locked securely onto one of the little cylinders of bronze siezed to the luff of the sail; each was smooth, perfectly formed, and about the size of a Goldfish cracker.

"This is great," I said. "How much?"

"Fourteen apiece," he said. "Forty-two dollars."

"Phuuuuuck," I exhaled quietly, softly enough that he might not have heard it, and a feeling came over me reminiscent of the one I had when Michael Ashmore threw a crab apple in fourth grade (as I held a basketball over my head, in mid-pass) and struck me a short distance below the waist.

"Okay," I said, wishing I hadn't liked him to begin with. "Thank you."

I wouldn't be going out to dinner for a week, or taking a paper. But I had 'em! No time to waste looking elsewhere. Now it was into fabrication mode. I drove home on back roads, past cranberry bogs, used-car dealers, basket shops, and glimpses of Buzzards Bay through the trees, my heart thumping in my chest at the thought of building the new hoops.

Back at the cottage, after a brief lunch of peanut butter and honey between two slices of tough old sourdough from the back of the fridge, I set to it, out in the shed. It was a pleasant afternoon, with sun, a little haze, and the breeze cool off the water out of the southwest. It was about three-thirty in the afternoon.

By rolling the middle sized of the three old hoops along a tabletop, I found that the strip of oak that formed it was about forty inches long. It was half an inch wide, and three-sixteenths of an inch thick, planed down to nothing at the ends. It was a tapered slice of a board rolled into a wheel, with the grain running all the way through it. I needed five new strips of oak just like it.

I found a promising oak board, and took six slices off it on the table saw. With my block plane I tapered each end of each strip down to almost nothing. If I got two good hoops out of the lot, I'd be doing well. I decided to steam one strip first, and was just getting the steam box going, with a wisp of steam coming out the hind end, when my friend Coop walked in the shed door. I had heard a truck ease into the drive a moment before.

"What're you doing?" he said.

"Getting ready to steam a strip of wood, see if I can make a mast hoop out of it."

"Fuckin' A," he said. He stood about six feet tall, with shoulders broad and thick from many years of carpentry and windsurfing. He was about fifty, with thick dark hair cut short, wearing dun colored overalls and a blue work shirt. He didn't stand up quite straight, but had a relaxed way of moving his large body through the world. He stood now just in front of the bow of *Daphie*, looking up at her, his long arms at his sides.

"This fucker ever going to float again?"

"Yup," I said. "That boat's gonna be the belle of the ball. I'm about to make the mast hoops for her, and then I've got another couple of months of work to do on her, and then she's going in."

He looked her over, stooping to look at the keel, and then standing on the edge of the cradle to glance into the cockpit. "She looks like shit," he finally pronounced.

"Give me a chance to put a coat of paint on her, and maybe you'll change your mind," I said. I knew Coop's way sometimes was to charm through absolute offense.

"All right, I'll wait for the paint. I like the shed," he said, glancing around at its frame. "Feels like we're in the belly of some old whale. You got time for a cup of tea?"

"Sure," I said, and went inside for the kettle, which I brought out and put on the second burner, next to the steam box kettle. Coop and I had worked on many carpentry jobs together, and I knew he was blustering for the fun of it, and trying to shake me up, the way friends do, keep me loose.

Once I had the kettle going, we sat on stumps I'd brought into the shed.

"Not enough wind to sail today?" I asked, knowing already there wasn't by the calm at the tops of the trees.

"Nah," he said, disgusted. "Not even blowing ten. It was cappin' this morning, out of the west, maybe blowing twenty-five, but it died around lunch just as I began to think it might hold, and I've been moping around ever since. Was framing in a dormer two stories up, looking out over the bay as the wind died, and just feeling sorry for myself."

"You are sorry," I said.

He smiled at this.

"How many days of sailing do you need to call it a passable year?" I asked. He turned this over in his mind for a moment, then said, "A hundred, and I'm alive. A hundred and fifty and that's a good year."

I knew that Coop was apt to sail in January and February, along with the rest of the hard-core windsurfers in Woods Hole, despite the water temperature being in the high thirties, and despite the bulky wetsuits one had to wear. Wind was wind, and it often blew hard in winter, and it had to blow at least fourteen knots to push their low-displacement, high-performance boards to speeds at which they would hydroplane. In low winds, the boards just plowed through the water, which felt like driving a car with flat tires. No fun.

"Yeah, and it hasn't blown much all week," he said. "I'm beginning to forget who I am."

"You need a boat to work on," I said.

"Now maybe that's true," he said.

I had brought some green tea out with me, which I put into a cast-iron teapot. I filled it with the hot water from the kettle, and we sat there for a few minutes while the tea steeped, and didn't say much.

Then when it was done I put some milk and sugar in mine. Coop had his plain. We drank it sitting on the stumps.

"What's the longest day sail you've done on your board?" I asked him.

"I guess around the Vineyard, across outside Cuttyhunk, over to Padanaram and back. That was about sixty miles, when you figure in all of the extra tacks I took, but I was going fifteen knots a lot of the way. I've sailed farther in a day, but that was the biggest voyage."

"Did you go through Canapitsit at all?" I asked, referring to the channel between the islands of Cuttyhunk and Nashawena.

"Yeah, I came through on the way back from Padanaram,

did a loop around Nashawena, and then headed back through Robinsons."

"You have any trouble getting through Canapitsit?" I asked. Here I was referring to the narrow channel between the islands of Cuttyhunk and Nashawena, where the current is ferocious at flood or ebb.

"Nah. I made sure I got down there well after noon, when the wind was up and strong. I whaled through there," he said. "It was more heading up the bay later, as the wind died, and I had to tack downwind to keep enough boat speed to plane. That was touch and go. What about in this thing?" he asked, nodding toward *Daphie*.

"Farthest I've sailed this is: down the sound, through Robinsons Hole, down to Cuttyhunk, and then back up the bay," I said. "All told, that's probably forty miles of bottom under the keel, and I remember it felt like a trip, coming around under those cliffs, and then through Robinsons, down past Pasque and Nashawena, and then the long run home afterwards."

"That's when you know where you are, during a day like that," said Coop.

We finished the tea, and he left soon after, his truck's power steering yammering slightly as he backed out of the drive. He knew I didn't want to make my first hoops with him looking over my shoulder. Once he was gone, I took the first slim piece of oak out of the steam box, and slid another one in.

The steamed piece came out of the box wavy as a noodle. I wrapped it around a form of four sixteen-penny nails driven into a piece of plywood, and promptly made a square of wood, splitting the strip at one corner in the process. Clearly I needed to refine my mold.

In my second attempt, I took an old canning jar of the correct dimension, wrapped the next strip (once it was steamed) around the bottom of this, and then grabbed this new hoop, which wanted to spring away, with the jaws of a Vise-Grip pliers and held it. It looked good.

Then I drilled holes for rivets through the hoop in two places. One rivet would just catch the inner tail of the strip before it ended, and one would go through the thickest part of the hoop. Then I drove copper nails through each hole from the inside, and nipped the nails off so an eighth of an inch of their shafts poked through. I then put a copper washer over the end of each stub in turn, held the hoop against the anvil that stood in the corner of the shed, and peened over the stub to spread it against the washer. A rivet! Two rivets! By Toutatis! By Leviathan's breath! A hoop near completion. I then released the pliers, riveted the remaining end of the strip, where it slimmed to nothing against the outside of itself, and moved on.

In an hour I had four hoops, all of which would serve, although one was a bit large and a little off-round. Clearly I'd been thinking of something else as I made that one. Then it was time to mix the goo. This meant three squirts of resin, three of hardener, and then enough low-density filler to give the epoxy the consistency of peanut butter. I filled every gap in all the hoops, new and old, with this fudge, and coated them with it as I could, and let it harden while I made some dinner.

The next day, once I'd sanded everything down to smooth, I had five good new hoops. Then I fastened a new bronze fitting to three of the hoops with small bronze screws, put a couple of coats of varnish on each hoop, and reminded myself to put the hoops on the mast before I stepped it. [To "step" a mast is to secure it in an upright position ready for use]

This is hard to remember, and it is always frustrating to realize (after you have stepped the mast and rigged the shrouds and gotten everything else set) that the hoops are back home in a drawer, and that you have to pull the mast out again, and put the hoops on it, and then, finally, finish rigging.

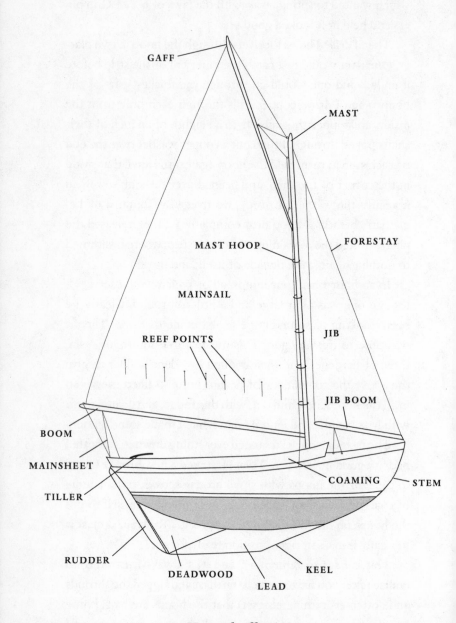

GAFF

MAST

MAST HOOP

FORESTAY

MAINSAIL

JIB

REEF POINTS

JIB BOOM

BOOM

MAINSHEET

TILLER

COAMING

STEM

RUDDER

DEADWOOD

KEEL

LEAD

Herreshoff 12½

38. July:
The Bulkhead Grille

IT WAS THE FIRST Wednesday of July, about nine o'clock in the morning, when I hauled myself up the stepladder into the boat, and began to think about the bulkhead.

Originally, *Daphie* had been made with a watertight partition just forward of the mast. This bulkhead created a sealed airspace in the bow. The gases inside were supposed to keep the boat afloat in case of swamping, and were needed to counteract the inclination of the seven hundred and fifty pounds of lead in the keel, which wanted more than anything to go to the center of the earth, taking the boat with it.

When I first took the tarp off *Daphie* a year and a half ago, she had a large rectangular opening in her bulkhead just forward of the mast step, rendering it quite a bit less than watertight. Inside this little forepeak were a bunch of horizontal boards, loosely installed, which had walled off a pile of Styrofoam that (you may remember) had long since been converted to apartments by mice. I had cleared all of that out of the bow. What I contemplated now was a square opening in the bulkhead, with the empty space of the forepeak beyond.

I'd run into Bill Mayhew a few days before at the supermarket and he'd asked how the boat was going, and if he could stop by and check it out. I'd said "yeah" fast and told him to come by any morning he liked. He called last night and said he'd swing by around nine, as he had to check out an old S-boat in a barn out on Penzance, and so would be going right by. He would arrive any minute, and I was looking forward to his visit, as there were several matters I hoped to discuss with him, among them the bulkhead. As I waited for him, and looked through the opening into the forepeak, several solutions occurred to me.

I could make a grid of oak laths—thin pieces of oak about an inch and a half wide, woven into a latticework to cover the opening—that would both be strong and allow for ventilation. Most local H-12½'s had this feature; it was the accepted solution to the problem, like white shorts for tennis. But to my eye it was fussy. Froo froo. And it wouldn't match the mahogany coaming and seats whose varnished color was dark, more sanguine. I threw that idea over.

Another option was to make something out of marine plywood that would cover the opening, yet still provide ventilation. The foredeck, afterdeck, seat supports, and bulkhead were all made of marine ply. It was not the most romantic of woods, but it was, like it or not, a big part of this "traditional" wooden boat. I was leaning toward that when Bill pulled up outside in his pickup.

I climbed down out of the boat in time to hold the door for him as he came into the cottage. He headed straight for the coffee pot, which sat on the counter by the sink with its red light glowing, along with a carton of milk, a bowl of brown sugar, and a couple of mugs. He poured himself a mug, took nothing else, and then sat in an old rocker on the postage-stamp deck outside the front door, next to the big lilac. He exhaled as he sat down, and seemed to relax.

"So how's the boat comin'?" he asked, as soon as I'd sat down in the other rocker with my own cup of coffee.

"Getting there," I said. "I guess you haven't seen her in a while. I've got her back together, frames are done, refastening's done, so now it's small stuff, mast hoops and deck canvas and bulkhead vent, along with caulk and paint and varnish."

"Sounds good," he said. He stretched his feet out in front of him, and then propped his feet on the low rail that ran around the edge of the deck, and took another deep breath.

"Air smells good down here in Woods Hole," he said, and he closed his eyes for a moment.

"Same air you have up there in Senegansett," I said.

"Almost," he said. "Something different about it here, though, something easier about it. I don't know. Maybe it's just being away from the shop."

"Rafey getting on your nerves today?" I asked.

"You know, it's probably a lot of things. Rafe is a great guy, but he thinks he's got a lock on good sense. He was going on about the conservation commission today, how they're screwing up the whole river question, how much of it to restore. And he's right. They're talking about 'wise use,' which means let the developers do whatever they want, and they're the *conservation* commission, not the chamber of commerce—it's the con com's *job* to be tough on the regs. But they aren't anymore. It's foxes in the henhouse." He said all this, and then said with mock incredulity, "Hard to believe, ain't it?" At this he raised his eyebrows, and took a two-handed swig of his coffee. Then he went on.

"But Rafe comes at it so strong from the other side that it doesn't leave any room on his side, either. Even for me. I agree with him, but I'd just like him to give it a rest."

"You guys finish that Rozinante?"

"Oh yeah. You should see the interior work that Rafe did on that. Just spectacular. But that boat's another sore spot," he said.

"How so?" I asked. Bill and I had been building a bit of a friendship over time, as I talked to him about the boat, and it seemed he'd decided I was to be trusted, more or less. I'd wondered about this, and thought maybe it was because I was prepared to see his craft as an art, rather than just a skill. His family had been at it a long time, and I knew too many people had seen them as labor to be hired, rather than as equals. To me Bill was a master of his craft, an artist, a wise person. Perhaps he sensed my respect.

"Well," he said, "We agreed on a price with the client a year and a half ago, and that was fine, but then the guy goes nutty, and starts saying stuff about 'You came in ahead of schedule,' and that he priced some of the material and thinks we overcharged, and so he wants to cut ten percent off."

"Screw him," I said, a little too suddenly. Then, after that had sunk into the morning, I said, "Was your price fair?"

"Course it was," he said. "And you know, when I figure out Rafe's and my hourly wage, and figure in the extra time it took to find just the right materials, he's getting a bargain. We probably made about ten bucks an hour apiece."

"So what are you going to tell him?"

"I'd like to tell him to go fuck himself. He thinks I'm a rich guy he can dicker with, or one of his grandfathers told him he always had to haggle, or something. But I was raised to be honest, not a horse trader. That's what he doesn't get. It's a cultural thing. When you live around the people you trade with, you can't be anything but fair. But he's a city guy, and doesn't get us down here at all."

We drank our coffee in silence for a minute. The wind had come up slightly, and was moving the treetops a little, and I could see it moving through the grasses in the wetland down at the end of the street.

Then Bill spoke up again. "You know, you can kind of feel what Woods Hole used to be like, on this little street, with these normal little houses, when it was regular people who lived around here. Not that there's anything wrong with the summer people—Christ, they're my living these days—but back when everybody didn't have to have an enormous house and a palatial master suite and marble countertops and all of the bullshit, back when people came here to live, and they were fine with a simple house and to have their kids in school, didn't need all the immensity. Or they'd just been here forever, you know. Even the summer people were different then, some-how—they had a bit of a feel for the place."

"You mean like Fay?"

"Exactly, old Joseph Story Fay planting the beech forest with seeds from his saddlebags, and the guys who refounded the yacht club insisting that it would be a little cottage on the beach, without a ballroom, et cetera." He took another swig of his coffee here, and contemplated *Daphie* for a moment, then went on.

"Those guys raced the local boats for years—the sprit-sails—and then they had the knockabouts—simple boats—and at Quissett they had boats like yours—none of the flash. But it's changing now. Everybody's footprint has to be enormous. I just wish they had enough class to keep it in perspective."

"Like the Rozinante?"

"Precisely. A simple boat. No engine. A bunk up forward for two, with sitting headroom, a simple stove, a simple head. Seaworthy as a boat can be, and fast, a ketch for balance and flexibility—if these idiots all had Rozinantes, the world would be a better place."

"And you'd have work for a while," I said.

"Amen, I would. And I'm a bit of a hypocrite, since at the prices I have to charge, only a millionaire can afford one anymore. But anyway, what's the deal with your boat?" He swung his feet off the rail. "What are we looking at today?" he asked.

"Today, I'd just like to ask you about the bulkhead," I said.

"Oh, man, I don't even have to look at the boat in order

to tell you about that," he said, and settled back into the chair with his coffee, put his feet up on the rail again.

"That was a problem from the get-go," he said. "Originally, there were different treatments of that bulkhead, but way back there was a general movement toward airtight compartments as flotation, which came out of the surfboats the old lifesaving service used—they'd launch them off the beach, and they wanted those things to float no matter what.

"Herreshoff started building his small boats with airtight flotation at some point. But it never really seemed to work out. It did the job in terms of flotation, but at least around here we found that all the paint would peel off the forward part of the boat where that box of stale air was, and that it just seemed to cause the boat to deteriorate. Everything needs to breathe." After saying this he took a deep breath and breathed it out slowly as if to demonstrate.

"This was all before my time," he went on. "But the different yards all had different ways. Charlie Eldred at Quissett boatyard started cutting a big square opening in the bulkhead to let it breathe, and then he'd make that lattice out of oak, and screw that on there, and fill the whole forepeak with Styrofoam flotation. Some places they'd just cut a square out, and leave it open, and gussy up the woodwork in there so that it looked on purpose—polished up the floor timbers and varnished the frames. That's how a lot of other boats are done. So there's different ways to go there."

The morning was warming up as we spoke, the thin white haze that had been over us was beginning to clear, and there was the tang in the air of a cool sea and seaweed fresh and damp on the beach. Ted had come out of the boat shed and was looking at us from its doorway, where she sat on her haunches. Birds were working over the thicket across the street, as I posed my question.

"How would you treat that detail in a 1939 boat?" I asked.

"If I owned it, or if someone else was telling me what shade of lipstick they wanted on it?" he replied.

"If it was yours," I said.

"I guess whatever I had time to build that would serve and not look like cheese." he said. "It's got to be whatever you think is appropriate." There was the answer I'd been looking for.

Next I asked, "Would you take that watertight fitting out of the bulkhead and patch it up?" I was referring to the bronze port on the extreme starboard side of the bulkhead that had been original equipment on *Daphie,* for access to the water-tight compartment.

"Nah. I'd just leave it there. It's original. Let it be. So let's take a look at her."

He heaved himself up from his chair, and walked the ten steps off the deck and over to the boat shed, and started examining her hull, running his hand over the seams between her planks. I could feel my heart beating.

"She looks like she's got a ways to go yet, but I can see the planks are fit, not too fair, but fit. You took the broad planks and the garboards off, right?" he asked, referring to the bottom two planks on either side.

"Yup," I said.

"They go back on okay?" he asked.

"Yup," I said.

He peered over the gunwale.

"Hey!" he said, "look at all those new frames! They don't look half bad. Looks like you need floorboards, though, and the seats reinstalled—you still have those?"

"Yup," I said.

"Well," he said, turning to me, "it *is* coming together. Once you have the floorboards in, and you get the seats back in, then it'll start to feel like you're getting close. You got any other questions for me?"

"Well, I know I've got to redo the decks," I said. "I went down to Barnum House [a small local historical museum] to talk to the guys there the other day—" I started to say, and Bill cut me off.

"Whatever *those* guys said will work," he said. "They know their stuff as well as I do—Art Burgess and Dave Ash and that whole crew. Better, even. They'll steer you right. And I'd rather not give you too many of the answers—the whole thing begins to feel less organic then."

He headed out of the shed as he said this, handing his empty mug to me as he went by. Ted had left the shed by now, and was sitting on the corner of the deck railing. Bill reached out his hand and ran it down her back as he went by, which she enjoyed and stood up for.

"I gotta go and look at this old S-boat, keep on with the morning," he said.

"Whose is it?" I said.

"I'm sworn to secrecy," he said as he climbed into his truck. "Guy doesn't want anyone to know he has it. I think it's been in there for four hundred years, and I think it's hogged pretty good, don't know if there's a chance to bring it back, but we'll see."

"Thanks, Bill," I said.

"No worries," he said as he pulled his truck's door shut and turned the engine over. "I'll be back."

I was set. Bill had given his blessing to whatever I came up with. So be it. I had a scrap of half-inch marine ply that would serve. I got to work.

I would make two plywood panels, each fourteen by twenty-four inches, each mounted against cleats so that they sat flush with the rest of the bulkhead. First, I made the cleats out of half-inch white oak—four of them—and sanded them, drilled holes in them for screws, primed them with good white oil paint, and then screwed them to the inside of what was left of the old bulkhead so they jutted out and gave me something to screw the panels to. Then I cut the panels out of the half-inch ply, and drilled twelve one-inch holes in each of them. Through each of these holes would pass the restorative breeze. I painted the panels with white oil primer, left them to dry on sawhorses on the little front lawn, and went in the house for a snooze.

39. First Thursday in July: Decks

I ʜᴀᴅ ʙᴇᴇɴ ᴛʜɪɴᴋɪɴɢ about the decks for a while, the way one thinks about a pile of wood that must be cut and split before winter.

My unspoken thought was, What will you find when you take the old canvas off? Will the plywood beneath be shot? Will a terrible rot be unleashed, which will spread to all wooden boats in the harbor, and all wooden structures in the town, the state, the nation, finally boring into the legs of the president's desk in the Oval Office, little piles of sawdust appearing beneath it on the blue carpet, portending the final collapse, only stone structures remaining, the implosion by rot of the White House and the Pentagon, slowly, piece upon piece, and the panicked, sawdust-covered citizenry fleeing into hills covered with toppled lifeless trees, their bark peeling and grey, leaves withered, a million families making their last stands in gasless minivans strewn along the shoulders of country roads, as the paper in their journals and magazines was consumed by the strange rust, the end of cellulose being the end of all economy, of the dollar as driven by housing starts, enabled by numberless and now-disintegrating two-by-fours, once sustained by toilet paper and paper towels and Post-it notes but now rendered unto dust. And this all begun when I first peeled the old canvas off the foredeck to expose the pathogens in the wood beneath. Rot? Or not? It was time to know what the canvas would reveal.

Finally, on the morning of the first Thursday in July (making four days in a row of high production), I climbed into the boat and began to tear away at the old canvas. The first came away easily, and I saw what lay beneath: slightly weathered grey marine plywood in fine shape. No rot.

The old canvas, I knew, had likely been bedded with thick white lead paint. For advice on this topic (as I had mentioned to Bill) I'd gone down to the shed behind Barnum House in Woods Hole one Saturday morning a couple of weeks before. I knew in that shed I was likely to find some of the leading lights of local boatbuilding.

Barnum House is one of the oldest houses in Woods Hole, converted thirty years ago to house the Woods Hole Historical Collection. Within are files, and more files, and dioramas of the old treeless Woods Hole (when sailing ships and sheep were king) and models and greeting cards. It is a treasure. Behind it is a temporary shed, much like mine in the style of an elongate Norman arch (although it is larger than mine and has an L attached), which was my true target this day.

Within were two boats—an old dory, and a Beetle Cat— that were being restored by volunteers. Three of the people within generally knew what they were doing.

One of them was Art Burgess, who had been building and repairing wooden boats for fifty or more years around here. Another was Dave Ash, who had been doing the same. A third was Jim Shaw, who among other things, was once a mate and bo's'n on the *Ti*, the *Ticonderoga*, the legendary ketch built by L. Francis Herreshoff.

I went in that morning with Garth, an old friend who wanted to see what they were doing with the Beetle Cat, as he had one at home he'd been sailing for years. He met me at the cottage, in his big Dodge pickup, which had a reel of blue hose and a large white plastic tank in back.

"How you doin', Pal?" he said out the window. We had worked together as carpenters occasionally, in past summers, and the banter of those times came back easily.

"I'm doin' fine, Pal," I said. "How is it?"

"Ready to rock," he said. "Listen," he went on, "are these guys just going to make a fool of me if I ask a question?"

"Not at all," I said. "They're interested in getting the information out. Relax."

It was about 8 A.M. We drove around the back way, past Stony Beach, where I glimpsed the bay, still flat in the calm morning air, and then Woods Hole harbor, where the wind was barely up. Across the Hole (where the current showed as a band of dark blue water moving east) Nonamessett looked close, sharp in outline.

"What's all the stuff in the back?" I asked Garth, as we rolled along Water Street, where a guy was sweeping the sidewalk in front of the Cap'n Kidd.

"It's all for sugarin'," he said. "I had to get down here fast this weekend, and I didn't have time to drop it off, so it stayed in back."

"How'd you do this spring?" I asked him. Garth lived in the Pioneer Valley, in western Massachusetts, and had learned to sugar several years before.

"We got almost too much. More you get, more you gotta cook, so we were tending the fires for days. Finally got through it at the end of May, but I almost threw in the towel."

"How many feet of hose do you string?"

"Feet? Try miles. I think I had a mile of hose out this year. A freakin' mile."

"Pull in here," I said, as we crested the hill by the library.

An old, dark-shingled house was in front of us, with a barn off to the right.

"Where the hell're the boats?" asked Garth, who never feigned patience.

"They're in a shed behind the barn there," I replied.

"Are they makin' moonshine back there?" he asked, half serious.

"No, man," I said. "But here, let me go first."

We walked back to the shed, which, like mine, was covered in plastic sheeting. Art Burgess was just inside, sitting on a stool, a lean man with a strong jaw, talking animatedly to Dave Ash, who stood at ease, an athletic man of seventy with thinning hair, holding a Styrofoam cup of coffee. Both men were brown from being in the sun, and had the expressive, strong hands that came with a lifetime of boatbuilding. Art wore green cotton work pants and a matching green button-down shirt. Dave wore jeans and a heavy khaki button-down shirt.

"You guys come to complicate the morning?" said Art to us as we walked in. He was smiling broadly.

"Yes," I said. "Art, Dave, this is my buddy Garth. He's interested in your catboat, how you're restoring it, because he's got one of his own which might need some attention soon."

"They all need attention soon, if they been around for a while," said Art.

There were a few big power tools in this first part of the shed, and a long workbench with bins of screws and fastenings above it. In the next part of the shed was the catboat, up on sawhorses, with a couple of students leaning over it. Each was pounding on a tool with a mallet, the object of their ministrations out of sight down in the cockpit of the boat.

"Jim over there knows what's goin' on," said Art to Garth. Jim Shaw, tall and lean, probably well into his ninth decade, was standing at the stern of the cat, his arms crossed, watching the activity in the boat intently. "Go ask him anything you want," said Art, "but don't ask him about the tattoos on his arms unless you got a coupla hours."

Garth looked a little doubtful, until Art said, "Go ahead, he don't bite." With that he walked near Jim, who put out his hand and greeted him. Soon they were deep in discussion, leaning over the gunwale of the little cat as the sun came through the wall of the shed behind them, lighting up the sawdust that hung in the air.

"So I've got a question or two for you guys," I started in.

"Want a cup of coffee?" Dave said.

"Sure," I replied, and he poured a cup of dark black coffee out of an urn they had going in the corner of the shed.

Art had been surveying me in the moments that I waited for the coffee, appraising, I imagined, my stance, how much force I might be able to put behind a brace and bit, how callused my hands looked and how much work they might have in them.

"So you're going to restore your old Herreshoff?" Art said at last.

"How'd you know that?" I asked, not offended that he knew, but curious as to the source.

"Small town," he said.

"Well, I'm already a ways along," I rejoined. "Replaced thirty frames so far, all new fastenings, reconditioned the broad planks and garboards, planning to renew the transom—"

"Whoa," said Art. "Renew the transom? I've never heard of that. You mean replace it?"

"No, I'm thinking I'll just cut out the nail-sick wood around the drifts, clean up the drifts, and scarf in some new wood, epoxy it right in there." Art rolled his eyes.

"Geez, I never know what you guys are gonna do. How long you think that's gonna last?"

"I don't know, maybe a few years. I don't feel like I have the time to get into the whole transom," I said.

"You know, Art," said Dave, "I don't think that sounds like such a bad idea."

"It ain't a *bad* idea," said Art. "I just don't think it sounds like a *good* idea. How's it gonna look?"

"It'll look like there are three patches in a mahogany transom," I said.

"Patches!" said Art. "You sound like my mom with a pair of my dungarees."

"I'm not trying to hide anything, Art," I said. "I want the boat to work, to have its original dimensions and everything, but if I don't have to fix everything right away, if the old dog will hunt—that's okay with me." Art sat quietly with his arms crossed, and thought for a second. Clearly this rubbed him the wrong way.

"I don't want to give her a facelift, just get the body healthy underneath," I went on. Art was quiet for the moment, so I took the opportunity.

"Dave," I said, "it does look like you've had a little work done, huh."

Dave looked at me, not comprehending for a moment, and then got it. "You're darned right! Had the pullback done," he said, laughing and pulling the skin at his temples back toward his ears with his fingers, "and I had the neck tightened up a bit 'cause I was startin' to look like an old rooster."

"You still look like an old rooster, and you act like one by god," said Art, laughing. Dave laughed, too.

"You know, the main thing is to keep those iron drifts from getting moist any way you can," said Dave, returning to the topic. "If they aren't takin' water out of the wood, and if water isn't getting to them, the rust will slow way down, and maybe that transom will hold for a while. I mean, replacing that transom is a bear of a job. I'd rather go sail as soon as I could, rather than replace that whole thing."

"That's what I was thinking," I said.

But Art was shaking his head, his visage suddenly taking on a new depth, as if he were channelling a sea god of the old world. He said, "Here's the thing: If you get into that transom, and dig around in there, and find that those drifts are just corroded down to nothing, then you *have to* replace the transom—there'll be nothing holding it together. On the other hand, if there's something left of the drifts, then you could cobble together some scarfs and glue it up, and it'd probably hold up for a while. But as long as it's like that it'll never be right in my book."

He said this last phrase with feeling, as if we were debating scripture, which in a sense we were.

That was fair enough. I decided to steer the conversation onto another tack.

"I hear you, Art," I said. "I'll have to go back and rethink the transom. But what I wanted to ask you guys about most was the canvas decks."

"Most of the guys are using Dynel these days," said Art, pivoting neatly onto the new topic. "It's a synthetic fabric, it's tough, and you paint your deck with clear epoxy—mix it a little thin—and then you lay that Dynel down, and then you paint the top with epoxy, too, and squeegee the stuff right down through the fabric so it soaks through, and then you've really got something. But make sure you got slow hardener going, and don't mix it stiff, 'cause you need some time to get that goop down smooth, and if it goes off before you're ready, well, it's got the grip of God. You're in trouble."

"L. Francis says in *Compleat Cruiser* that he recommends cotton canvas bedded in white lead paint," I said.

"Yup, that's the way we used to do it. I got a feeling there's a shop across the bay that might sell you some white lead if you approach them right," said Art. "You been reading L. Francis, huh?" he went on. "He knows what he's talking about, so you won't go wrong there."

"Would you use canvas anymore?" I was curious in part because my cousin had given me twenty-five yards of heavy white canvas in a four-foot roll.

"It worked for years," said Dave. "I don't see why not."

"You think I could bed canvas with epoxy?" I asked.

"Sure, goop it up," said Dave. Art nodded assent. "But remember," Dave went on, "When that stuff goes off it's all over, so get everything set before you mix your mix."

Jim Shaw came over then, wearing a watch cap. He leaned in. "Canvas will work," he said slowly, giving each word weight. "Canvas will work fine. Worked for years. Will work for years. Not a blessed thing has changed about how canvas works on a deck."

"The voice of the prophet," said Art, smiling.

I was reassured. I had seen Garth stalk past me and out the door a minute before, so I knew it was time to go.

"It looks like my chauffeur there is ready," I said. "Many thanks, guys, for the kind words and the coffee. I'll be back soon."

I shook their hands, and turned to go. As I walked out the door, Art yelled after me, "You'll have to pull the toe rails off and spline the canvas under them." I waved in response to this. Garth had the pickup turned around when I got to it, and as soon as I was in he was gunning it into the road, heading back through the village.

"How'd it go?" I asked.

"That guy was great," he said. "Told me everything I need-ed to know about refastening, and replacing frames. Really felt like I could trust everything he said."

"How often does that happen?" I said.

"Not a lot," he replied.

"Worth coming all the way down here?"

"Heck yeah."

We rode in silence back to my place, past the old schoolhouse on the bluff above Eel Pond, and then past the old bell tower.

As we pulled into my lane, I asked him why he cared about the old boat so much.

" 'Cause it's something that was my family's that's mine that I can give to the kids," he said. "It just goes way back, and it's how we get out on the water, to be the hell out there, you know." He paused here, and then said, "It's just awesome."

"What is?" I asked.

"How that thing has held up, seventy years, and she's as good at what she does as she's ever been. Where are you going to find something like that? Everybody's looking for the new flavor, and it's the old flavors they ought to be looking at."

"You got time for a cup of tea, Garth?"

"Tea?" he said, "I haven't had time to drink tea since my first kid was born. You gotta be kidding me. I gotta get back, put a coat of paint on the old girl's interior, get a coat of varnish on the mast, get the summer rollin'!"

"Okay, Pal," I said, and climbed out. "Take care."

"Be seeing you," he said out the open window as he pulled out. "Come on out for a sail later in the summer, when I'm back on the Cape. That's the only time I calm down."

I went in, made a cup of tea, and sat on the deck for a few minutes while Ted walked around my legs, bumping her head into my shins.

40. Canvas Decks

ALL OF THE INSTRUCTIONS from Art and Dave sounded good, but it wasn't until today that I had the guts to start ripping the rest of the old canvas off the decks. It came up easily, was brittle, and tore into strips of sand-colored cotton. It was ready to leave.

Underneath lay grey plywood: pristine, strong, and well protected all these years by the old canvas. I finished ripping up the front deck, and then did the stern deck, slicing along the edges with a utility knife.

Then it was time to make a template. I taped several sheets of heavy paper together, and carefully traced the shape of the foredeck. I repeated this for the afterdeck. Then I laid each template in turn on the canvas, traced each carefully with a carpenter's pencil, and cut the canvas with a big pair of shears.

It was time to mix the goo. I made a big batch, nearly a pint, and painted it on the plywood of the foredeck with an old brush. It soaked in well, so I put down a second coat, and then laid down the canvas on top of the plywood. So far so good.

I then began to paint the top of the canvas with the goo, and in places the cloth seemed saturated, but not everywhere. The canvas was heavy and thick. I was suspicious. I peeled back some of the canvas, looked underneath, and saw that even where I thought the canvas would be well bedded in epoxy, the goo hadn't soaked into the fabric. Son of a gun! I would have to paint all of the bottom of the canvas as well, and then somehow make sure that the cloth was completely saturated with epoxy. At this rate I was going to run out of resin before I could finish. The grip of god seemed to be closing in on my canvas deck.

I jumped in the truck, drove to Wood Lumber, bought another quart of resin, and levitated home. Round trip: twenty minutes. *I might have ten minutes before the whole damned batch goes off,* I thought. So I mixed more clear epoxy. Squirt-squirt-squirt into the old tuna can, mix-mix-mix with a scrap of cedar shingle. Then I spread more epoxy on the underside of the canvas, and then spread it on top, using my rubber-gloved fingers as squeegees until the canvas was entirely permeated with epoxy. Then I smoothed the canvas out, sealed it along the edges, got it just right, no bubbles, and then waited with relief for chemical reality to turn the goo to rock.

I observed the transformation along with Ted, who was sitting on a crate at the corner of the shed. The process—watching glue dry—was accompanied by satisfying gluey smells, and then everything stopped suddenly, an avalanche setting at the end of its slide. The foredeck was done at 3:34 P.M. on a Saturday—beautiful, flat, impregnable. Time to start on the rear deck.

The rear deck was a simpler shape, a parallelogram, and it went easily, the process now clear to me, and there being an adundance of epoxy. I had the grey plywood deck sanded, the epoxy mixed, applied, and done in an hour.

The last conundrum was the little piece of deck just forward of the mast, aft of the coaming. It was a chevron, hardly a folded handkerchief of canvas, and Bill had ripped into it on his first visit, getting the point of his awl under it through a small hole and tearing it up.

"That's gotta go!" he had bellowed at the time, and I had had to restrain him.

"Okay, Bill! Hold on. I got the message! I'll tear it up from here," I had said.

I could see he wanted to dig away some more with that awl, get some peace by demolishing my boat, and that wasn't going to happen. It was about that time that I convinced him of the good sense of a cup of coffee.

Now I was faced with Bill's nasty tear. The canvas there also disappeared sweetly under the coaming, and was clamped under a piece of mahogany edging. Much of the original fabric was okay, and I decided, instead of ripping it out, to slice it down the middle, fold it back, rebed it with epoxy, patch it with a small piece of new canvas, and then overcoat any blemishes with clear epoxy. Which I did. It came out fine.

So the deck was done, and one of the most notable things about it was that the plywood underlayment, installed in 1939, was still strong, hardly worn, its plies still well glued.

41. *Floorboards*

ON THE FIRST FRIDAY of July, I got to the floor-boards. They were three-and-a-half-inch mahogany planks, arranged in panels along the fore-and-aft axis of the boat, supported by a web of spidery white oak joists that held them up about eight inches above the bottom of the bilge. The little oak joists that supported these panels of floorboards, made out of the same stock as the ribs, seemed hardly strong enough to support a cat—yet ably supported a two-hundred-and-fifty-pound human.

I had the five panels of floorboards in a stack at the side of the shed, and the task with them was easy: I had to sand them to wood, replace some of the screws that held them to their backing (short lengths of three-quarter-inch board), and then repaint them with a coat of primer and a couple of coats of a traditional "buff" (a sort of desert sand color) exterior marine paint.

I liked the whole system of these floorboards, because it was so straightforward (you can remove any of the three panels down the middle of the boat in order to have easy access to the bilge for pumping or retrieval of beer) and because, other than refastening the boards to the cleats that held them together (with new bronze screws) and replacing two short joists and several little posts, I didn't have to do much to them.

Almost everything was original, and still strong. I did coat the joists with a lick of clear epoxy, which hardened up their surfaces some, and sealed them, but other than that they are as they were circa 1939, and they serve.

"And they serve." Those words are problematic. Do they

serve with distinction? Do I? I believe the floorboards do. But what about the new canvas and epoxy I laid on the foredeck? As I walked out the door of the shed behind Barnum House that day, Art Burgess yelled after me something like "Be sure you take off the toe rails and spline the canvas underneath them."

By this he meant that I should first take off the narrow strips covering the edges of the foredeck (which come to a point at the bow) and carefully *wrap* the new canvas over the edge of the deck, so that there would be a continuous piece of canvas going right over the edge, like water over a falls, and that I should then refasten the toe rails over the edges of the new canvas.

Well, I didn't do that. And I have to tell you, I may have sinned in this. But those toe rails were original, and fastened with so many screws (still well fastened, I might add) that it was clear to me that to remove those old toe rails would be to destroy them. They were sealed under sixty years of varnish. I couldn't bring myself to dislodge them.

Moreover, it seemed to me that to cut the old canvas an eighth of an inch inside the edges of the toe rails, and to lay down the new canvas right alongside the remnant ribbon of the old canvas, and then to join the two layers of canvas with a generous layer of epoxy, and then to paint them with a stout deck paint, would be barrier enough against infiltrating water.

And on top of *that*, every one of the eighty-odd screws in the new toe rails would have pierced that splined canvas, providing egress to water even through the new canvas folded over the edge. So I punted, and left the old toe rails alone. Besides, I like the looks of the old toe rails. They bear the scars of collisions and time, like my face. But I felt a little uneasy about this decision. I feared the judgment of the men in the boat shed.

So far, all looked bulletproof. I could see no flaw in the new decks where water might penetrate, and there was no sign that it had. Still, I worried. Did I commit a sin? Are the boatbuilding spirits riled with me about this issue, even in a small way? Will the wrens carol once again over the cockpit of *Daphie*?

42. Monday, Second Week of July: Transom

I AWOKE THIS MORNING at 3:53 A.M., wandered downstairs, and heated old coffee in my battered white tin mug with the blue rim.

I was thinking full bore about the transom, and what I would find when I began to repair it later that day. This made my heart beat faster, half with anticipation, half with dread. That's what had awakened me. The boat at turns cajoled and bullied me, even in sleep. That was part of the deal.

Often a rebuild of a 12½ consisted of three big-ticket repairs:

1. Replacing frames as needed (which I had done)

2. Refastening (replacing screws/rivets/bolts with new) (also done)

3. Replacing the transom (not done)

So, back to the transom: its repair was my charge, and after my early wake-up I dozed for a while on the couch until the sun was up, made oatmeal and tea, and got out to the boat shed around eight. There, I began to dig around in the transom.

In *Daphie*'s transom there are four drifts, and the outboard ones, nearer the edge of the transom, were largely fine. I could see a trace of vertical blackness on the surface of the wood here and there along their paths, but it seemed that these two outer drifts weren't deteriorating much.

The inner two, however, were in real trouble (although not along their entire length). The real corrosion in each of them was near the center of the transom, along the horizontal edges of the planks they held together. Water had gotten in there, with predictable results.

What this looked like was two patches about the size of the bottom of a beer bottle where the wood was blackened and brittle, looking almost like charcoal. Bill had dug his awl into one of those spots (before I had a chance to stop him) and pulled out a chunk of dark iron-oxide-impregnated wood, exposing the shaft of the iron drift within. The drift itself was black, flaky with corrosion, and about the width of a pencil.

I knew, however, from my time chipping rust off the iron rigging of schooners, that iron can rust and rust, expanding to something like sixty-four times its original diameter before it is entirely gone. Which meant that these drifts, if they had only rusted, probably had plenty of strength left at their core.

So I commenced with my own awl. Gradually, as I dug away at the wood around each bad spot (as if I were digging into the wooden tailgate of a pickup truck from the outside), I saw that the drifts were really okay, if slightly corroded. If I could stabilize them and fill the voids I'd created, first with epoxy, and then with wooden scarfs to fair out the surface of the transom, I might buy myself a decade or more with the old transom. Happily, none of this damage was visible on the inner side of the transom. There the wood was pristine.

So as the sun climbed over the trees shading the shed, I chipped away at the transom. By the time I had both cavities cleared, exposing the drifts (each passing through its cavity like a stalactite in a cave), and had sanded and painted the drifts, and allowed the paint to dry, and encased all in epoxy mixed to the consistency of paste, it was late afternoon.

I left the epoxy to cure, and cut a couple of scarfs to fit in what remained of the holes, shaping each new piece of mahogany to the slightly eccentric shape of its hole. I epoxied those in place that evening, and went to bed.

In the morning, I again made oatmeal, and tea, and then went out to the shed brandishing a random orbital sander, and sanded down the scarfs and the little border of epoxy around them, so that they were flush with the surface of the transom.

And it looked a bit odd, a couple of patches in what is supposed to be one big tablelike surface of mahogany. But it looked strong, and I had also sealed the gaps between the panels that made up the transom with epoxy—no more water would infiltrate there. I could move on, happy with a version of perfection. Once I had varnished the thing, and it had taken on the deep brown glow of varnished mahogany, the whole scenario might not draw a lot of attention to itself.

43. Second Thursday in August: Elf

THURSDAY EVENING. I SIT outside under an over-cast evening sky. Next to my left hand is a glass holding scotch and water. Not far to the left of this is a blue ceramic bowl which holds twenty or more oyster crackers and two Fig Newmans. In my left hand, held between index and middle fingers, rests a small passable cigar that I bought at the filling station. There are three ice cubes in the drink. This is my third scotch of the year, second of the night.

I am just back from a visit to *Elf.* She was the second 12½ built in a line of more than 450 extending down through the years. The Herreshoff Manufacturing Company built 364 up until 1943, and then the Quincy Adams shipyard subsequently built 50 or so, and then Cape Cod Shipbuilding right up the road in Wareham built another 35 in wood. Others have built them here and there, no doubt, and perhaps in other countries; but *Elf* was number two, and for me to see her, and to sit on her, pump her bilge, look at her details, was rather like seeing an original canvas by Grant Wood.

Elf was built in 1914 for Mr. P. H. Monks, of Bourne, who (it is said) asked Nat to build him a boat he could sail with his grandchildren. *Elf* was later sold by Mr. Monks to a Mr. Jackson, the grandfather of Rebecca in whose kitchen I sat just an hour ago.

Smoke, exhaled, from my cigar, is going down under the picnic table. There is weather coming, a strong low, Katrina by name, and this cigar smoke warns of her. It is cowering.

Let me back up a little. The other day my mother phoned and said, "I met the woman who owns number two."

"Number two?" I said, and she said, "H-two."

"Ah, H-two," I said, comprehending.

"Herreshoff two," she said.

"The second one built? You mean *Elf*?"

"How'd you know her name?" she asked.

I had been reading production records from the Herreshoff plant, and I remembered *Elf* was the second one built. I told her that.

"It's moored at Monument beach," she said.

"Really," I said, intrigued.

"I played tennis with her owner. We got to talking, and I told her about your project and she said she had number two. She says you can go look anytime. Call her."

"I will," I said.

"And don't forget who got you on board," she said.

"I won't," I said.

I called her. Rebecca, who is my mother's age, was cordial on the phone, and asked me out to the house that evening before dinner.

I met her and her husband on a small island connected by a causeway to Bourne. I pulled up in the old Saab and they greeted me at the back porch. Soon we went to pump the boat.

This meant a stroll to a beach where there was a narrow pier with a dock at its end. We climbed into an old flat-bottomed rowboat there, and rowed out to *Elf*, which sat fifty yards offshore, among seven or eight other sailboats.

As we approached I could see she was extremely fair, her hull so smooth I could hardly tell she was planked. And her brightwork, reflecting on the calm water, was flawless.

But her seats were what caught my attention.

They were hard yellow pine, beautifully finished, and arranged differently than *Daphie*'s. Rather than being just two long benches on either side of the cockpit, her bench seats ended about three feet short of the forward bulkhead, and a thwart (a seat running across the axis of the boat) shot across the cockpit there.

This was, I knew, the original configuration of the H-12½ seating (much the same arrangement as on a Woods Hole spritsail), but I hadn't seen it before. What did it mean?

In those early days of the design, *Elf* was closer to being a truck. She was part fishing boat, part station wagon. She had to be able to be rowed, and the only comfortable way to row such a large and relatively heavy boat was to sit on a crosswise seat. In *Daphie*, with her two bench seats, there was no comfortable way to row with two oars, though I have done so every once in a while by kneeling on the floorboards, which after a time is painful. (More often I rowed with one oar, and countered its turning action with the rudder, which worked pretty well.)

Elf had been well cared for over the years, and as soon as I was able to poke my head over the gunwale, it was clear she'd been rebuilt even more thoroughly than *Daphie*. Her floor timbers were thick and solid and new, and her frames were beautifully full dimensioned, tight to the planks, and freshly painted.

I noted that she still had her original airtight bulkhead forward, and seemed not to be losing any paint because of it. Her decks were white and new, and her spars were bright with polyurethane, unscarred by time. In fact, she looked like a new boat! Which was both lovely to behold, and somehow not quite right. She was ninety, after all, and hardly showed her age, the Jane Fonda of Herreshoffs.

I did sense that this family had strong stories about *Elf*, that she held power for them the way *Daphie* holds power for my family, but after two soft inquiries ("So how do your children feel about *Elf*?" and "Was *Elf* a big part of your growing up?"), which were subtly deflected, I didn't dig further. *Elf* was part of their family, had been with them down through time, and it was not my place to intrude.

After several minutes of observing the subtle differences between *Elf* (her floorboards rose up in a little platform at the back of the cockpit) and *Daphie*, I pumped her out, and we rowed in, and then strolled to the house. They gave me a scotch and we talked for another little while.

And now, after a careful drive home (after sitting at the bottom of their driveway for half an hour until my head was clear) I sit among the sounds of crickets and tree frogs on my deck, writing. The second big scotch, from my own seldom-visited bottle, is gone, the cigar is gone, and I am nearly gone. I don't know if I found out much of anything tonight. I saw a beautiful old boat, and spoke with a couple of charming people who have had many good times in their old boat. *Daphie* sits in the shed, is not yet done, and will never reach the perfection of *Elf.*

What the hell. I wish I had never seen her—number two. She's beyond perfection! I want to get through this project, make my old boat *live* again (for I love her), and move on with life. Yes, *Elf* is a beauty, but far more perfect than I will ever make *Daphie,* or would want to. Let's hear it for rough beauty! Time for bed.

44. Stories

THERE IS A STORY my father has told me many times. He and his mother lived in Falmouth. It was 1943 or so, a grey spring day, and a friend of theirs, a man named Jim, had been given a Beetle Cat, which lay not quite derelict on a beach in Mattapoisett, on the far side of the bay.

Jim had decided it was time to bring the boat over to Falmouth, weather or no, so he and my father (who was ten or so) hitched a ride, as one could in those days, over the bridge, found the boat on the beach, launched it, and raised sail as they were pushed off by a west-northwest breeze. They were dressed warmly, and Jim, who was no slouch, had brought along four bailers. As they shoved off, they noted that clouds were gathering to the north, and that the wind seemed fresher.

The Beetle Cat, as built by Crosby (as well as Concordia), is a strong little boat, seaworthy, fast, fickle. It has relatively low freeboard—there are no seats to speak of—so one sits on the floorboards or the gunwale. It has one large gaff-rigged sail, a centerboard, and a big shallow rudder that works well unless one is skating down a wave face with the sail in too far. Then, if the rudder comes out of the water, the boat will head up into the wind faster than seems possible, all forward motion ends, and the boat slides sideways across the wave and comes to rest heading upwind, in irons. Which is just a momentary setback, but disconcerting nonetheless.

From what I can remember, this Beetle Cat on the beach had seen better days, but felt seaworthy enough to them as they headed out into open water. I imagine them swinging through several small freighters lining up at the top of the bay, gathering for a convoy that would take munitions or food across to Liverpool, or Murmansk.

Jim was in the navy, an experienced mariner, and this was a bit of fun for him. For my father, it was his first time offshore in a small boat, and as the cat fairly flew downwind, the big sail rocketing them through the smooth water, he was, to say the least, wide-eyed.

Once they had crossed the shipping lanes and were getting out into the center of the bay, however, the seas became steeper and the little boat's seams began to work as the wind came up to eighteen knots, and twenty, and twenty-two. She hadn't been in the water for some time, so hadn't swollen as one would like a boat to swell before making her work, plus the occasional comber dumped itself right over the gunwale. Jim steered on a broad reach for Penzance Point in Woods Hole, which was a dark line on the distant horizon, and told my father to bail. Which he did. He bailed and he bailed and he bailed, and seemed to make little headway. And then he lost the bailer over the side, watched it bob away in the wake.

"Keep bailin', man," I imagine Jim saying. "We gotta keep bailin', or we'll be sailing her across the bottom. And your mother wouldn't like that."

So my father grabbed another bailer and kept at it for another ten minutes, the water sloshing around their feet, until that bailer too went over the side.

"That's all right, man. Here's another. Keep at it, kid. We'll be all right," said Jim in my mind, and my father did, kept scooping the water out, staying even with it, until after only five minutes this time, and with still another five miles to sail, the third bailer was lost overboard.

"Boy, you don't like those bailers much, do you?" said Jim,

his big hand reaching inside his jacket pocket, and coming out with a long piece of heavy twine. "Hold this," he said to my father, and handed him the tiller, which my Dad took.

"Push the tiller a little more toward me," said Jim. "That's it, hold her there," and then, putting the mainsheet under his left foot, Jim grabbed the last bailer and tied it neatly with the twine to a cleat under the gunwale.

"There," he then said, handing the bailer to my father. "Now, we can't lose that one. I've got to sail the boat, and get us into Woods Hole all right, and I'm counting on you to bail. It's very important, what you're doing, and I'm relying on you. I know you can do it, and so does the boat. She can't do it without either of us working at it. Now let's go, kid."

My father bailed for another forty-five minutes, and kept the sea out until, in winds gusting to thirty knots, they were finally just off a fine little crescent beach on the outer shore of Penzance, where my grandmother had by chance gone to look for them, or their wreck.

Jim saw her, a young woman in an overcoat standing on the beach and waving, headed in toward her, ran the little boat up on the beach on a swell, the two jumped out, pulled her up farther, dropped the sail, and took a scolding from my grandmother, who then observed the weather worsening, the sky darkening further, as they made the sail neat and invulnerable to wind, and coiled the lines. Then they all got into her black Ford as the rain began to come down in sheets, drove off the point and into Woods Hole, and stopped by the drawbridge at the Cap'n Kidd, where they had clam chowder, and sausage and bread and cheese, and hot tea with whiskey, and just whiskey, and warmed up by the woodstove, while Leonie the owner leaned on the bar and held her pet skunk, who had a leash on and fell asleep in her arms as she told them stories of coming back from Tarpaulin Cove in a gale once, and how their boat had sunk just as they came up to the dock, had gone under just as they stepped off it.

They went back to Penzance on the next good day, and waited for the tide, and then pushed the cat out into a fair current in the Hole, raised sail, and brought her around to Falmouth, into Siders Pond, where she stayed the rest of the summer.

That was my father's first time offshore, afloat, and at risk, and not the last. I think about half of that story is true. If my father were writing this he could tell you which half. The part about the catboat is about as I heard it, and Leonie did have a skunk. But I don't know what she said to them once they were in the bar, beyond what I have heard other people say from the same stools in the same bar forty years later. That's the story as far as I know it. It's the story I tell.

Another story that comes up for me is of a sail my father took in a boat he acquired when I was three, called *Capella*, which was a 12½. Except that it wasn't. It was close, but no 12½. Everyone wondered, as they sailed by, "Is that a 12½?"

It was sixteen feet long, six inches longer than *Daphie* (which was by then in my uncle's barn in northwestern Massachusetts), and had been built by a guy in East Falmouth who wanted a 12½ but either didn't have the drawings, or felt he could improve on the original. I don't know. But the story, as I recall it, is that Dad took his boat, *Capella*, for a sail in October of 1971, the last sail of the season.

It was a beautiful, high, Indian summer day, a Wednesday, and he just took off out of Great Harbor, beating up the sound. The wind was good and strong, a little west of southwest, so the going was easy, in the lee of the islands. The sun was strong, too, and he had a sandwich and a beer or two with him, and the day stretched out. By midday he was most of the way to Cuttyhunk, so he thought he'd try to make it there, see how the water was in Canapitsit channel. If there was a swell in there, and the tide was low and flowing against the wind, it would be easy to bottom out there, break the boat on the bar.

But the water was high, and he zipped through on the flood, and then was able to beat right up the gut into Cutty-hunk harbor on one tack, and sail around a little in there, and then drop the hook, and snooze for a bit on one of the seats.

And then he heard a shout, and saw that a gentleman on a cabin cruiser, a nice old Lyman, was pushing off in a skiff and rowing toward him. It was the only other visiting boat in the harbor.

When he had come alongside, it was to invite Dad over to watch the World Series, that year contested between the Pittsburgh Pirates and the Baltimore Orioles. My father was quick to accept, and they spent the remainder of the day eating hot dogs and drinking cold Budweisers and watching the '71 Pirates win the seventh game of the series behind the pitching of Steve Blass and a fourth-inning home run by Roberto Cle-mente. Manny Sanguillen caught the game and Willie Stargell contributed a single, and all of this unfolded on a small black-and-white TV.

When I was four, and we still lived in Pittsburgh, Willie had visited my school, and I had gotten his autograph. He was a huge man, with a huge hand into which mine disappeared when he shook it, and he had signed his name on a blue index card, and smiled down at me, and patted me on the back, and said, "I see you in the outfield, son."

I took those two words he wrote and have them now in a box which I can see across the room, where I write. He was my first hero, and always will be, for the sweetness he showed that day, and for the vicious hacks he took at the plate on behalf of his team, and all of Pittsburgh, and me. How strong it was to see Willie hit one out of Forbes Field, when I was six. There was a stillness at the plate, followed by an explosion of strength, and then the high arcing trajectory of the shot (so high that it climbed above the limits of the lights, up into the dark night), with El Señor Clemente already on base.

By the time the game was over, it was well along into evening. My father's kind host brought him back to *Capella*, and Dad set out on the long sail home, reaching down the bay. Halfway back, after he'd come through Robinsons Hole in the dark, into Vineyard Sound (threading the narrow channel by looking for the silhouettes of the cans and nuns against the moonlit water) the wind died, and he started rowing.

And he rowed. And rowed some more. Six miles lay before him, with the tide pushing from behind at half a knot.

The evening became night, the moon now behind him, the islands stark in the pale light, and the ocean quiet in their lee. He rowed with one arm and then the other, and then drifted a bit, and rowed some more, and felt his back tiring. It was work, to row *Capella*. Occasionally he'd hear a fish rise, or see a boat passing in the distance—a green light crossing, a red light fading.

At eleven or so he was crossing the Hole. The tide was slack. No boats in sight. Just him in the dark little sloop, under the heavens, the creak of the oars coming occasionally, and the slap of the small waves in the confused waters as they waited to be moved again by the tide. And then he was across the Hole, and moving into the outer harbor.

At eleven-thirty he was on the mooring, made the boat neat, rowed in, walked back to the house, and fell into bed, rarely having lived a better day.

45. Third Monday in August: Covering Boards

THERE WAS SOMETHING SAD about putting on the covering boards this morning. They are the light mahogany boards that cover the sheer strake and the sheer clamp, right along the gunwale of the boat, from the transom to the foredeck.

They are delicate pieces of wood, so it was incongruous how solid they made the boat look when they went back on, and I was made melancholy when they did, as I would likely not see the boat that way again—in pieces—see the tops of the new frames as they rose inside the boat. It meant we were getting close to being done.

On Saturday we had a service for my cousin Chick, who died four years ago at fifty-seven. He was a big man who loved to cook and eat and drink, a retired commander who had headed the bomb-disposal school for the navy. He was a father of two girls. His mother was my mother's sister. He had a heart attack. And when he was young he had sailed *Daphie*, as had his brothers Ben and Pieter. They had sailed her as much as I, and loved her as hard, the second generation to have her.

Chick's ashes, as he wished, were committed to the great, booming channel in the middle of the Hole. On Saturday, because there wasn't a marker for him anywhere, we dedicated a stone—a big block of granite with his name and dates on it—to his memory on the shore of Little Harbor, at the back of a pier there. I have a picture of that pier with a spritsail tied to it, dating from 1900.

And somehow, putting these covering boards back on the boat feels like something significant to Chick. If it is a new beginning for *Daphie*, it is a continuation of the old as well. These are the same boards Chick and Ben and Pieter and my mother and his mother leaned on, pushed off from, scarred. There are forty screws in each, forty holes to be bunged, then layers of varnish to apply.

By noon I had both boards screwed back on, and was commencing with the bungs, which is the hard part. First I had to cut the bungs, which I did with a heavy-duty handheld Porter Cable electric drill, drilling down into a new piece of mahogany with a Fuller bung cutter and cutting ninety bungs three-eighths of an inch wide. I dipped each in varnish, inserted each one in a screw hole so its grain ran parallel to the board's grain, and then left them to dry. Later, I returned with a sharp chisel, and trimmed each bung off just above the board; then I sanded each bung down till it was fair.

46. *Story*

MY MOTHER TELLS ONE about being out on the Joneses' boat, with her friend Derek. It was a wooden sloop, maybe thirty-five feet long, named *Mallie*, or something like that.

They were teenagers, seventeen, and having a hell of a good sail out in the bay, when they saw a squall forming to windward. They tried to run before it, beat it home, but it came on fast, overtook them with the sails still up, and before they knew it they were struggling to keep the boat upright. The sky was very dark in the midst of the storm, and the rain came down hard, and then *Mallie* was knocked over, and the sea was in the cockpit, was disappearing down the companionway. Mom was thrown hard onto the deck and against a winch, bruising her ribs and knocking the wind out of her, and the sea was wild, and *Mallie* was booming through the water, and then Derek was gone. Gone!

My mother knew he was back behind them somewhere. Her thoughts were, "I've got to handle this boat well enough to get to him back." She struggled to bring *Mallie* into the wind. She braced herself how she could, and put the tiller down, and slacked the sheets. Slowly, *Mallie* began to right herself; Mom could see that there was a lot of water in the bilge.

And then she could see Derek, back in the wake. He'd managed to grab the mainsheet, which had gone overboard and was streaming along behind. He was pulling himself hand over hand back to the boat. She put the tiller down hard again, and the boat responded slowly, heading farther up into the wind, which blew so hard that it made the sails crack as they flogged, and she thought they would surely tear. And then he was alongside, and she was pulling him on board, and he was all right.

They pulled the boat back together. The wind moderated. They pumped out the water, took her into the mooring, put her to bed, and rowed in. The sun was out by then, and the breeze was light. They walked to Derek's house, and went inside, and had a seat at the kitchen table, surprised to be alive, and his mother asked as they sat at there trembling, "How was your sail? What a lovely day for it." She was perplexed when my mother and Derek said nothing, and just looked at her, still shaking.

And then there is another short story. She tells it quickly. She was in a race. The whole fleet rounded a mark leaving it on the wrong side. She was the only boat to round the mark correctly. And although not first around the course, she won.

I am not sure, that I have these stories exactly right, but that's how I've recollected them for a while now. That's how I tell them.

47. Three Tillers

THE TILLER OF MY father's near-Herreshoff *Capella* was square in cross section, not round. That I do recall, suddenly. I hadn't thought of that in years. I can feel that tiller in my left hand, as I sit here in the cottage at the table.

Odd. I last steered that boat when I was seven or eight. *Daphie's* tiller, on the other hand, was—is—round, with a smooth knob at the end. I can feel both of those tillers in my hand, like ghosts, as well as a third—that of *Sandpiper,* my old fiberglass goldeneye that is in the water now.

Daphie's tiller is shorter and less robust than *Capella's* or *Sandpiper's,* which is appropriate, as *Sandpiper* is the bigger boat.

But the last time I steered *Capella* was thirty-two years ago. When I imagine reaching for her tiller, I reach up.

As I think of that old tiller, I remember too going out to a boat meadow at Barlow's Boatyard in Pocasset, Bourne. It was April or May in 1972 or 1973. I was seven or eight, and we would drive out there, my father and I, he at the wheel of his old three-speed Jeep Cherokee, drive out along the sandy back roads to a meadow that ran down onto a little salt river, the Back River, and the two of us would work on *Capella*. He would sand or paint or caulk, and I would run around in the tall grass, perhaps take a swipe or two at a plank with some sandpaper. And as I watched him he would put in a new screw or two, or press in some new underwater seam compound with a caulking knife, or talk with the men at the boatyard, who wore green work pants and brown work boots, and who would stand with their feet apart and their arms crossed while he talked to them, and laugh and nod their heads, and then sometimes produce something that he asked for, for which he paid them money or signed a piece of paper, and then we would go back to the boat, and sand something some more, and paint it or caulk it. I saw that this was how one had a boat.

You did the work yourself, that was one thing. And I saw how good my father was at talking to these men, how he often seemed to say something that they enjoyed hearing; they would always stop what they were doing for him, and chat, and stand in a way which said they weren't threatened by him, or made uncomfortable by him, even though they worked with their hands, and he only did sometimes. There were no airs. Now, all these years along, I see how special his talent was, at finding where their commonalities as men lay, reaching across the gulf of profession. I have worked enough with my hands, undercover, as it were, to see this clearly now.

And the grass in the meadow grew, and the boat came together, and it was clear to me that this was a good thing, this working on the boat. Afterward we would eat fried clams at a little restaurant on Barlows Neck Road. I have rarely had days so good.

48. Third Tuesday in August: Seats

THE SEATS ARE THE last major interior component to be reinstalled. There are other cosmetic details to be taken care of, but the seats are the last big item. Looking into *Daphie*'s cockpit without seats is about like looking into a car without seats—it looks empty and unfinished.

It was cool when I got up this morning; the sky was a deep, clear blue. Ted came out to sit on the picnic table, under the black cherry tree in the front yard, while I drank my tea.

It was about seven-thirty when I went and found the seats in the back shed, where they'd been leaning for more than a year—two curved mahogany planks, each with nine holes for the screws that held them down. They were in fine shape. What really needed work were the parts of the boat that supported the seats.

When installed, the two ends of each seat would sit on simple blocks of oak screwed to the aft and forward bulkheads. Under the middle of each seat would be a curved bracket made of plywood and oak that was screwed to a frame and curved up to meet the bottom of the seat. It was a simple, solid way to support the seats.

Renewing the end cleats wasn't needed—they were still sturdy. The center supports, however, needed refurbishing. They were still sitting, like a couple of odd boomerangs, on top of the seats in the shed, right where I'd put them eighteen months before.

So I took each of these center supports apart, each consisting of a fourteen-inch girder of two-inch oak that ran along under the seat, which was screwed to a curved buttress of marine ply that held the girder up. Once I had the screws out, I sanded everything, and primed everything with good white oil marine primer, and let that dry.

And then I thought some about Jan Hahn, my mother's sister's second husband, who'd had a heart attack while racing *Daphie* in the early '60s. He was a relatively young man—in his forties—when he'd died. I didn't like to think about that when I thought about *Daphie,* but there it was, another part of her history. I see his daughter once in a while around town. I ought to take her sailing and have a talk about her dad.

After lunch the paint was dry, so Ted and I went back out to the boat shed. I drilled new holes for screws that would pass through the oak into the curved plywood struts, mixed a batch of goo, glued the girders to the top edges of their plywood struts, and screwed them together. This took about an hour, all told, and then it was time again to do something else.

Since the weather looked like it would be okay for a few days, I decided to bring the spars out (they'd been hanging above my living room for a year and a half, suspended from beams on loops of string).

I laid them out side by side on some yellow steel sawhorses. The mast, the boom, the gaff, the jibboom, and the tiller—five spars, all needing light sanding and then varnishing. Once the seats were back in, they would be next.

When they were laid out, I took a few minutes to look them over—they were all spruce, light, straight, and in fine shape—while I waited for the goo on the seat supports to set up. When the epoxy had hardened, I sanded down the rough spots, and got to work bolting each bracket to the rib which supported it.

This was a nice time to use my right-angle drill, one of the specialized tools which years ago I never imagined I would own. I drilled holes with it in the starboard and port midships frames so that the seat supports could be bolted to them. This whole task consumed about forty-five minutes, and once the supports were bolted in place it was time to put the seats in there, and see how they looked.

I laid each seat down in its place. I put nine bronze number twelve inch-and-a-half screws through each seat and down into the same cleats and supports they'd sat on for sixty-eight years. They were firmly held, and the last thing I did was sit on the port seat. The boat was now wholly back together.

I then cut eighteen half-inch bungs in a piece of mahogany, glued them into the screw holes in the seats, and let them dry, then went out for a run to Nobska Beach, where the crowds had vanished with the evening. I could see the light at Tarpaulin Cove, four miles away, just beginning to blink as the evening came on.

49. *Third Wednesday in August*

THE DAY BEGAN OVERCAST, and I was up at seven-thirty, making oatmeal and tea, and wondering if it would clear later, as it was supposed to. There was not much happening on the road. Ted and I had breakfast in the shed on the stumps, and then she sprinted off around the back of the cottage. I for my part was focused on the holes in the sides of the boat. There were about nine hundred holes in the painted planks, all with fresh new screw heads just within, and all needing seam compound to be spread into them, and smoothed, so that I could paint over them.

And there were the forty or so holes in the mahogany sheer strakes, the topmost planks on the hull. All of those needed mahogany bungs in them, all of which bungs needed to be cut, glued, trimmed, and sanded.

So, I got to work around eight, and listened to the radio. Iraq was coming apart at the seams—no surprise there, as the territory in question was one the Brits had cobbled together eighty years before as a nation of arbitrary lines and dissimilar peoples. Now we were trying to forge a new nation of the same strange bedfellows. I turned the radio off and wondered what I could do from this shed to make things better in Iraq. We had a policy based on the mendacious use of flawed intelligence, poor judgment, and folly. I didn't know what to do. I kept on cutting bungs, gluing them in, trimming them off.

50. *Third Thursday in August: Spars*

SPARS ON A 12 1/2 take some time each year, because unlike most parts of a boat (which need at most two or three coats of paint) they require many coats of varnish: at least five, perhaps eight or nine, as many as twelve. Which means that one spends time with them.

On *Daphie* the mast, being the biggest spar, requires the most time. I don't know how big the mast is on *Daphie,* but that's because I don't care to; mythologically it is just *big* to me and that's how I want it to remain.

I guess it is the size of a small tree—four and a half inches in diameter, perhaps—and straight, tapering toward the top, maybe fifteen feet tall.

I shinnied up the mast of *Marlin* (a Herreshoff 12½) the other day, when her peak halyard escaped and went to the top of the mast. This is a particularly disheartening way to end a sail—having one's halyard, for one reason or another, end up out of reach up there.

There is usually no good way to get such a halyard back down, other than to climb the mast, which I did for my friend, who was tired of staring at the figure-eight knot way up there, stuck in the maw of the pulley. If you have a long pole with a good pincer on the end you can sometimes grab a halyard and pull it back down; otherwise, you must ascend.

I was still able to pull my body up and up again, until I could reach the line and haul it back down with me. The mast didn't budge, didn't even consider breaking—stout piece of spruce.

Daphie's mast was identical to that one, or nearly so. It was a solid cudgel of wood, mottled dark here and there where a little water had crept through, which had not damaged the wood, but had discolored the varnish. Today it was my task first to look it over, there under the black cherry tree, next to the shed, lying on the yellow horses.

All of the tackle looked good. The "gooseneck," a bronze fitting that allows the boom to swing in four directions while remaining attached to the mast, looked fine. And the other tackle looked good, too: the pulley about twelve feet up the mast (which received the throat halyard) looked strong and well attached, and the two blocks near the top of the mast through which the peak halyard ran looked fine.

The stainless-steel cables that were the stays (the H-12½ has three stays—a forestay, and two sidestays, or "shrouds") all looked good where they looped over the top of the mast. I took off the bronze cap that held them there, removed them, and set them aside.

The other spars all had less gear on them. The main boom (about eleven feet long, and thick as the barrel of a baseball bat) had no attached lines. Rather it had the other part of the gooseneck tackle that attached it to the mast; a bronze track (for mounting the sail) that ran down its length; a block or two for the mainsheet; and a small cleat or two.

The jibboom (about as long as a baseball bat, and as thick as the handle of one) also had some old bronze tackle on one end, to allow it to attach to the bow, as well as a bronze track where the jib mounted. I particularly liked the jibboom, because the jib was self-tending, and did its job without much supervision.

Then there was the gaff, which ran along the top of the mainsail, and was two-thirds as long as the main boom, narrower, and was fitted at one end with "jaws"—two bowed pieces of wood that wrapped around the mast like arms and served as an old-fashioned gooseneck with the added ability to slide up and down the mast. I had broken these jaws in a big wind twenty years before, and had replaced them.

The last spar was the tiller, a tapering piece of ash about as long as an axe handle, but much narrower; it fit through a hole in the transom (its squared base fitting into a square hole in the top of the rudder) and curved nicely into the cockpit, becoming progressively more narrow as it did so, with a rounded end that fit in one's hand.

I began to sand the spars lightly, with 120-grit sandpaper, just roughing up their varnish a little. Thankfully my cousin had kept the spars undercover, and only the mast needed to be sanded down to wood in a few places. The rest of the spars were in relatively good shape. I sanded them all, and then wiped them down with a cloth to take off the dust. This took about an hour, and then I got a can of spar varnish, didn't shake it (bubbles in varnish are not good), opened it, and began to brush it onto the mast.

Immediately the old spar jumped back to life, the new varnish bringing out the gold highlights of the wood, and as I moved to each of the other spars, brushing the varnish on smoothly and evenly, each piece of wood seemed to awaken.

By the time I was done with that first coat, it was 5 P.M., and a couple of dry leaves had blown and stuck to the varnish on the mast. No matter. I would repeat this process eight times in the coming days, and on the coaming and seats and transom, too. Much of my life in late August would be spent varnishing.

51. Third Friday
in August: Paint

I HAD BEEN VARNISHING, but there were other things to do. Such as paint. For me, boats are divided into sections, in terms of maintenance. It's the only way to manage preparing them for summer—to break them down into their parts. This approach may date from when I was hired as a boy to maintain the Quissett Yacht Club fleet during the winter.

Starting when I was twelve years old or so, in the afternoon, after school or on weekends, I would walk up the road to the Coffins' house, an understated place set back in the woods, and in the basement I varnished tillers and paddles, and painted rudders and centerboards right through the winter. There were fifteen sets of four each: the gear from eight sloops, and seven prams, which meant sixty pieces, each needing at least two coats of something and maybe five or six. I was twelve and thirteen and fourteen, and made a couple of bucks an hour, and listened to WMVY (the Vineyard's radio station) down there, music of the '60s and '70s—the Grateful Dead and Curtis Mayfield, Dylan, and Taj Mahal.

Now, when I paint or varnish, I can't let go of how I was trained to it by Mr. Coffin. He was sixty or so then, a quiet, thoughtful man who always wore a blue button-down shirt, jeans, Top-Siders, and glasses with grey plastic frames. He smoked his pipe nearly continually, lighting a sweet-smelling leaf with a Zippo, all of which smelled like work to me, and let me know, as he smoked, that he was thinking hard, that when he did speak, that I should give it weight.

He taught me how to open a paint can (carefully, so as not to get paint in the groove where the lid seals, or on the label), and to stir the paint (carefully, so as not to get paint in the groove where the lid seals, or on the label), and how to clean a brush (slowly and carefully, so that it is truly clean, and can be used again), and how to clean up when I was done (slowly and carefully).

I also think about how I came to respect those boats I was busy preserving, the O'Day Javelins and Optimist Prams, which I later taught sailing in, and ran the sailing school with. I relied on them, well maintained, to keep my students safe, and they did.

The Javelins were heavy fiberglass sloops, sixteen feet long, and could pound through a sea or two, as well as go over one. They would capsize under duress, but for the most part they were stable and hardy—excellent boats for teaching seamanship, racing, and especially for teaching young sailors. When the club decided to replace them (bowing to the pressure of those who wanted to keep up with the racing teams of richer clubs) with 420s—little rocket ships that were far inferior as teaching boats—I turned the teaching program over to my assistant head instructor. He was a great guy and deserved the chance to head up the program; I, for my part, was too saddened by the capitulation to fashion to remain.

It seemed to me that it had eluded those in charge that although the 420 was an exciting boat to sail (and I had sailed them plenty, at other clubs), there was nothing inherently better about learning to sail one well than there was in learning to sail a Javelin well.

Or a 12½. Or a Woods Hole spritsail. To win in any of these one had to excel, one had to drive the boat better than anyone else presently could, which in each boat required different subtleties. But the Javelins lacked front-page sex appeal.

They were stolid, reliable, seaworthy. They were what I hoped I was. Clearly, the club's use for one with such old-fashioned values had come to an end. What does that mean with regard to *Daphie*'s interior and topsides paint? It means I admire substance over style. Just as I admire the whole boat. But to some extent it means that I like to paint, having been trained to it by a master.

In the interior of *Daphie*, the floorboards, the interior of the hull above the floorboards (including the new ribs), the bulkheads, and the decks needed paint. All of that got two coats of flat white oil-based primer, one coat in the morning, and then another in the evening when the first had dried.

The floorboards and decks then got two more coats of paint, once they had been primed. I painted them buff, a sand color traditional on wooden boats around here for decks and floorboards. The rest of the interior—the sides of the hull and the ribs above the floorboards, and the bulkheads—got two coats of flat white oil-based paint. The bilge got nothing, as its best friend would be the salt water it would marinate in once I launched the boat.

On the exterior of *Daphie*, the hull above the waterline got a coat of good white oil-based primer, and then two coats of flat white oil-based topsides paint.

All this happened during the last days of the third week of August, and the first days of the fourth week of August. I got out there every day and varnished spars, and painted, and varnished. There was a stretch of good weather, which helped.

52. *Wednesday, Fourth Week in August: Bronze*

IT WAS, REMARKABLY, TIME to put the bronze back on the boat.

I began at the bow, on Wednesday morning, after a cup of strong coffee and another illicit look at the *New York Times* from up the street.

When I was in the process of disassembling *Daphie,* I put all of her bronze fittings in a clear plastic bag, and put that at the bottom of a tool satchel, and forgot about it. Now I wondered what I'd done with all the bronze fittings. The thought occurred to me that, like a squirrel storing nuts, I would have put those fittings in the satchel where I typically put fittings, so I went to the back of the Saab, and opened the hatch, and found the satchel where it sits on top of the toolbox, and pawed through the strata within, and (lo!) found that plastic bag at the bottom of the satchel, and so began to reassemble *Daphie's* bronze tackle. (So, when you find a filing system that works, stick with it.) With an old wood-handled flathead screwdriver that had belonged to my mother's father, I set to work.

First came the chocks, two bronze fittings designed to hold a mooring or anchor line at the bow while allowing it to run freely. The chocks fit on either side of the stem right up at the bow, and they went back on easy as pie. I set them in a thin layer of bedding compound, which would keep the water out, and I used their old screws, one-and-a-half-inch bronze screws that I'd taped to the chocks when I removed them, and which were in fine shape.

Then came the forecleat, a bronze cleat made to Nat's pattern many years ago, which bolted with four bronze machine screws down through the deck. That also (once I had crawled under the deck, and punched pilot holes up through the new canvas) went right back on as if it had never left, with a little bedding compound beneath it to make it snug.

Then at the back of the foredeck on the starboard side there was a loop of bronze to install, where the bitter end of the jib sheet would be tied, and on the port side of the deck another loop with a bronze block attached. This was a fairlead for the jib sheet, and routed the line back to a cleat in the cockpit. Both of those loops went right back on in their accustomed places, as the forecleat had.

Then there was a smaller bronze cleat in the cockpit. This was a jamb cleat, designed to hold the jib sheet with just one turn of the line around it. It mounted under the gunwale on the port side, and it went right back on with a couple of new one-and-a-half-inch bronze screws.

Then there were two identical bronze cleats that mounted to the covering boards, outside the coaming, three feet forward of the transom. These were for spinnaker lines, and any other lines needed for docking. They too went right back on with their old two-inch screws, which I had taped to them with duct tape many months ago.

There was just one other cleat—a plain bronze cleat that mounted in the center of the aft deck. That was for the mainsheet. This too went on without any mischief.

The very last of the tackle to note was a bronze loop and pulley that slid back and forth on the bronze traveler bar mounted to the transom. I had left that on the boat, and it was still there, as were the four cleats for the halyards, which were still screwed to the forward bulkhead by the mast step. There had been no reason to remove them.

My main talent in this part of the reassembly had been in remembering where I had put the parts nearly two years before. So, in an hour I had reassembled the boat's bronze tackle.

I sat there in the shed on a stump after I'd completed this task, and sipped at my coffee, now cold, its surface a haze of various dusts and several drowned gnats, and reflected on how much this particular task really meant to me: like a knob on a telescope, this task seemed to have brought things further into focus.

When I removed all that stuff eighteen months before, it felt like a huge risk. When would I ever get the cleats and loops and chocks back on? I asked myself. Was it folly to remove them? Would I be the guy who takes his motorcycle apart and leaves the parts strewn on the garage floor, where they remain for twenty years because he never got around to putting it back together? Would I be the fool of whom a grandniece would ask, "Hey this old boat in the picture—whatever became of that?" To which someone would reply "Oh, yeah, that was a pity. That was Uncle Dan's boat. He took it apart years ago, and just never got it together again. He kinda cracked up after that, moved out to the desert, lived in a yurt . . . and then he just faded away."

But today the pieces went back on. I am not that guy. The family still has the boat. You hear that, generations to come? I am not that guy.

53. Thursday, Last Week in August: Caulking

I FIND, AT THE end of the work required to put a wooden Herreshoff 12 ½ in the water, that my right hand is usually in tough shape, because it is the hand that braces the putty knife as it presses underwater seam compound into the seams between the planks.

This is one of the more sublime tasks in the catalog of "what must be done," one of the last stations on the pilgrimage, in order to float a 12 ½.

The topsides, interior, and brightwork (varnished wood) are all straightforward. One might as well be painting a house carefully. But the bottom of the boat, the section below the waterline, and near it, requires another sort of special attention, which is given at a stoop, kneeling, or reclining, for the cradle is low to the ground.

First, in the spring (or in this case, in August), during the week of the pilgrimage, you sand the bottom. Then you scrape and chip away at the loose paint some more, and remove any loose seam compound from the seams. This operation takes a couple of hours of concerted work, and leaves one splotched in odd places, like the top of one's head, with blue or green paint dust, and contorted, stiff, and oddly satisfied.

The hull's surface has been deconstructed. All of the loose surfacing agents have been banished. Open seams and old scars glare. And then it is time to make the newly rough smooth again. So you prime the few bare patches of wood with bottom paint, and then it is time for the underwater seam compound. And the putty knife.

This year it was a beautiful cool morning, the fourth Thursday in August, when I finally pulled the can of seam compound down off the shelf in the paint section of the back shed. It was with some anticipation that I opened the can with my favorite old Stanley flathead screwdriver, which has a big black wooden handle.

The can was a quart, which is the smallest amount they sell underwater seam compound in now, and I'd given the can a good squeeze when I bought it to be sure the contents were still soft and pliable within.

Upon opening the can on the sawhorse in the shed, and lifting off the lid, which let go of the edge of the can with a metallic "tink," I knew we were going to be all right. Within lay the great unction, colored a deep iron-oxide red, red as ochre, red as dried blood, red-brown, smelling richly of oils almost to the point of fishiness—a paste the consistency of bread dough, or good peanut butter. Very thick. Substantial. Yet workable.

I took a dollop on the putty knife, and began systematically to work it into the newly clean seams, filling voids and eliminating cracks. It is as if one were filling the slots between old floorboards, when one does this. With a couple of exceptions: (1) you're doing it from underneath, and (2) these boards will be immersed, and will swell, and if the paste were to dry to inflexibility, the planks would buckle out and pop away from the hull, so strongly do they come together when they swell.

However, the underwater seam compound stays limber. This is its great talent, along with adhesion to wood and smelling mysterious. Rather than hardening, it pooches out a bit under the pressure of the planks, and forms a watertight gasket. It is miraculous stuff.

Beneath it, at the very inside of the seam (beyond which lies the interior of the boat), is a thin band of cotton caulk—a line of rolled raw cotton that forms the innermost defense against the water. So there is cotton, and then this dark unction, and paint, and then the sea.

One of the signal pleasures in caulking is the slow, systematic progress one makes along each seam. No millimeter can be ignored, for a leak even as big as a pencil's lead will sink the boat in a couple of hours. So progress with the putty knife is careful, slow, and measured, with excess compound scraped off and reapplied farther down.

At the end you go back over the seams and check again, and finally, after a glass of lemonade and a nap you check again and are satisfied, and you've got a boat that now looks vulnerable and oddly fortified all at once; the bottom, mottled blue or green after a winter of idleness, is now striped dull red along the seams, as if surgical work had been done and sewn up there, and she is good as new.

Then, after allowing the compound to dry and skin over, I did a final light sanding to fair it, added a little more compound here and there, and then . . . she was ready for bottom paint, at about noon on Thursday. By Jove!

But I wasn't ready to paint the bottom yet. Anyone who has put a few boats in the ocean knows that bottom paint is an afterthought. You have to have it, but once you get to that stage, the hard work is over—the boat is practically in the water. I would paint her bottom tomorrow, or on the morning of the launch; for now, I needed to reflect on what this whole deal had been about. I needed to sit in the shed for a few minutes and stare at my shoes.

For the most part I had backed into being the protector of

Daphie. She, in my mind anyway, is a symbol of the family, just about the only physical one still extant. Therefore, someone in the family had to be her protector, determined enough to see her through her restoration.

When I sat on that roof a year ago and more, in December, I didn't feel I was up to this—taking the lead through this difficult country for the family. But perhaps I have been walking point for myself, trusting myself to reassemble the metaphorical cleats, blocks, screws, and chocks.

There were some other things going on, however. Even as friends, some of them, had allied themselves to causes that promised remuneration, I had turned back, once again, to carpentry, and the Cape, and a boat. It was an odd way to go about a career.

Ten days ago I went to a cousin's home. He is of a different family than the one that commissioned *Daphie*. He had a couple of buckets of local oysters he'd raked, one bucket from West Falmouth harbor, the other from Quissett. He said, "Eat a couple and tell me which is from where."

I said I couldn't, and he said, "You can. It's a question of sweetness," and he was right. The two fish were quite different, one more tart, the other sweeter. Cast away on a strange beach, he could have located himself by tasting the shellfish. Perhaps I am seeking similar discernment through the wind.

54. Friday, Fourth Week in August: Sails

I HAVEN'T SAID A word about the sails.

Of course, *Daphie* has two—a mainsail and a jib—as well as a parachute-like sail called the spinnaker that is only set when the wind is from behind, usually in a race. The spinnaker billows out in front, and is hard to manage, but does add speed downwind, unless it gets away from the crew, and goes down into the water and then under the boat, and gets caught in the rudder, three feet below the surface. This happens from time to time, and when it does, that is the end of the race for that boat.

I knew the sails were around somewhere. I looked in the closet in the front hall of the cottage, and then in the closet up in the loft, and then looked under the bed, where I keep some things, and then in the front hall closet again, and they were there the second time, in their green canvas bag under a coat. Right where I'd looked before.

They were Dacron, a synthetic fabric much like nylon. The main and the jib were white, and the spinnaker was purple and yellow, those being the colors of Williams College. The boat had been in my uncle's care in Williamstown, and so the spinnaker was made in the colors of his town and the college there.

I took the spinnaker out of the bag to see how it was. It is a big gossamer three-sided sail with a bronze ring at each corner. One has to fold it so when it is hoisted it will rise cleanly to the top of the mast, and not be twisted or snag. This folding is called "flaking the spinnaker." I began without thinking to flake it in the front hall as I had several hundred times before. Then I found myself sitting at the kitchen table, looking out at the backyard, folding the sail, my hands working it into shape.

My uncle Phil (the steward of *Daphie* for years) was the kind of guy who, when he greeted you at the back door of his house, and brought you through the doorway with a powerful grip on your hand, made you feel you were exactly the person he'd been waiting for, the one guy he needed to speak to.

And then there was almost immediately the offer of a beer and food, and a chair by the hearth, and perhaps a walk out to the barn to look at the boat.

He was a true uncle to me, deeply caring, solid as oak, whimsical enough to bring *Daphie* to a barn in the mountains of western Massachusetts to restore her.

He once told me, as we sat by the fire in his kitchen, that when he raced *Daphie* he would gather the spinnaker into a long narrow bundle, tie it like a sausage with rings of light thread, and then join those rings of thread with a sturdy piece of twine. Then during the race he'd hoist the sail as he rounded the windward mark, tug hard on the twine to break the rings of thread, and watch the spinnaker fill with wind in an instant, setting far more quickly than anyone else's. He told me that was part of how you won. And he won a lot. Not with this spinnaker but with another, earlier one. His daughter Hilary made this new spinnaker, and these sails. I'd like to win again the way he did.

55. Fourth Saturday in August: Bottom Paint

BOTTOM PAINT: IT SMELLS bad. I like that bad smell. It means we're getting closer to floating. The old bottom paints I grew up with were vehicles for cuprous oxide— toxic melanges of copper in an oil base. Sea creatures and slime were poisoned by it and stayed away. Nothing grew on the ground over which the boat sat in winter. I hate to think how that paint affected the ocean.

Now the paints are "ablative," which in my youth I knew as the fifth form of a declension of a Latin noun, as in the question from Mrs. Phillips in ninth grade, "What is the ablative of 'girl'?"

We could all answer that: "That would be *puella*, one of us would say," after raising a hand and being called on, "meaning 'from by with at on or in the girl.'"

Mrs. Phillips would nod solemnly, oblivious to the scandal that it caused us to wonder what "in the girl" might mean. In her mouth? In her presence? In her what, exactly? Even Latin grammar was freighted in those days.

Now, apparently, *ablative* means a paint that flakes slowly off the bottom of the boat so that marine organisms that affix themselves there, like rock climbers scaling rotten sandstone, fall back into the abyss, their pitons useless and their climbing ropes trailing behind them as they tumble out of sight. I would call such a paint "exfoliant." But what do I know?

What I do know is what that this morning I deconstructed the shed. Which was a little hard to do, after the struggle I went through a year and a half ago to build it. But there was no other way to get a trailer to the boat, and no other way to feel like this project was truly nearing its end. It took a couple of hours to take it apart, and I was met with stare-downs from Ted, who clearly didn't appreciate losing her outdoor shelter and high-napping spot. What could I do, though, Ted? The boat was ready—nothing left to do but de-shed, paint the "boot top" stripe along the waterline, paint the bottom. I started to paint.

There was a lot of birdsong going on—a couple of vireos were down at the end of the street in a little oak, and a pair of juncos were across the way in a honeysuckle thicket.

The hull below the waterline looked rough as a seventy-year-old surfer's face. Along with being green with old bottom paint, and mottled red along each seam by the underwater seam compound, it looked *impossibly* rough. But perhaps I was looking too closely. I eyed the broad stripes of red caulk sweeping along each seam, consciously blurred my vision so that they would look smooth, and started painting the bottom, at the bow.

The paint manufacturers say to apply two coats. I used to believe them. But *Daphie*'s planks were still sealed well for 90 percent of their length by old paint, even after all this time. The 10 percent of wood that was bare I would hit twice. For the rest of the bottom, one coat would suffice. It was late in the season, after all, so there was little time left for slime to proliferate before the sea turned cold.

The work went fast, and the blue paint flowed on smoothly as I cut up to the old red boot top stripe. And one side was done. Done! Suddenly one side of her looked *good,* not because of my particular skill, but because a fine form reasonably dressed will look good. And suddenly she seemed solid again, youthful, no longer a collection of beat-up planks but again a hard carapace, a hull strongly capable of resisting the sea. That is, until I walked around to the other side, and knelt down next to *those* beat-up planks and began to paint again.

Finally I stood back, at 1 P.M. or so, and looked at her. Man, was she *lovely*. How could I have failed to understand that climbing into the old Saab one day a year and a half ago, and driving a while (past Slocum's ground zero, which admittedly I didn't think about at the time) and debarking and hauling my carcass and my hammer up onto that roof in Marion would lead to this moment, to the renewal of this small portion of beauty?

The guy from Quissett boatyard, Jack, was due to arrive around nine on Monday (two days hence) to launch her, so I still had time to kill before beginning to feel freaked about how little time I had. The next task was to paint the boot top, without which a boat looks odd, much the way a man is not dressed without a belt.

But I couldn't paint the boot top yet. I had to allow the bottom paint to dry first. Instead, it was time to get some gear into the boat.

First I put together the tools I knew I'd want on board (pliers, Vise-Grips, screwdrivers, wrenches, wire cutters, a good knife, etc.) by rummaging in several boxes of idle tools (tools not currently in use at Robb Construction). I put these in an old black plastic toolbox, and went and found the rest of the stuff *Daphie* would need to be properly equipped for sailing: anchor, anchor rode, life jackets, horn, compass, charts, oars and oarlocks, a bottle of water, dock lines, extra lines, first-aid kit, pump, bailer, twine, a flashlight, a bucket to pee in.

I went over this pile of stuff, and checked a few things: the mousing (safety wire) on the shackles connecting the anchor to the anchor chain, and the anchor chain to the anchor rode; the integrity of the bottom of the bucket; the suck of the pump; the supplies in the first-aid kit; the life in the flashlight batteries. This was one of the joys of preparing to leave shore—the provisioning of one's own small planet.

In the past I'd always launched *Daphie* on my own, with a pickup and a trailer at one of the town's public ramps. But I didn't have that trailer anymore—it was rotted out back at my cousin's place—so this time I'd enlisted Jack. I had a day to rest. Except that I still had to paint that boot top.

I got to that Sunday, just after noon. I put strips of blue masking tape along the top and bottom of the old red stripe at the waterline, positioned so the new red paint would just overlap the new blue bottom paint, and meet the new white topsides paint at a faint groove set into the planks. Once the tape was on, I gave the old red boot top a light sanding, and smoothed on the new red paint, which was fire-engine red. It went fast, taking about forty minutes to do both sides.

When that was done, I made a pile inside the front door of other stuff I couldn't forget, such as the sails (which I had inspected, and found in good shape), and then enjoyed the rarity of being ready far before the morrow by walking into Woods Hole and buying a large vanilla ice-cream cone. The last of it was gone as I returned across the pitcher's mound on the ball field on the other side of the marsh, and so I arrived home empty-handed, though I felt I had celebrated the end of the work on the boat in a meaningful way.

56. *Last Monday in August: Launch*

ON MONDAY JACK WAS on time, his white pickup coming down the lane, with his low flatbed trailer behind. I felt my pulse pick up a few beats. Twenty months of labor, on and off, was done. I wouldn't have the old boat to rely on anymore as a buffer between myself and subsequent dreams. I briefly contemplated telling him to go home, that I was going to replace the ten ribs (out of forty-two) that I hadn't replaced yet, that I was going to rebuild the transom after all. But I kept quiet.

He was efficient, had the boat pulled onto his trailer in ten minutes, and was gone. I followed a few minutes later, but by the time I had piled the sails into the Saab and driven down to the harbor's edge in Quissett, *Daphie* was already on the marine railway there, and Jack had disappeared. No one else was around.

I remembered the first time I saw such tracks, when I was three or four, and how confusing that was. There at the edge of the sea was a train track that disappeared into the waves! How tremendously strange! Were the trains here also submarines?

Now, it was a gentle summer morning, and I stood alone under the trees that rose on either side of the little boatyard. The tracks disappearing into the sea still seemed odd. I stood there for quite a while with my arms crossed, twenty yards off her port bow on slightly higher ground than she. There she was—the only physical artifact anyone could inhabit from the previous generations of my mother's family. There were the steel mills of Worcester, and the house on May Street, and the big Cape summer house, with its windows thrown open to a summer breeze. There sat my grandmother before the fire in a green and white overstuffed armchair, watching *What's My Line?* There was the hotel in Barbados one aunt had disastrously tried to start, and afternoons of racing and picnicking on islands near here, whole reams of conversation lost to time, and the boat the only extant vessel for those words. What of it?

She held much the same weight in my veins for my father's family, being the double of the boat I first sailed with him as a boy, worked with him in spring, a boat to which he had brought his own boyhood.

"Hey buddy," a voice said from behind me, and I knew it was Lawrence, my childhood friend, who'd come to rig her with me. He'd grown up with a 12½, too.

"How you doin', bro'?" I said to him, and shook his hand, and then Jack appeared out of a shed off to the side, and told me to climb into *Daphie* and put a bow line on her, and as soon as I had he took the brake off the car and we slid into the water, boat and cradle and rail car together.

The car stopped when the cable tightened to its stern hook. *Daphie*'s cradle, tied to the car, stopped at this point too, and *Daphie* and I kept going, drifting backward slowly. She floated right on her lines, as if she'd never left the sea.

I heaved a line to Lawrence, who had walked out on an adjacent pier, and he hauled us over to the dock there, where we made her fast, and then noted how quickly she was sinking.

"It's coming in fast," he said.

"Yeah," I said, as I watched the water weep through several seams and stream into the bilge.

"You remember to put in the bung?" he asked, referring to the wine-cork-sized plug that stops up the drain hole in the bilge.

"Yeah," I said.

"Good," he said, with fine understatement.

We both watched the rate of leak for another minute.

"You got a pump in her?" said Lawrence.

"Yup," I said.

"It seems normal, the rate it's coming in," he said after watching for another twenty seconds. Nearly half the bilge was full by now.

"I agree," I said. "Let's get her rigged."

Which is what we did for the next hour, taking turns pumping, and sorting out the various halyards, and then stepping the mast, attaching the stays, rigging the gaff and the two booms, and then bending on the sails, rigging their sheets.

We worked nearly silently, stopping now and again to pump. He knew the rig as well as he knew the house he'd grown up in—he could find his way around it in the dark. I knew it as well. And it was as if in putting the boat in order, each of us was putting something in order in his mind. Each line had a function and a cleat where one end was belayed, and a spar to which the other end was made fast.

We worked quietly. I trusted him to know where things went, and how, and why, though he probably hadn't rigged a 12½ in twenty-five years. These things were in our bones.

And then we were done, and the hull, though very much alive when it came off the railway, was now somehow articulate, a fully realized craft, capable of expression, deed, personality. The mast, with its distributed lines of tension, vectors descending to the boat in shroud and halyard, stiffened her, slowed her motion down to something considered. A mast has, after all, a lot of mass—a lot of torque is required to move it back and forth across the sky—and a boat slows down to do this, steadies up, becomes wholly herself. *Daphie* was awake.

She looked good. And she was still leaking like a sieve. Which was normal. It would take her a day to swell, and another day or two to really set up.

Soon I was alone on the pier. Lawrence had gone home to lunch with his family. I knelt to the pump, and nearly emptied her, and then watched it come in again. And then Jack was offering to tow her to the outer harbor, where her mooring was.

"You don't want to sail her till she's set up, right?" he said. "That'll just work her seams before she's ready. I'll give her a gentle tug out there with Boomer (his diesel launch) and you can row out to her when you like."

That sounded good to me. I watched him pull her slowly out through the crowded little harbor, thick with small powerboats, daysailers, and cruising sailboats. The water was sun-spangled. Eight or nine Optimist Prams with small children in them struggled for a little beach on the far side of the harbor—not much had really changed since I'd run that same sailing program twenty years before—and I felt a little crazed. I felt as if I were watching my little daughter vanish into a crowd in the city, with a strange man leading her by the hand.

So, I went home, grabbed some food, a fleece, and a yoga mat, and headed for the boat, prepared to spend the evening on her.

57. Launch Day Cont'd: Pumping

I SPENT YESTERDAY AFTERNOON (once I'd returned to the boat) pumping every fifteen minutes, about a hundred strokes on the handle of the old grey plastic "Thirsty-Mate" hand pump. *Daphie* lay at her mooring in Gansett Cove, in bright sun. I pumped, and sat there, and pumped, and sat there. I had dinner aboard around six-thirty, and watched the evening come on. At eight-thirty, two osprey chicks made a clamor atop their pole on Tick Point (across the cove, a lump of rock and *Rosa rugosa* and a few low red cedars). At 8:45 a large osprey, their mother by the size of her, flew in with a considerable fish held below her. The noise in the nest grew, and then subsided wholly. The sky was blue-rose to the west, above the trees.

Soon after, a great blue heron glided in on a long gentle approach and settled into the marsh just on the other side of Tick Point. It touched down in a foot of water, folded its wings, and then took careful steps, hunting slowly.

The evening came on further. The light died down in the bay to the west, seeped less and less through the trees on the western side of the cove. The light over the sea was at turns faint rose, then slate, then grey.

I lay back on the transom, and watched the stars come, first pricks of white in the pale blue sky, and then brighter in the dark sky, with thin clouds passing overhead. The light fell more, darkness came on, and then lights from three houses on shore reflected on the water. I heard an occasional voice from a dinner table, and a fork clanking on a plate, and then it was dark. The trees along the shore became more idea than image. I could hear the wind moving through them, though, their silhouettes faintly visible over the shore.

Every fifteen minutes I pumped, and the grey plastic foot of the pump rested on the keel down in the bilge. My bare feet braced the down pipe, gripping it clumsily between their soles; my right hand held the hose on the coaming; my left arm rose to pull the plunger up, push it down. At first it had taken about a hundred strokes to clear the bilge. After the first four pumpings—the first hour—I was down to ninety-five strokes, five strokes fewer, or about a gallon less. This trend continued, so that by the time it was dark I was down to about sixty strokes, pumping steadily, the clear seawater a solid tube jumping in spurts from the grey nozzle out over the water and landing as a mass with a thump.

And then when the bilge was empty I would recline, my head on the transom, and listen to the tree frogs and the cicadas, the frogs sounding birdlike with their regular trills, and the cicadas buzzing, a gentle high-pitched, many-voiced whirr. The wind was southwest, maybe seven knots in the bay, and just enough in the cove to keep the mosquitoes down.

The rowboat was tied astern, and wandered around, bumped the transom occasionally, and as the sky darkened there began to be lumps of light moving beneath the surface of the cove— bluefish accelerating after silversides and jostling ctenophores, which glowed yellow through a fathom of seawater.

Soon, all was exceeding dark, and the summer triangle stood out bright overhead, with Cygnus the swan in its northeast corner, wings outspread. There was another constellation overhead, a small bright box of stars with a tail leading away. I had no name for it. It was not Cassiopeia, or Orion, or the Pleiades. But I knew it well; an old friend.

With darkness the bioluminescence grew brighter and more numerous, with single flakes of planktonic light winking from a wavelet, or a deep glow emerging near the bottom, twelve feet down, as a school of menhaden or snapper-blues turned fast.

Then, without warning, the clouds thickened at eight or ten thousand feet, and the wind cooled and shifted quickly north, banging at fifteen knots right into the mouth of the cove. *Daphie* turned to face the new wind, and the moon rose unexpectedly, three quarters and waning. As we began to rock, it became cold. I became quite cold.

At 10 P.M. I unrolled the blue yoga mat on the floorboards and lay down. The wind was blocked for me now by the bulkhead at the bow, and the mast (at my left ear) rose straight into a vast star field framed by the hull. Occasional clouds scudded over.

It grew colder, but out of the wind I was warm enough. I still pumped every quarter of an hour, and when I did so I sat in the wind and shivered, and was thankful to lie down again when I could, out of the wind. At the ten o'clock pumping I needed I fifty-five strokes to empty the bilge. By 11 P.M. fifty was enough to empty her; by midnight, forty-five; at 1 A.M., forty; and by 2 A.M., thirty-five.

From 1 to 4 A.M. as I lay on the floorboards between pumpings, looking up at the star field, I leafed through lives and school years, walked around homes, saw lovers, roles in plays, classes, long hikes in the desert. I walked into campsites, recalled wrong turns, bears in the distance.

By 4 A.M. I was shaking with cold. I hadn't expected to stay with her this long, but the night had lain a hand on me—the constant shifts of her motion in the water and the moods of the harbor were mesmerizing.

She would hunt around on her mooring; the wind would

pick up; the texture of the dark water changed; moonlight played on it; gusts came down and passed with a rush as her halyards slapped the mast. The night was interesting without letup. But by 4 A.M. I was too cold to be any good any longer.

She *had* taken up, though; I could feel by her motion that she had begun to gather herself: feeling this was like the feeling one gets after a period of training, after a time of inaction. One day, muscles grow taut, are ready to bear one efficiently over the ground again. This was how she felt: she had begun to *knit*, become one hull again.

I lay down once more. The moon went down behind the trees, and the stars moved closer. Two satellites passed overhead, one after the other, their passage slow, unblinking. Then three twin-engine propeller planes, separated by some minutes, came over low on their approach to the Vineyard, their red navigation lights a-blink; two jetliners, high and thin in the moonlight, passed over, soundless, on a course diagonal to the others, bound east, bound out, to slip across to Spain.

Heading out.

Around 4:30 I rowed in, hands cold on the spruce oars, content the boat would not sink before I could sleep a couple of hours, eat some breakfast, and return. In another day she would take up entirely, and would not leak more than several gallons a day. I knew she was well paid—her seams had been caulked carefully.

58. Shakedown

FOR THE SHAKEDOWN, THREE days after the launch, I thought we'd sail to a nearby place called Hadley's Harbor. I walked the half mile to the boat, up the hill on the back road, and through the woods, oars over my shoulder, and observed as I came down the hill to the harbor that the wind was from the southwest at twelve knots. A fine breeze.

I rowed out to *Daphie,* saw that she was fine, climbed aboard, pumped twenty strokes, and then raised the mainsail, the blocks squeaking a bit as the throat tightened. Then I pulled the jib up (always second, so that the main kept the boat pointed into the wind while on the mooring), coiled the halyards, dropped the mooring buoy into the water, and we were off.

We made good time on the fresh breeze, going tack on tack across Gansett Bight, and passed under Penzance Point in twenty minutes. We then balled the jack across the Hole at slack tide, roaring along on a beam reach through the mile of calm water there, and came down fast on the can and nun at the west end of Nonamessett Island. Then, after making the turn into the narrow channel between Nonamessett and Bull Island, we came slowly into what is a holy place, like Chartres or Notre Dame: Hadley's Harbor.

We ghosted in, along the western side of the channel, which was barely fifty feet wide, through green water that was light green in the shallows along its edges, with granite boulders lining the shoreline on all sides, and trees above that. Then the wind died, and we sat there, the sails slatting for a minute or two, before a wisp came up and moved us along into the body of the harbor, which is a safe enclosure of low green hills coming down to the water.

And then a twenty-four-foot inboard cabin cruiser roared through the way I'd just come. A heavyset man leaned on the steering wheel as his lady sat florid on the poop in a blue canvas chair.

His big right hand was on the throttle as he came in, and as he made the turn at the start of the harbor, three snowy egrets rose from the shallows. They had been standing and leaning toward the water with their heads just submerged, scanning slowly like men who'd lost their glasses and were searching for them on the bottom.

But they straightened up with the rumble of his engine and the hissing of his bow wave and launched themselves into the air. They are long birds, stupendously light in design, buoyant on the wing, and from standstill they are quickly in full flight, wings long and rounded, cupping the air as they rise, their necks retracting from serpentine to an in-flight posture so tight that in profile their heads look like blocks with beaks pasted on.

They wore rapidly away on strong wing beats, their stick legs with asterisk feet trailing lightly behind.

·   ·   ·

The harbor felt animate to me, lined by pleasant and over-hanging oaks that might reach out a limb, if one were too loud or crass, or perhaps in friendship. Occasionally the woods along the shore gave way to higher ground—sometimes rocky meadow, sometimes more woods seen in the distance down a wagon path. It is a landscape similar to parts of coastal Scotland.

The harbor is shaped like an L, and as I approached the vertex of it I jibed and headed toward a dock along which lay four old wooden 12½'s. I read their names as I coasted by.

Clethra. Midget. Agouti. Kinglet.

The boats looked well cared for. Like *Daphie,* they were not very fair, showing seams between their planks where age had brought out the lines. For that they looked the better, I thought.

And their sails were faded. These four boats were the communal property of the Forbes family, who own the nearby islands in trust. I knew that many in the trust felt when they arrived in the spring that the condition of these four boats—*in* the water and *ready* to sail, or not—was an indicator of the island's condition and of life's tone in general. This may be so, although I would be inclined to give more weight to the feelings of the local rabbits and mergansers on these matters.

I coasted by a tall motor cruiser, on the flying bridge of which a woman of twenty-eight or so dried herself with a towel, her hair in cornrows. As I passed she saw me, slipping along her stern, and waved and smiled, twelve feet above me in a swiveling navigator's chair. I was soon in the lee of a high-sided, plumb-bowed Beneteau sloop of forty feet. Two older gentlemen sat on either side of the cockpit, each shirtless, with short white hair, a ruddy complexion, looking well fed. I'd been able to hear their murmur for several minutes, but now I began to be able to make out what they were saying.

"I remembah right where I was when they hit Pearl," said the man sitting on the port side of the cockpit. "Right where I was. Walking into Hannibal Confection on Roscoe Street, and it was on the radio on the counter. Old man Hannibal's listening to it like he's never seen a radio before, and we was the only ones in the store, him and me."

"I know it," said the other, sitting to starboard. "I'll always remember it, too. I was at my uncle's farm, and we was doing somethin', getting the cows in for evening milking, most likely, and my Aunt Tildy comes out and says the Japanese had done it, and FDR's taking us to war for sure now. I knew right then I was goin' in. I spent the next two weeks milkin' cows morning and night, and next thing I know I'm on the train to basic."

The wind had died, and I had begun to drift sideways, toward the rocky shore thirty feet away, at about a foot a minute. They went on.

"I remember when we went onto the beach, and the guy takin' the anchor off the bow of the LST gets it from an eighty-eight—he just disintegrates, and we're goin' anyway, through the water, onto the sand, diggin' in," said the guy to port.

"Thank God for the guy who come up with the bangalore, huh?" said the man to starboard.

"You bet your life. The bangalore was a beautiful thing," said the other.

"How long'd it take us to walk to Haye-du-Puits?" said the man to starboard.

And then I was out of earshot of the two old gentlemen, and was looking ahead to the end of the harbor, which ended at a little cove with a dark-brown boathouse and dock in one corner, a marine railway next door, and beyond that a rocky meadow where idle horses grazed, swishing their tales in the sun, their heads down in the grass.

I drifted closer to the trees at the very end of the cove, my sails close-hauled, faking a beat to windward over the mirror of the cove, and then I tacked, twenty-five feet from shore (or I made the motion of tacking, pushing the tiller far to starboard, and watching as slowly, slowly, the bow began to come around). Straight southwest, right at the end of the harbor, I could see a path mown in the grass of a meadow, leading up to the woods.

If I ran the boat aground and jumped out, I thought, I could get on that path and move down the island before anyone could waylay me, and then keep moving, running south and west, seven miles over dune and through forest and upland, past the old World War II bunkers, where men had watched for enemy subs and for invasion, and past West End Pond, until Robinsons Hole ended the island, and I would have to swim, or be caught and asked to leave. I wanted to make that trespass, have that jaunt.

As I thought of that I thought of the boy, sent by his father from Tarpaulin Cove, halfway up the island, to run at night down to this end of the island, and then to row across to Woods Hole, to warn the village of the impending British attack. What a night for the kid, first running on wagon tracks or perhaps cross-country to avoid pickets, and then having a tough row through hard current to Penzance Point, then more running, down the point, across the cut to the mainland, and then banging on someone's door to be let in, and relating the story, of such importance, and all of this in winter, when to go overboard on the way would likely be to die, and when to be caught might mean the same thing.

But the kid made it, and the attackers were turned away the next morning by slush and obstinate small arms fire. I ought to run down to the far end just in that kid's honor, I reflected. But instead I continued coming about, pushed the boom out, spun slowly around, and affected running back the way I'd come. The boat turned slowly, and began the ghost home.

It is an odd thing, ghosting. Sailors know that in a calm a boat can act as if intention were enough to create movement. This is how it seems at times when there is too little wind to be felt. Set the sails for the wind you *think* might be there, point the boat where you *want* it to go, and sure enough . . . you *ghost*. Is it the dark energy of the universe pushing on the slack sails that moves you, or perhaps the emotion of intention? Wherever you want to go, set your sail.

Working by this principle, I again approached, quiet as a water strider, the gentlemen with the short white hair on the Beneteau. I began to hear them again. And then I heard them clearly.

"Remembah the guy we saw in that wrecked cafe?" said the fellow to starboard. "The whole place had come down aroun' him, and he was still sitting at a table in the rubble, and he wasn't touched. Just kept sitting there, like if he moved he'd wake up dead."

"He was gnawing on his bread, wasn't he, covered with dust," said the gentleman to port.

"Yes, he was," said the other. "I'd forgot that. Jesus H. Christ, that's right. There were some strange things over there."

I ghosted along. A woman in a thirty-six-foot wooden cutter called out, "What sort of boat is that?"

I told her.

"Lovely lines," she said.

"Thank you," I said. "Where do you hail from?"

"England. The Dover coast," she said.

"Your boat is lovely as well," I said. "Who made it?"

"David Hillyard. It's one of his twelve-tonners," she said. And I admired the boat as I went by, which was a sturdy wooden double-ender, with a center cockpit, clearly heavy and built for the crossing.

Then at the vertex of the harbor there was a cat's-paw on

the water, and a sudden gust of northwest breeze. As I made the turn I headed down, away from the fierce little piece of wind, braced my feet on the opposite seat, sheeted in, and soon was moving fast, on a beam reach, with the sails taut and *Daphie* lowering her shoulder into the warm water. Then that wind died, and just as quickly another came up hard behind, southwest.

I let the sails out, and ran out the narrow harbor entrance into the mile-wide bight formed by Uncatena and Nonamessett on the south side of the Hole. I could see a flag on Penzance a mile and a half across the Hole, flying at the head of a great long house, starched out away from me. I ran for it, and made good headway for several minutes until the wind collapsed again, and I lolled in a light greasy swell, as voices came from Uncatena Island, a half mile upwind.

A woman's voice said, "Goddamnit, no! Not now! You are such a shit!" Then I heard a splash, and saw a woman walking up a lawn toward a big house. A man seemed to be swimming below the pier, and then was climbing the ladder to the dock, in what looked like a full set of clothes, but it was half a mile away. I couldn't be sure.

All was quiet again. Presently I reclined, my head on the transom. The sails slatted, the boat gurgled noncommittally. I lolled in the sun, shirtless, and traced the lines of the rigging upward with my eyes. Such a simple machine, each stay and line expressing force and tension in ways that canceled each other out, and resulted in force being applied to the hull when there was wind. It calmed me to trace the lines up to the sky and back down again with my eyes. No complications here.

In the back of my neck, resting on the transom edge, I could hear the high-speed screw of a powerboat heading west in the Hole. It faded.

A cormorant surfaced twenty yards away with a five-inch

scup in its bill, making a splash as it surfaced. After a moment the bird flipped the fish into the air, where it somersaulted and then vanished headfirst down the gullet of the bird, which paddled around for several minutes, looking uncomfortable and distorting its neck, and then dove away.

After twenty minutes of calm, during which I'd ghosted several hundred yards downwind, the wind rose again suddenly, sweeping down in a broad dark band on the water, and we were moving fast again across the Hole, reaching hard. Several twenty-five-foot sportfishermen roared by, giving me their wake to cross, and then a hundred-foot ferry—a catamaran—steamed past at twenty-five knots, leaving almost no wake, and then we were across, hugging the coast and zigzagging among lobster pot buoys, reaching toward the elbow of Penzance again. Once there we beam-reached across Gansett Bight, as the old family house stared down at us from the bluff—the penultimate station on today's saunter. Finally we hardened up under the light buoy at the mouth of Quissett, tacked into Gansett Cove, and shot the mooring head to wind. *Daphie's* sails luffed and then dropped as I loosed the halyards, and I reached forward into the warm water to grasp the mooring line where it lay, and made it fast on the forecleat.

And then I sat there for a while, and listened to the water slap at her hull, occasional birdsong, and the snap of bluefish tails on the surface as they chased silversides, which jumped en masse out of the water as the larger fish rose beneath them, and then fell back en masse into the water, sounding like rain. And then I made her neat, and rowed in.

59. *Proposal*

I GOT A CALL from Bill Mayhew yesterday morning. It was just after 7:30. He sounded a little out of breath.

"Listen," he said. "Rafe and I want to talk to you. Can you be at the pier at the harbor at nine tonight?"

"What for?" I said.

"I can't say," he replied. "Would that work? It'd just take an hour or so."

"Yeah," I said, and hung up, and went sailing—a long beat up the bay following the shoreline of Naushon Island, and then between it and the biggest of the Weepecket Islands, right up to a shallow harbor called Kettle Cove. The sun was hot, the wind at about fourteen knots, and after a close pass along the beach—a long crescent of white sand—I turned and headed for home. As I approached the channel between the Weepeckets and Naushon again, I couldn't resist stopping for a little while, and so tacked up under the lee of the largest of the three little islands and anchored.

I dropped the hook (a ten-pound Danforth) over in three feet of water, and let *Daphie* drift back till the anchor tugged and buried itself in the sand. Then I jumped in the water, which was cool and reached my hips. I waded to the beach, had a nap, and upon waking wondered if what my friend Jim Mavor said—he thinks there is a Norse burial site at the center of the little island—was correct. When I arose, now in shadow, it was an hour later, and the beach had shrunk. I swam back out to the boat (lying now in a fathom of water), raised sail, pulled up the anchor, and ran the rest of the way home. I was on the mooring at six, and had some time before heading over to Quissett. I wondered what the two boatbuilders wanted.

The harbor was dark when I arrived, with no moon, and the cicadas were making a low hum in the underbrush. As I came out on the dock where the dinghies were kept I could see Bill hovering just off it in his flat-bottomed Westport skiff.

"How you doin', Bill?" I said quietly.

"Good, Dan. Hop in."

He rowed easily, and once the boat's course was established and we had some way he used the oars only occasionally as we coasted toward Rafe's boat.

Once there, we climbed aboard and then down below, where Rafe sat in lantern light, looking over a chart. He got up and shook my hand, took my jacket, and handed me a tumbler of Talisker. It seemed this was the way in his boat and I did not object.

Things looked different below: There were extra blankets, and more books, and several boxes of food on the sole. The boat seemed fairly stuffed with gear—extra sails in bags sat on the starboard berth up forward, lines and various tackle crowded the shelves above the settees, and there was a thick pad of new charts at the nav station. In short, the energy of the boat had shifted. Once Bill was settled on a settee, and had his tumbler, I spoke up.

"So what's going on? Lotta new stuff down below here."

"I'm goin' for a sail," said Rafe. "And Bill and I have a proposal."

"Where you headed?" I asked, and in the moments of silence that followed Rafe held my gaze, and I could hear the halyards whupping against the mast in the light breeze. Finally he said, "Outbound," and then, "leave it there for now."

"Okay," I said.

"I'm going along, too," said Bill. "I'll be gone for a couple of months more or less, and it was all looking smooth as glass 'til yesterday this guy calls up, wants to drop by, then makes *us* a proposal."

"Yeah," Rafe broke in. "He says he wants—thinks he wants—three twelve-and-a-halfs, new. He's got a cove up in northern Maine, and a whole lot of family, and he wants three daysailers, but the pinch is he's never been on one, and needs to know the boat before he can commit."

"And you guys set sail . . . ?" I said.

"Tomorrow," said Bill. "That's the thing. We need you to explain the boat to him, help him know if he wants keels, or centerboards . . ."

"You'd build him Havens if he wants?" I said, referring to the Haven 15, the shoal-draft adaptation of the 12 ½ drawn by Joel White.

"Absolutely," said Rafe. "At fifty thousand apiece we'll build him one with an outhouse if he wants."

"We were thinking," said Bill, "we'd give you a commission of seven hundred a boat, assuming you land him, and we get a contract signed. It would be a good piece of work for us, get us through the winter, that's sure."

"We figured we'd better ask you now," said Rafe.

"You mean instead of tomorrow morning as you raise sail?" I asked.

"It's short notice all around, we know," said Rafe. "We were just trying to ease out of here, not have to do a lot of explaining. Sorry to be so mum about it, but sometimes you just like not to have to answer a lot of questions, you know? You just want to go ahead."

I understood that.

"It'd just mean taking the guy sailing a few times, three or four, getting him familiar, no real selling, just let him see the boat, let it sell itself," said Bill.

It was easy to say yes to all of this, which would consist of little more than having some company on a few sails. I told them this, and we clinked glasses, and they both relaxed considerably, a reasonable prospect of work through the winter easing their minds.

"Of course, I don't know if I'll be back," said Rafe.

Bill looked at Rafe steadily for a few moments after he said this, expression neutral, and the subtle sounds of the boat— halyards slapping softly on the mast, and water flowing past the hull—filled up the sudden quiet. Then he said, "Well, you need to let me know that by December, Rafey, so I can get someone else to help me plank these things up if you're not back."

"Oh, I'll let you know," said Rafe. "But I'll feel no obligation until December."

"That's fine," said Bill. "December one."

"December one," said Rafe.

"Where you headed, Rafe?" I asked again from where I sat on the port settee, near the forward bulkhead.

"Should I tell him, Billy?" he asked his friend.

"Why not?" said Bill. "He ain't gonna tell anyone."

"France," said Rafe. "The Azores, then the Canaries, then the Med, and finish up somewhere in the south of France, find a place to moor *Altair* for a while, then head into the hinterland, once I get rid of Bill."

"What's the draw?" I asked.

"He met someone," said Bill.

"Lady?" I said.

"You're doggone right, a lady," said Rafe.

"Yeah," said Bill. "A vintner. Rafe says it's the same thing as boatbuilding but with grapes."

"I never said that," said Rafe.

"She's got a vineyard?" I asked.

"It's an old family deal," said Rafe. "About seven hectares. Small, but they've been back up there two hundred and eighteen years, making wine. I figured I might as well get the hell out of here, let *Altair* do her thing."

"Where'd you meet her?" I asked.

"At the Kidd," said Bill. "At the bar. Where else?"

"In the spring. March the seventeenth," said Rafe.

"That's still winter," I said.

"Whatever," said Rafe. "She was visiting friends, and they came through for a meal, and I was just having a quiet bowl of chowder, and before I know it she's telling me all about her grapes."

"This was after Rafe had already given her the lowdown on the cranberries around here," said Bill.

"Yeah," said Rafe. "So then she tells me all about her *terroir*."

"Her what?" I said.

"Yeah," said Rafe. "It's this French thing, where the grapes grow in a place, where the soil has a chemistry, and there's weather unique to there, and specific rain, minerals in the soil, the exposure—all those things. When you take them all into account, then you have the *terroir* of the place, and . . ."

"The character," said Bill. "He's trying to say that that's what gives the wine its character."

"Say the word again for me, Rafe," I said.

"*Terroir*," he said, pronouncing it "tare-warr."

"So you're going to see this gal?" I asked.

"I gotta get the hell outta Dodge," Rafe said. "This place is getting to me."

"How old is she?" I asked.

"She's two years younger than Rafe," said Bill. "And it's not the place, man, it's the people that're getting you down," he went on.

"Some of the people," said Rafe.

"Yes, some of them," said Bill.

"Yeah, in summer there's too damned many of them," said Rafe, looking at me intently, "and in winter it's the ones who are trying to turn the place into a suburb who disturb me. Half the time they don't know they're doing anything wrong, but the grit's gone out of the place. Million-dollar homes everywhere, conservation commission run by a bunch of builders—I mean, if you don't have an income better than a hundred grand, you don't even consider living here. And the biggest businesses around here are the pavers! The shortsighted assholes who pave! I can't even quahog or oyster anymore half the time— because it's so polluted because of all the runoff comin' off all the freakin' pavement!"

"You're overstating it, Rafe. Not everyone disagrees with you," said Bill.

Rafe sat with his back against the cushions of the starboard settee. He'd clearly let himself feel a little more of his frustration than he'd meant to.

"Well," he said, "I gotta take a leak. And I can't wait to shove off out of here tomorrow, get out in the gyre where things mostly make sense. On the Cape the *terroir* is shot to hell." He climbed up the companionway, and once he had cleared the ladder, I spoke to Bill.

"So you're heading out with him?"

"Yeah," he said. "I figure we'll need two months to get well across. We just finished the Prudence we started right after the Rozinante, so we've been going hard for eighteen months without a breather, so it seems like a good time for a bit of a romp."

"I'm envious," I said.

"Well, maybe Rafe will give you a call when he's ready to sail back, or maybe I'll be calling you to see if you want to help me build those boats if Rafe decides he ain't coming back."

"That might not be all bad," I said, and then we lapsed into silence for a little while, and listened to a halyard whupping the mainmast—a light line in a light breeze, not making a lot of noise.

There were other signals coming through, too—the constant low sound of the wind moving through the rig, and the slight motion of the boat as she hunted around her mooring. I took a swallow of the whiskey, as did Bill, and then Rafe was coming back down the companionway.

"The other thing that's shot to hell in this country right now is habeas corpus, and it's killin' me," he said, and sat down on the starboard settee again.

"You know I was thinking about it the other day," he went on. "I got a friend, young man I met when I was a counselor at a camp in New Hampshire. Kid's from Gaza, and I was thinking I might just reach on through to the Suez Canal, zip down to the Red Sea, drop the anchor in Aqaba or wherever you drop an anchor over there, and take the bus across Jordan to see him—we correspond still—and then I realized King George can declare me an enemy combatant if he feels like it, at his whim, and throw my ass in jail and throw away the key, no trial, no jury involved. That's what he says he can do. That makes me think twice about visiting a friend. I mean, that is not what I fought for."

He was quiet for a moment here, and Bill and I exchanged a glance.

"Why don't you give him a call, see if he's around, see if he can meet you in Jordan?" said Bill.

"Give him a call?" said Rafe, incredulously. "I can't give him a call. They've already got my line tapped. If I give him a call, they'd really think we were up to no good. They'd probably track the boat."

"Your line's not tapped, Rafe. You're going a little far," said Bill.

"I think it is," said Rafe. "I hear the weirdest things on the line, snippets of conversations, and clicks."

"C'mon, Rafe, you're paranoid. They'd have to get a warrant to do that, and nobody's gonna get a warrant to listen to an old boatbuilder."

"Listen to what I'm sayin', Bill," said Rafe. "I've still got a file on me over at the FBI from after the war. And the line started to sound funny when I began talking to France a lot."

"When do you guys sail in the morning?" I asked. I really liked Rafe, but I'd heard it all before.

"First light," said Rafe, brightening up.

"Good," I said. "Then I'll leave you to it."

"Here's a packet of information, and a contract for the guy, and his number," said Bill, handing a manila envelope to me. "He's in town until the end of next week. If it's a yes, get him to sign that contract, and drop it in the mail to me. Jenny'll let me know when it comes in."

"I'll see what I can do," I said. "Bon voyage, Rafe, and thanks a lot for your help with the boat." I shook Rafe's hand, and he shook it back hard, and nodded meaningfully, and then looked away. And then Bill and I climbed back into his skiff, and he started to row us in.

When we were partway in, he said, "Yeah, Rafe's pretty angry. But I can't blame him. He did two tours, in '67 and '68, the last one ending after Tet, and he was in the thick of it. I think he feels he did his part, and he resents feeling like his rights to privacy are gone."

"You feel like he's all right to sail with?" I asked.

"Oh yeah," said Bill. "He's fine. He'll be fine. I think it just brings a lot of emotion up in him. He's thinking of leaving the country for good. He loves it here as much as anyone, but he's seeing what we stand for dumbed down, you know? Maybe he's taking it too far, but he's a survivor."

"You were over there too, right?" I said.

"Yeah, but I was a couple of years earlier. I sort of missed the real tough part."

"Well," I said, "I hope you guys have a great sail, and I'll see what I can do to convince this guy your boats are for him."

"That's fine, Dan," said Bill. "Don't work it too hard. I don't want to build him the boats unless they're right for him. If it's right for him, then we'll have a job. Maybe the *terroir* up there calls for a different boat. I don't know."

He kept rowing. The stars were out, bright, and there was a light wind. His oars made glowing whorls in the dark harbor.

The next day when I went for a sail in the evening, *Altair* was gone, her mooring vacant. And I had a feeling I might not see Rafe again unless I went to France. Or unless the midterm elections here changed the way things were going. I did follow the course I knew they would have taken, for a while, tracking southwest toward the end of the bay, where they would have worn off on starboard tack, and reached for Ireland. "Hell," I thought, "with a couple of bags of food, thirty gallons of water, a tarp stretched over the cockpit, and a little luck, *Daphie* and I might arrive not so long after them."

60. *October*

WINTER WAS ABOUT TO come on in earnest, and I needed a sail to cap the year. Two days out with provisions for a night sounded good. I left three days ago and planned to return late the next day, then haul the boat soon after.

I listened to the computer-voice loop on the grey plastic weather radio ("the marine forecast for southeastern Mass-ach-u-setts as far south as Watch Hill Rhode Is-land") the day before I left and found two days of fair weather ahead, with ten to twelve knots of wind out of the southwest—a last taste of Indian summer.

I packed a sleeping bag and pad, a heavy green tarp, several cans of soup, a loaf of sourdough, a block of cheese, several apples, a flask of wine, a pipe and rough tobacco, a camp stove, a large stainless mug, a few teabags, a couple gallons of water, a cell phone, the weather radio, a couple of charts, two strong flashlights, extra batteries, warm clothes. In short, way more than I needed. If the weather held I would be in no real danger from cold or exposure. Unless I fell overboard.

The morning was cool—about forty degrees—and clear when I stepped from the dinghy onto the starboard seat.

I laid my tarp on the floorboards, stacked my provisions on it, wrapped them up, and tied the bundle to the bulkhead so it wouldn't shift.

I had a plan: beat up the bay fourteen miles to Penikese, the seventy-five-acre island where I'd spent three years as a teacher at the school for delinquent boys.

Although it was fourteen miles to Penikese, it would be farther for me because it would be tack on tack all the way. I'd laid out several possible routes in my head the night before, one going inside the Weepecket Islands, hugging the shore of Naushon, and another a course of broad tacks out into the bay, where I might meet a container ship or fuel lighter. Either way we would sail twenty-three miles, maybe twenty-five or more, depending on how I managed the current. If we were able to average three knots an hour over the bottom, I knew I'd need at least seven hours, maybe eight or nine, to make it to the shallow anchorage at Penikese.

I pulled out the yellow copy of the *Eldridge Tide and Pilot Book* that I kept in the lazarette, under the stern deck, and read there that the current would be against us most of the day along the islands, and would run slightly less hard out in the bay. I would head out, then, and see what I could see. I raised sail, cast off, and pulled in the sheets. *Daphie* leaned over with taut sails, and surged ahead.

The wind was steady, and we were soon well offshore, a mile and then two miles and making good way. I found the breeze was about fifteen knots, and that she went best a little off the wind, so I eased her down a bit, eased the main sheet out a touch—this gave her a better angle to ride over the waves, and made up for any loss of heading with greater speed. We were making good time, and only occasionally did the bow send the top of a wave back my way.

Braced as I was, with one foot against the edge of the opposite seat, the tiller balanced and no strain to hold, and the boat solidly held by the force of the wind on her sails, I didn't think much for a couple of hours as we worked to windward, making several long tacks out into the bay.

At the beginning of the third tack, already having covered seven or eight miles upwind, I glanced under the headsail and saw a tug approaching with a barge in tow, probably carrying fuel oil.

There are many dire cirsumstances to imagine at sea, but among the worst is being run down by a tug, as this offers the opportunity to be caught in its hawser, and then run over by the barge. I was wary of tugs, much as I admired their brawn.

This one wasn't coming fast, I could see, and its bearing to me wasn't changing. Which meant that we were on a collision course. Each time I looked under the mainsail, the black hull with the bright red rail was hovering over the oarlock mount on the starboard gunwale.

The day was bell-clear, and the sea was dark blue, having cooled and lost the plankton that make it green in summer. The land, low along the sea as it looked to my eye from four miles offshore, was a mix of green and increasing brown— roan trees, rufous thicket, russet underbrush, with some blond where there was grassy meadow.

We bounded on, and I began to see that the tug was pulling slightly ahead, and that the barge had a good bone in its teeth. Soon I could see the dark line of the hawser, which was a quarter mile long, curved down from the tug and disappeared into the bay, and then rose again to the barge. I was now on a collision course with the hawser.

I began to wonder if I might sail between the tug and the barge, over the submerged section of hawser, and on through to the other side. I did have the right-of-way as the vessel under sail. What would it be like to misjudge slightly and have the hawser rise under *Daphie*, saw her in half, and then flip her just before the barge crushed her like a nut?

When it was clear that no wind shift would come and enable me to foot past the bow of the tug, I tacked, still a quarter mile off, and headed back for the eastern shore of the islands. The tug plodded on, her big diesels making a low thrum that faded as I sailed away from her.

This tack brought me as far south as the middle of the island Pasque, just beyond Robinsons Hole, and after the next long zigzag I was well southwest along the coast of Nashawena, beyond Quicks Hole. From close in both islands were remarkable for their hues—brilliant reds where staghorn sumac leaves were still on the low trees, bright yellows of beech leaves, reds of maples in wetlands and of upland oaks that still had their leaves, blonds of occasional rocky meadows, and plenty of brown underbrush, all coming down to the pink and tan granite boulders along the beaches.

It was midafternoon by now, and I decided on a series of shorter tacks, the last of which would keep me quite close to Nashawena, in order to avoid a reef near Penikese called Gulls. Gulls may be the best place-name around here. It is a place where gulls often *seem* to stand on water in the midst of the bay. But they're standing on sand.

I have a chart circa 1776 that shows Gulls as Gull Island, a place with substantial land, but now it is just Gulls. The land is gone and the birds remain.

I still had a couple of hours of daylight, so my thought was to sail a little beyond Penikese to Cuttyhunk, get a look at that island which I like so well, peer through Canapitsit channel at the Vineyard and Gay Head, and then beat over to the cove at Penikese for the night.

So I sailed close to the blocky mass of Cuttyhunk, stolid and sure out there at the end of the archipelago. And as I crept closer to the island, the wind died. So I watched the sun set and wasn't worried by the darkness; rather, I was concerned about getting to Penikese without an engine.

I rowed with one oar through the twilight, which was an affair uncomplicated by clouds or humidity, just a big disc settling down into the water in a wide band of red. I compensated for the one oar's push to starboard by holding the tiller to starboard with my foot, and rowed like this for forty-five minutes on smooth water, and then anchored about 150 feet off the pier in the cove at Penikese.

I had approached quietly and at such a quiet hour that it seemed no one on the island had noticed, although I knew there would be folks sitting on the deck of the single house that was the school. Someone would be having a mug of coffee after dinner, and would note the little boat in the harbor. A kid would say, "Who the fuck izzat?" And a staffer would say, "Hey, John, can you rephrase that for me?"

And John would say, "Yeah. Who the fuck is that asshole in the sailboat?" and he would laugh. the staffer would say, "Just someone pulling in to anchor for the evening, John, but let's have a little talk about appropriate modes of expression, huh?"

And after a long discussion ("Fuck you with your appropriate modes of expression, is what I got to say to you, pal," might be John's riposte) as they sat in battered Adirondack chairs, John would be nudged inside to work on an essay for a while, after which there would follow some cribbage at the dining table by the woodstove, and then bed at a reasonable hour.

At anchor, with the sails furled, I heated a mug of soup on the stove, which sat on the afterdeck by the tiller, and ate some bread and cheese, and had a cup of wine, and a pipe, and watched the sky lose its western glow and go black, and the stars come out.

One day, ten years before, when this was my home, a kid named Jeff and I found a clay pipe in a kitchen midden close to the beach, not far from where the pier pushed out into the cove. We dated that pipe (as you can do by measuring the diameter of the hole in its stem) to the 1820s.

"Whoa, dude, that's really frickin' old," was his comment at the time, and I could see him in my mind, crouching down to dig some more in the litter of crockery and pebbles that spilled onto the beach.

Reclining against the transom in the boat, bundled in a Windbreaker, I could hear small waves breaking on the far side of the isthmus that joins the main island to its peninsula, Tubbs. The cove itself was a mirror. The only glint of light from the house was from two kerosene lamps in the big window of the kitchen. No one had come down to the pier to see who I was, which was fine with me. I was home, and they were home, too.

After a while, once I was sure that the staff and students were in bed, well after midnight, I went for a swim. It was clear out, and cool, and the moon was coming up over Nashawena to the east. After packing a shirt, jeans, sweater, hat, flashlight, and sandals in a drybag, I threw that in the water, dove in after it, gasped at the cold, swam to the pier, climbed the ladder, and after drying off and dressing, went for the nighttime walk that I'd been craving for some time—one I had not taken in several years.

I was walking in moonlight, as I had many times when I worked on the island once the boys were asleep and I could walk out across the old meadows and paths alone. This time I was careful not to go near the house or where I might run into someone on a late-night trip to the outhouse. I figured it was unlikely anyone would be out for a stroll on the far reaches of the island.

I walked up the main hill, rising a little less than eighty feet above the water, to two deep old brick cisterns, and looked out on the ocean all around, grey-white in the moonlight, with the breeze soughing through the grass and blackberry thickets—how many times had I come up here to watch the sunset with four or five students?—and then I walked down the hill, and out to the western end of the island, tracing a quarter-mile track along an old stone wall, out through old pasture, to the leper cemetery (Penikese was a leper colony from 1903 to 1921).

It is a melancholy place, with two rows of small stones naming the lepers who ended their lives on the island. But it is a peaceful place, too, from which one can see up and down Buzzards Bay. From the edge of the low bluff there I looked across toward the distant lights of Westport, Massachusetts. Further west, beyond the lights of Point Judith, lay Narragansett Bay, reaching north into Rhode Island. Four hundred years ago, that was the realm of Massassoit and then of his son, Metacomet, or "King Philip," the sachem who had led the Native Americans in their uprising against the English in 1675. Penikese was an easy two days from there in a canoe, and I could see faint lights on the peninsula where a man named Church had lived. He had become an officer in the war, and led the small party that killed Metacomet and ended the war.

As I turned and looked back at the low bulk of Penikese behind me, her old sheep meadows stretching east toward Cuttyhunk and rising to the central hill where the cisterns were, it was easy to imagine one of the Mayhews out there—a farmer in the 1700s—or John Anderson, the New York City financier who had owned the island in the 1860s, strolling up that hill. Or a Wampanoag fisherman, say in the 1200s, out for a walk and thinking about the fishing he would do in the cove the next day. A war axe was found in the sediment of the cove not so long ago, and was dated to the 1400s. It was hard to say, as I looked back toward the hill, with the moon beyond it, if there was a person walking up the hill. It looked, the longer I stared, as if there might be. I would have to be careful not to surprise someone out for the same walk I used to take.

And then I walked north, down through old meadow now

gone to wild grassland (and likely little changed in the process) to the narrow isthmus, and along the cobbles of the steep winter beach there. The moonlight was bright now, and once I had crossed the span of the isthmus, I climbed the low hill of Tubbs—the Kansas-like far side of the island, grassy and low, home to a least-tern rookery.

I stood on a great boulder perched at the edge of the western shoulder of Tubbs and looked back across the cove at the main island, and at the hill rising there. I could see *Daphie* floating in the barely rippled cove, silhouetted against the moonlit trees on the far shore, and I could see two sharp boulders set on the distant ridge, between which I knew the winter solstice sun went down, if one looked for it, on December 21.

Native Americans, long before Bartholomew Gosnold came through here in 1602, had set those stones up as part of a calendar, and I liked to see them when I came to the island.

And then I walked back across the isthmus, back along the foot trail, detoured around the house and went down to the little schoolhouse where I had held school for several years, and stopped at an old black ash that stands in a sheltered spot there.

Ten years before, a couple of kids and I had studied American government in school, and one day we copied the Bill of Rights, each taking roughly a third of the text.

Then, "In the name of the freakin' Minutemen," as one of them put it, "And so that it will be preserved 'til kingdom come, or at least till I get outta this wack joint," as the other intoned, we put our several pages of scrawl in thick plastic bags, and then into a little steel box, and wrapped that in lead flashing, and wrapped that in rubber roofing membrane.

Then we buried our trove two feet down, and made a map

Approaching the dock.

of its locale, in triplicate, each taking a copy, with a dark X marking the spot.

Now, in the moonlight, the ground there looked undisturbed, as far as I could tell, with the grass growing over it. It was good to see that place. I sat under the tree for a few minutes, and then walked back down to the pier, retrieved my drybag, stripped to my suit, and swam back out to the boat.

I slept on the floorboards that night, on a pad, in my old down sleeping bag, as *Daphie*, cradling me, swayed lightly in the swell.

61. November

I HAD A LETTER from Rafe the other day, which Bill brought over to me. He showed up in his pickup, his power steering yammering a bit as usual as he turned in; a minute later he banged on the door.

We had a cup of tea on the deck while the sun went down, and I read the letter.

Dan,

I put Altair up in a little harbor about a hundred miles from here. You'd like it—not too crowded. We had a hell of a good sail. Just one bad gale as we approached the Brittany coast, but other than that, all went smoothly. Bill's a good crew, by and large, and by the end my starsights were coming in inside a mile. I knew you'd appreciate that.

I am up in a region in South-eastern France called the Vaucluse. It's in low mountains, and it's nice here. A very small village. They've got a terrific sense of themselves here, as you might imagine, with everybody knowing everyone else for so long, and Catherine and I are getting along first-rate. She has fields scattered all over the place, as does everybody else. I'm learning that I have a nose for wine, and I'm liking it here, so I think I'll stay for a while.

Listen. Thanks for taking that guy out in your boat and selling the project. I guess it worked great. What I'm wondering is would you be willing to pitch in with Bill on those 12 ½ s? He needs a hand and mine ain't gonna be around. I think he's going to be building three.

Well, let me know, and let Bill know, and come visit (once the boats are done)!

Best,
Rafe.

Bill looked at me when I looked up from the letter.

"So?" he said.

"So what?" I said.

"So, how would you feel about pitching in with me on those boats?" he said after a moment, raising his eyebrows, and fixing me with a stare.

"Are you serious?"

"Yeah," he said. "How many people do you see around here who know the insides of a twelve-and-a-half intimately who are unemployed who might be able to afford to be hardly employed?"

"How hardly?" I asked.

"Well, we can talk about that," he said. "You have any interest?"

"Yeah, I've got some interest," I said. "How long are we talking about?"

"To build four?" he said.

"I thought it said three," I said.

"He wants four. All centerboard," he said. "It's pretty shoal where he is, and he thinks it'll fit the region better. I think we could do it in fourteen months."

"Fourteen months," I said. "Let me think about it for a couple days." Which is where it stands now. If I accept, then Rafe was right—you can't just fix the one.

Tomorrow, *Daphie* gets hauled out. The other day I built a shed to store her in for the winter. It only took about four hours once Coop showed up to help, and we didn't snap one piece of strapping.

Plus, when I was leaving the lumberyard that morning, before we built the shed, I let Lenny know that I'd taken his schedule into account in planning the day, not wanting to inconvenience him by arriving at the yard too late.

"I got here on time just for you, Lenny," I said.

"Bah humbug, guy," he said, looking in the car window with a grizzled grin. Then he punched my receipt with his little machine so that a punched-out image of Mickey Mouse landed on my lap.

What will happen in the spring is anybody's guess, but I'd like to put her in the water a little earlier next year, if everything works out.

Glossary

Beam width of a boat at her widest point.

Beat a heading on which one sails as close to the wind as possible, which usually points one's bow into the waves, against which one beats.

Beetle Cat a shoal-draft, centerboard, gaff-rigged catboat with a single mast stepped in the bow; a popular boat developed from the traditional types of small fishing and freighting craft on and near Cape Cod.

Bell buoy a large navigational buoy equipped with pendulums that strike a bell as the buoy is moved by the seas.

Bent keel the curved timber that forms the topmost part of the keel immediately beneath the floor timbers.

Bight an embayment formed by a curve in the coast.

Bilge the bottom of the inside of the hull, where water and anything else collects.

Block and tackle a combination of two blocks (pulleys, often with multiple *sheaves*, or pulley wheels) joined by loops of rope, and used to haul something up a mast, tighten a halyard, or shift a big weight. Often the blocks have a hook at one or both ends.

Boom a spar attached to the mast at its forward end that runs along the bottom of a sail. On *Daphie* both the mainsail and the jib have booms.

Boot top the stripe (red on *Daphie*) that runs around the boat at the waterline.

Bow the front of the boat.

Bowline the best knot invented by humankind. It forms a loop in the end of a rope, and will hold indefinitely, but will not jam.

Bowsprit a spar that sticks straight out (and often slants up a little) in front of the boat, in order to increase the distance forward at which one can set a sail or sails.

Broad plank the last plank but one at the bottom of a hull on either side. Beneath the broad plank is the garboard which is the last plank before the keel.

Bulkhead a partition, watertight or not, between two sections of a boat.

Cap rail on *Daphie*, the flat, narrow mahogany board that covers the top edge of the hull, protecting the tops of the frames, and joining the sheer clamp and sheer strake, just outside the coaming.

Carvel another name for plank-on-frame construction in a boat. Also called "clinker."

Catamaran a two-hulled symmetrical vessel, offering (in well-made vessels) great stability, increased speed, and high excitement. Drawbacks include the difficulty of creating a strong joint between two hulls so that in heavy weather they do not rip apart, and righting a catamaran when it has capsized.

Catboat a sailboat with one mast in the bow. Such boats have one large sail, allowing for simplicity of operation and much room at the center of the boat for work. A drawback of a large single sail is that it can be difficult to control in heavy weather. Such boats are called "una-boats" in England and elsewhere.

Cat ketch a catboat with a second smaller mast (and sail) stepped aft, but in front of the rudder post.

Cat's-paw a disturbance on the surface of the sea caused by approaching wind. Looks like the paws of many cats walking on a smooth surface, leaving the pattern of their prints as they run around. "Cat's-paw" also refers to a curved claw-like tool used to remove nails from wood.

Caulk to make a boat watertight by filling the seams between the planks with cotton, oakum, seam compound, etc.

Centerboard a hinged fin that drops down beneath the keel of a vessel to prevent the vessel from slipping sideways.

Center of effort that point on a sailing vessel that is the average of all of the vectors of force being applied to the hull by the various sails. If the c.o.e. is further forward than the center of lateral resistance, the vessel, when its sails are well set, will consistently head "down," or away from the wind. Which is not how you want it.

Chain plate the plate or bracket, strongly mounted to the hull, which anchors a stay or shroud.

Chine the ridge or corner formed when the vertical side of a boat meets (below the waterline) the flat section of the bottom of the boat. A boat is said to have a "hard chine" when these two sections of the hull meet in a corner. A hard chine can improve a sailboat's ability to sail to weather (into the wind) by keeping it from slipping sideways as much as it would if its chine were soft. It is also easier to build a hard-chined boat than a smooth-hulled boat. Drawbacks include decreased strength (this is a place where the hull is stressed), and less aesthetic appeal. Usually found in shoal-draft boats (boats meant for sailing in shallow water, and thus not able to employ a full keel).

Claw off a lee shore to sail away from a shore on which the waves and wind threaten to dash one. A desperate action, requiring a vessel to sail into the wind. A good sailing vessel will do this in any weather. Old freight haulers which were square-rigged and relied on trade winds and favorable winds for locomotion were often wrecked because they couldn't "point" high enough into the wind to escape a storm which pushed them onto a lee shore. The outer beaches of Cape Cod were the end of many vessels under these circumstances.

Cleat a device, usually shaped like a squat T, to which one can tie a line. Also, a piece of wood used to join two other pieces of wood.

Coaming planks or structures that form a raised edge around a cockpit or hatch in order to prevent standing water from entering. On *Daphie,* the coaming surrounds the cockpit, and forms a backrest for the passengers.

Come about, come around in sailing, to turn a boat, so that it moves from the condition of being under full sail on one tack to the condition of being under full sail on the other tack, with the bow passing through the eye of the wind.

Cradle a wooden superstructure that supports a vessel, allowing it to sit upright on land.

Companionway stairs from one deck to another.

Cutaway forefoot a gradual innovation in sailboat design, signaled most strongly by the vessel *Gloriana,* designed by N.G. Herreshoff, although he wrote that she was just the culmination of a trend which could be seen in many designs leading up to her. The cutaway forefoot refers to the hull at the bow being shallow, rather than biting deeply into the sea. Older vessels tended to have a rather more square profile at their leading edge. The cutaway forefoot allowed a vessel to turn more adroitly, as one needed less effort to push a shallow bow sideways through the sea, *and* it allowed the weight saved at the bow to be transferred to a deeper keel amidships, increasing the stiffness of the boat, while at the same time reducing a vessel's wetted area (and thus her drag) as well as her waterline length. However, as a boat with a cutaway forefoot heeled, she "put her shoulder down," burying more of her forward hull in the water, increasing her waterline length in doing so, and so gaining speed (as hull speed or maximum possible speed increases, as a matter of physics, with the length of the hull on the waterline).

Cutter a single-masted boat with one mainsail and two (or more) foresails. Much like a sloop, but with the mainmast stepped slightly further aft, or the sails balanced slightly differently.

Danforth a very effective type of anchor with two triangular flukes that hinge downward from the shaft of the anchor.

Deadwood the solid wood of the keel below the hull.

Dinghy a small rowboat.

Dory a flat-bottomed rowing boat, pointed at the bow and nearly pointed at the stern, originally used for fishing. On the great fishing schooners, the dories would sit nestled in stacks of four or five, and would set out each day to long-line for cod or similar fish. It was not unheard of for fishermen who became separated from their vessel to row hundreds of miles to shore. An extremely seaworthy boat when built deeply enough.

Draft the distance from the waterline to the bottom of the boat.

Fathom six feet; usually in reference to depth of water.

Fiddler crab *Uca pugnax*; small crabs, possessing one large claw (the fiddle) and one small claw, who commonly live in burrows in the sediment around spartina grass, and in mudflats in salt marshes.

Floor timbers the trapezoidal blocks of wood mounted at intervals along the top edge of, and perpendicular to, the keel. They are the "anchors" to which the bottom ends of the frames (ribs) are attached. They follow the flare of the hull of the boat as it widens out, starting at the keel, and so are narrow at their bottom edge (at the keel) and wider at their top edge. Each has a different shape (at least in my boat), depending on how the hull is shaped at that station. Toward the bow they are narrower. At the beam they become wider. Toward the stern they are narrower again. The ribs are riveted or bolted to them along their outside edges, and then curve up to form the hull's framework.

Foc's'le foreshortened version of the word *forecastle*, meaning the enclosed space at the bow of a vessel. In a freight or fish-carrying sailing vessel, the foc's'le was often the space (before the foremast) where the crew had their quarters. A dark, damp, nasty place to be.

Fore-and-aft refers to a rig which employs sails set fore and aft, with their leading edge attached to a mast or stay at the centerline of the vessel, then stretched aft, and controlled with lines ("sheets") attached to their after edge. As opposed to square-rigged, in which square sails are set with their centers pivoting on a mast, making them primarily useful for sailing down or across the wind, but not into the wind.

Forefoot underwater section of the bow.

Frame a rib.

Gaff on a gaff-rigged sail, a spar attached to the mast and stretching along the top edge of a fore-and-aft-rigged sail. Not a sprit.

Garboard the bottommost plank on a hull.

Gooseneck the joint at which a boom or gaff joins the mast. Easily broken in a flying (uncontrolled) jibe.

Groin see jetty.

Gunwale the upper edge of the side of a boat. Often pronounced "gunnel."

Gut, Gutter a narrow passage or gully, as of a stream or path. Around here, a swift-flowing passage of water, much like a small river, whose current changes with the tide.

Halyard a line with which one raises a sail.

Head a commode on board a boat.

Heel to tip sideways, usually occasioned by the wind.

Hole a large gut; a channel between lands, through which currents move swiftly.

Irons to be "in irons" is to be stuck pointing straight into the wind, without having enough "way on" (speed) to steer to one side of the wind or the other and begin to sail again.

Jetty a pier of rocks built out into the ocean to protect a beach from surf and erosion. Often jetties encourage erosion, rather than discourage it.

Jib a sail that sets forward of the mainmast.

Jibboom a spar that stretches along the lower edge of a jib.

Jibe to pass the stern of the boat through the eye of the wind, which occasions allowing the wind to push the boom or booms to the other side of the boat. If uncontrolled, this maneuver can break the gooseneck and even the mast.

Keel that part of a boat below the hull which provides both stability and reduced movement sideways through the water.

Ketch a boat rigged with two masts, the after mast (the mizzen) being shorter than the mainmast and stepped in front of the rudder post.

Knee an L-shaped structural member of a boat, such as one used to support the deck, as in "deck knee." The strongest knees are cut from limbs of trees shaped in this way.

Knot a nautical mile, or a nautical mile per hour.

Lazarette a sheltered compartment at the stern of a boat used for storage.

Leeward the side of the boat away from the wind.

Leg o' mutton refers to a standard (these days) triangular mainsail bent to a mast and boom, with a relatively high (taller than wide) aspect, which results in a sail shaped something like a leg of mutton.

Line a rope that is part of the running rigging of a vessel; really, there are no ropes on boats. Rope is what you find in a chandlery. Once you buy it, and assign it a specific task, such as "docking line," or "anchor line," or "halyard" or "sheet," or "extra," it is a line. Rope does not exist aboard.

LOA Length overall; the length of a boat from the tip of its bowsprit to the very end of its transom. Sometimes other structures (such as rudders and overhanging booms) come into play here.

Locust black locust (*Robinia pseudoacacia*) in this case. A tree with compound leaves that grows commonly on Cape Cod, and is notable in part for its deeply furrowed bark, its fierce thorns on its saplings, and its wood, which will commonly last longer than granite when used as a post.

LWL length on the waterline; the length of a boat in a straight line stretched from its stem at the waterline to its stern at the waterline.

Mahogany a tropical hardwood that is prized for its durability and rot resistance; a wood often harvested in ways which represent poor environmental practice, and which encourage deforestation, erosion, ruination of habitat, fisheries, and local economies, so that people like me can build outdoor decks, and boats, cheaply. Please try to research and buy mahogany grown in sustainable ways, or don't buy it. Use locust instead. It's great for decks.

Mainsail usually the sail mounted behind the largest mast. In a sloop, the after sail.

Mast a spar mounted vertically to which are attached the mainsail and various stays and shrouds.

Mast step the platform, slot, or place on which the bottom of the mast stands and is secured.

Marconi Rig characterized by a tall mast with a leg o'mutton (triangular) sail. So named because of the tall radio masts of the wireless radio innovator, Guglielmo Marconi (1874–1937), whose name was associated with the modernity that the new tall rigs with higher aspect sails represented. He received the Nobel Prize in 1909 for contributions to the development of wireless telegraphy.

Mizzen the smaller of two masts; the after mast in a ketch or yawl, and the foremast in a two-masted schooner.

Monohull a boat with one hull, as opposed to two (catamaran or proa) or three (trimaran).

Painter the short line tied to the bow of a small boat or tender and used to tie the boat to something (a dock, piling, pier, another boat, etc.).

Peak the top edge of a gaff-rigged sail.

Plank a board used to form the skin of a boat's hull.

Plank-on-frame a method of constructing boats in which planks are run horizontally across an inner structure of vertical ribs.

Plumb bow a bow that makes a straight line up and down.

Port the side of the boat to one's left when facing forward.

Reach to sail with the wind abeam (perpendicular to the keel) is a beam reach. A close reach means that the wind strikes the vessel on an angle just forward of abeam, and a broad reach means that the wind strikes the vessel just aft of abeam.

Red oak *(Quercus rubra)* a type of oak that rots quickly in boats if one end is submerged, and the other above water. Otherwise a very good sort of oak that grows in moist, slightly acidic soils in the northeast of the U.S.

Reef to "shorten" or reduce the amount of sail area one has up, by tying part of a sail or sails down.

Rib like the ribs in your chest, the ribs of a boat are structural members on which the skin of the hull (the planks) is hung.

Rivet one method of fastening a plank to a frame, or of fastening anything to anything. The rivet, looking much like a nail, is passed through both objects that are to be held together, and then has its tail flattened against the outside of a washer on the far side.

Rope any length of braided or woven line not on a boat.

Rozinante a twenty-eight-foot ketch designed by L. Francis Herreshoff. It is a slender, shoal-draft boat, easily driven, and modeled after lifeboats which were practically unsinkable. It has simple accommodations below for two, and is thought by many to be one of the most lovely boats ever drawn.

Rudder the movable fin submerged at the stern of a boat by which one steers.

Rudder post the vertical post on which a rudder pivots.

Run to sail with the wind directly or nearly directly behind one. In this situation, the sails are let out, and one (if one is good) pays close attention to the risk of jibing.

Salt Marsh a tidal ecosystem that when healthy teems with fish, mollusks, birds, crabs, plants, plankton, etc. A northeastern salt marsh is as productive as rain forest, in terms of biomass produced per acre, which places it at the top of global ecosystems in terms of productivity. The salt marsh anchors the oceanic ecosystems, and for every acre we destroy, fishing boats sit idle in New Bedford, men are out of work, and many families are impoverished, as is the great ocean.

Sheer the curve of the hull, usually from high at the bow to low amidships to a little higher again at the stern. Sheer is often an indication of both good looks and seaworthiness.

Sheer clamp the curved timber running along the top of the side of the hull, inside the ribs.

Sheer strake the topmost plank on the hull, running parallel to the sheer clamp, on the outside of the hull. On *Daphie* the sheer strake is made of mahogany.

Sheet a line used to control the trim of a sail in terms of its orientation to the wind.

Shoal shallow. Can also mean a particular shallow place, as in "Horseshoe Shoal."

Shroud a rope, wire, or cable supporting the mast from either *side* of a boat. Can also be called a sidestay when the word *shroud* cannot be remembered. One does not call a forestay or backstay a shroud. See "stay."

Sloop a one-masted vessel with two sails: a main and a jib.

Snotter the line tied to a sprit with which one raises the sprit up the mast of a spritsail.

Sole the floor inside the cabin of a boat.

Spar any pole used to to control a sail, or to which a sail is mounted for support, such as a boom, gaff, mast, or pole.

Spartina refers to *Spartina alterniflora* and *Spartina patens*, two grasses that grow in salt marshes; *alterniflora* grows in tidal waters, while *patens* grows just above the high-tide line.

Spoon bow a bow with a profile like that of a spoon, meaning a very shallow curve aft and down toward the water, and often a long overhang.

Spreader a small spar or rod that holds a stay out from the mast, often about two-thirds of the way to the top of the mast, thus increasing the leverage that the stay has on the mast.

Sprit in a spritsail rig, a spar holds the top corner of the sail back and away from the top of a mast, and is tied to the mast near the bottom of the sail with a "snotter." Not to be confused with a gaff, which runs along the top of a sail.

Spritsail a boat rigged with a spritsail rig on one or more masts. The Woods Hole spritsail was a Willys Jeep of a boat, a small truck able to sail well to weather with a load of fish, freight, or people. It was fast, stable, shoal (able to get into shallow water), and was easily derigged in order to slip under the many low stone bridges that spanned local creeks and gutters.

Spritsail rig a spritsail rig refers to a four-sided sail, attached to a mast along its forward edge, and held aloft by a sprit. A spritsail can have a boom running along its bottom edge, or can be "loose-footed."

Starboard the side of a boat on one's right hand when looking forward.

Stay a rope, wire, or cable supporting the mast from the bow, stern, or side of a boat. See "shroud."

Stem the leading edge of the bow of a boat; the timber of which the leading edge of the bow is made.

Stern the back of a boat.

Swamp to fill with water and wholly or partially submerge; as in, to make a swamp of the interior of one's vessel. Not a happy word, usually.

Tack to move the boat from one side of the wind to the other, with a concomitant adjustment of the sails. To come about. This results in a zigzag course. Also, the bottom forward corner of a sail.

Tender a small boat used to go to and from a larger one.

Throat the lower part of a gaff-rigged sail, right along the mast.

Tiller the lever that one uses to control the rudder.

Toe rail a low, raised ridge along the edge of the deck designed to give one's foot purchase on the slippery surface.

Topsides the deck of a boat under the sky (not down below), or the sides of the hull above the waterline.

Transom the back of a boat, where the tailgate of a pickup truck would be.

Trimaran a three-hulled boat, sharing many of the characteristics of a catamaran.

Trunnel a "tree nail," or wooden spike made of hardwood (often locust) that is used to nail other pieces of wood together. Highly effective.

White oak *(Quercus alba)* a species of oak that is tough and rot-resistant, often used around here for boat parts.

Windward the side of the boat that the wind strikes first.

Wrack line the line along a beach of seaweed and flotsam and jetsam and crap that we like to stroll next to because there is a chance to find something wondrous and strange.

Yard boatyard. Also, the spar spanning the top or bottom of a square sail.

Yawl a two-masted boat, with the shorter mast (the mizzen) mounted aft and behind the rudder post.

Acknowledgments

Thanks to Bob Bender and Johanna Li. Thanks to Jill Kneerim.

Thanks to L. Francis Herreshoff, for his writing and creation of sensible cruising designs. Thanks of course to Capt. Nat Herreshoff for his work.

Thanks to boatbuilders everywhere. When I have gotten it right, it is due to them. When I have bungled a boat repair, it is entirely my fault.

Thanks to Damien McLaughlin, Doug Cooper, Bill Cooper, Al Lunn, Steve Schaefer, Whit Hanschke, The Herreshoff Museum staff, and in particular John Palmieri for his time and help.

Thanks to Roger Billings, John Billings, George Billings, and Elliot Billings for their thoughts and energies as mariners. Thanks also to Frank Renna and Jack Wixted for their enthusiasm about boats and ridiculous projects in general. Thanks to Nick Bennett. Thanks to Atlas. Thanks to Jurgen Atema.

Thanks always to Jim Millinger, great teacher of all things maritime. Thanks also to Capt. John Wigglesworth, who really knows how to sail a vessel.

Many heartfelt thanks to my Uncle Phil Alton, the nicest sailor I ever met, who took care of *Daphie* for many years. Thanks also to Carey Alton, Marion Alton, Liz Alton, Robin Alton, Alison Robb, and in particular to Hilary Alton.

Thanks to Bart Nisewonger, Zach Alton, Wil Dix, Lawrence Peirson, John Vose, Jake Densmore, and all who contributed to the progress of the boat.

Thanks to Eric Little, who was generous with his knowledge.

Thanks to Jim Mavor, who understood the need to be on the water as often as possible, and to Barbara Little for the same.

Thanks to my old friends and allies at QYC, with whom I came to know sailing as a way of life: Doug Jones, Abby Armstrong, Mike Phillips, Mike Garfield, Buz Crain, Cathy Cook, Liz Bernstein, Hilary Davis, Liz Morse, and Hugh Montgomery. I learned so much from you all. Also, thanks to Janet Chalmers, Nancy Cloos, and Marge Crain.

Thanks to the waters of Vineyard Sound and Buzzards Bay, and the islands thereabout and the marshes and beaches, and to the coastal land abutting, in which church I and many others have practiced our odd faith.

Thanks to my parents, who taught me to sail, and who always said time on the water was time well spent.

Thanks to Maia Porter, for your steadfast clearheaded help, your encouragement, and for your love.

Thanks to everyone with the faith (and skill) to put to sea in small boats with sails, or oars, or paddles, or with just the will to go. May you voyage well.

Index

Page numbers in italics refer to illustrations.